Wisconsin for Kennedy

WISCONSIN FOR KENNEDY

*The Primary that Launched a President and
Changed the Course of History*

B.J. HOLLARS

WISCONSIN HISTORICAL SOCIETY PRESS

Published by the Wisconsin Historical Society Press
Publishers since 1855

The Wisconsin Historical Society helps people connect to the past by collecting,
preserving, and sharing stories. Founded in 1846, the Society is one of the nation's
finest historical institutions.
Join the Wisconsin Historical Society: wisconsinhistory.org/membership

Front cover image: *Dubuque Telegraph Herald*; back cover image: WHI Image ID 56515

Printed in the United States of America
Cover design and interior design by Brian Donahue / bedesign, inc.

28 27 26 25 24   1 2 3 4 5

Library of Congress Cataloging-in-Publication Data

Names: Hollars, B.J., author.
Title: Wisconsin for Kennedy : how a band of believers launched a president
   and changed the course of history / B.J. Hollars.
Description: First edition. | Madison : Wisconsin Historical Society Press,
   [2024] | Includes bibliographical references and index.
Identifiers: LCCN 2023024426 (print) | LCCN 2023024427 (ebook) | ISBN
   9781976600173 (paperback) | ISBN 9781976600180 (ebook)
Subjects: LCSH: Primaries—Wisconsin—History. | Presidents—United
   States—Election—1960. | Kennedy, John F. (John Fitzgerald), 1917–1963.
   | Wisconsin—Politics and government—1951– | United States—Politics
   and government—1953–1961.
Classification: LCC JK2075.W62 H65 2024 (print) | LCC JK2075.W62 (ebook)
   | DDC 324.2775015409—dc23/eng/20230925
LC record available at https://lccn.loc.gov/2023024426
LC ebook record available at https://lccn.loc.gov/2023024427

♾ The paper used in this publication meets the minimum requirements of the
American National Standard for Information Sciences—Permanence of Paper for Printed
Library Materials, ANSI Z39.48-1992.

For Meredith, Henry, Eleanor, and Amelia—
you've all got my vote.

"If history were taught in the form of stories, it would never be forgotten."

—RUDYARD KIPLING

"I suppose that there's no training ground for the presidency, but I don't think it's a bad idea for a president to have stood outside of [Oscar] Mayer's meat factory in Madison, Wisconsin . . . at five-thirty in the morning, with the temperature ten above."

—PRESIDENT JOHN F. KENNEDY, MAY 12, 1962

CONTENTS

AUTHOR'S NOTE

In the spring of 2020, I discovered a digital collection of rarely cited interview transcripts housed by the John F. Kennedy Oral History Collection, recounting the 1960 Wisconsin Democratic primary. As an author and a Wisconsinite, I was immediately drawn to these stories. President Kennedy famously remarked there was no better training ground for the presidency than Wisconsin, yet few scholars have fully explored the key role the state played in Kennedy's political rise. Before reading the oral history transcripts, I had been unaware of how Wisconsin helped propel Kennedy to the White House and how close the state's voters came to derailing his future political plans.

Much of this book relies upon these oral histories, as well as other firsthand accounts, personal letters, archival newspaper reports, an array of scholarly books and articles, records from the John F. Kennedy Presidential Library and Museum, and personal interviews I conducted. This work builds on the research of many writers and scholars—most notably Theodore H. White, David Pietrusza, Dennis L. Dresang, Carl Solberg, Ted Sorensen, Jeff Greenfield, and Robert Dallek, in addition to documentarian Robert Drew, who captured Wisconsin's 1960 primary with riveting authenticity. For more than half a century, so many people have given so much in the service of preserving this story. I am indebted to them all.

Creative nonfiction uses literary techniques to tell true stories; as a creative nonfiction writer, I have employed the tools of the genre (including point-of-view shifts and writing in scene) to write a character-driven account of this extraordinary primary contest. With this approach, I hope to brush the dust from this history, not only so that general readers might know it better but also so that historians and scholars might continue researching this pivotal moment from our nation's political past.

At no point did I sacrifice historical facts for a creative flourish. Quoted dialogue can be confirmed on the historical record, and the scenes recounted here are true. Yes, John Kennedy and Hubert Humphrey indulged *LIFE* magazine by posing awkwardly beside a barn in Clintonville in the thick of their primary battle. And yes, Bobby Kennedy trudged for miles through the snow when his train screeched to a halt outside of Eau Claire. Indeed, Ted Kennedy launched himself from a ski jump in Middleton to win over a few more voters. And Jackie Kennedy did, in fact, commandeer a supermarket's loudspeaker system in Kenosha. For me, each of these scenes glimmer with humanity, providing new insight into the personal nature of the Wisconsin primary. To bring these people more fully to life on the page, on occasion I have incorporated basic human gestures in line with their characters: a flipped page in a journalist's notepad, an advance man's anxious glance at a watch, a smile from a supporter.

While John F. Kennedy's Wisconsin presidential primary campaign is the center of this book, Kennedy himself is not entirely the focus. Instead, this is the untold story of the team of people who banded together to help Kennedy win the Wisconsin primary, setting him on course for the presidency. By every measure, they were an eclectic bunch: a cranberry farmer, a politician, a mayor, a union organizer, a journalist, an oil man, a friend, an architect, and a pair of Kennedy brothers, among others. Today, many of their names have become footnotes, their faces mostly recognizable from the fringes of photographs. We all know of Jack and Bobby Kennedy, but regrettably, few know of Philleo Nash, Pat Lucey, Ivan Nestingen, Jerry Bruno, Ira Kapenstein, Pete Dugal, Charles "Chuck" Spalding, Karel Yasko, and so many more. Yet their oft-overlooked contributions make for some of the most engaging stories.

Unquestionably, the most overlooked of all are the women who were involved in the 1960 presidential campaign, many of whom did not hold official leadership posts and whose stories, consequently, were not fully recorded. My research was hindered by this limited recorded history, and the stories included herein reflect that. But make no mistake: women played key roles throughout Kennedy's run for the White House and beyond, including Wisconsinites like Vel Phillips and Toni McBride, as well as Kennedy's female family members, including Jackie Kennedy, Rose Kennedy, and sisters Eunice, Pat, and Jean. For a host of reasons, these women deserve their own book. In their own ways, each of them shaped Jack Kennedy as a person and a politician.

Not included in this book is the story of Kennedy's eldest sister, Rosemary, who lived in Wisconsin from 1949 until her death in 2005. On the wishes of their father, Joe Kennedy Sr., Rosemary was institutionalized at the St. Coletta School for Exceptional Children in Jefferson, Wisconsin, eight years after a failed lobotomy. Rosemary's condition was a highly guarded secret; tragically, most historians believe the Kennedy siblings were unaware of Rosemary's location as they crisscrossed the state during the 1960 primary campaign.

Wisconsin for Kennedy highlights the courage and commitment of Wisconsinites who came together for a common cause, who risked their reputations in the service of a more perfect union, and who demonstrate the important truth that everyone has a story that deserves to be told. These were Wisconsinites who asked not what their country could do for them, but what they could do for their country. And they found their answer long before such a phrase ever left President Kennedy's lips.

This is their story.

Cast of Characters

Jerry Bruno: A former forklift driver and union organizer with a ninth-grade education from Kenosha, Wisconsin, Jerry Bruno was the executive director of the Kennedy for President Club of Wisconsin, overseeing logistics for Senator John F. Kennedy's Wisconsin primary campaign. Bruno later served as an advance man for President Kennedy's official travels.

Pete Dugal: A native of Cadott, Wisconsin, as well as Chippewa County's Democratic Party chairman, Pete Dugal drove Senator Kennedy to campaign stops all over northwestern Wisconsin during the 1960 primary campaign.

Hubert H. Humphrey: Dubbed "the Happy Warrior" for his cheery optimism, Hubert Humphrey served as the progressive senator from Minnesota from 1949 to 1964 and 1971 to 1978. At age forty-eight, he competed against Senator Kennedy for the Democratic Party's presidential nomination. Under President Lyndon B. Johnson, Humphrey later served as the thirty-eighth vice president of the United States.

Ira Kapenstein: As a young political reporter for the *Milwaukee Journal*, Ira Kapenstein covered Senator Kennedy's presidential run at close range. He declined an invitation to work for the campaign because of health reasons but later worked for Bobby Kennedy's 1968 presidential run.

Jacqueline "Jackie" Kennedy: A New York native interested in fashion, photography, and horseback riding, thirty-one-year-old Jackie Kennedy campaigned across Wisconsin to help her husband get elected: posing with prize hams, talking to shoppers over supermarket loudspeakers, and leading crowds in song as they patiently awaited Senator Kennedy's perpetually late arrival.

John F. "Jack" Kennedy: In January 1960, the forty-two-year-old senator from Massachusetts declared himself a candidate for president. The Kennedy campaign was the first to leverage the power of state primary contests—a groundbreaking strategy that ultimately helped to transform how future presidents were nominated. John F. Kennedy was the thirty-fifth president of the United States, serving from January 20, 1961, until his assassination on November 22, 1963.

Robert "Bobby" Kennedy: As a thirty-four-year-old lawyer, Bobby Kennedy served as campaign manager for his brother Jack's presidential run and helped assemble the team of Wisconsinites who were responsible for the campaign's success in the primary. Bobby Kennedy would go on to serve as US attorney general, New York senator, and presidential candidate before his assassination in 1968.

Theodore "Ted" Kennedy: At age twenty-eight, Ted Kennedy was assigned to help his older brother secure primary wins and delegates throughout the western United States. In Wisconsin, Ted pinch-hit for Jack at several events when his brother couldn't attend himself. Ted Kennedy later served as a senator for Massachusetts from 1962 until his death in 2009.

Patrick "Pat" Lucey: A native of La Crosse, Wisconsin, Pat Lucey rebuilt Wisconsin's struggling Democratic party and brought it back to prominence. As chair of the state's Democratic Party, Pat remained technically neutral throughout the 1960 primary, though his unflagging support for Kennedy was well known. Pat Lucey later served as Wisconsin's thirty-eighth governor.

Philleo Nash: Born in Wisconsin Rapids, Wisconsin, Philleo Nash was a guitar-strumming cranberry farmer with a PhD in anthropology who worked for President Truman before becoming Wisconsin's lieutenant governor. Nash supported Humphrey during the 1960 election until his withdrawal from the race. Nash later served as commissioner of the US Bureau of Indian Affairs.

Ivan Nestingen: The mayor of Madison, Ivan Nestingen served as chairman of the Kennedy for President Club of Wisconsin and helped lay the groundwork for Senator Kennedy's Wisconsin primary run. Jackie Kennedy was said to have nicknamed him "The Rock" for his steady leader-

Madison, Wisconsin, October 23, 1960. WHI IMAGE ID 8619

ship. In 1961, Nestingen left the mayorship to join the Kennedy administration as undersecretary of the US Department of Health, Education, and Welfare.

Vel Phillips: In 1960, thirty-six-year-old Vel Phillips was the first woman and first Black person to serve on Milwaukee's Common Council. Phillips would later become the first Black person to serve in Wisconsin's judiciary, as well as the first woman and first Black person to be elected Wisconsin's secretary of state. Though initially skeptical of Kennedy, Phillips eventually became a key ally, accompanying him to an NAACP rally days before the 1960 Democratic National Convention.

Charles "Chuck" Spalding: A writer, investment banker, and longtime Kennedy friend originally from Lake Forest, Illinois, Chuck Spalding dedicated much of the winter and spring of 1960 to helping Senator Kennedy win votes in western Wisconsin.

Karel Yasko: In 1960, Karel Yasko was the forty-eight-year-old Wisconsin state architect. He enjoyed two unique and memorable interactions with Senator Kennedy, whom he admired greatly. Later, Yasko served as the architect for the General Services Administration and credited President Kennedy for his impact on architecture and the arts.

From left to right: Robert F. Kennedy, Edward Kennedy, and President John F. Kennedy outside the White House, 1963. CECIL STOUGHTON, WHITE HOUSE PHOTOGRAPHS, JOHN F. KENNEDY PRESIDENTIAL LIBRARY AND MUSEUM, BOSTON

THE GATHERING

Bobby Kennedy
October 28, 1959

Five months and seven days before the Wisconsin primary

When thirty-three-year-old Bobby Kennedy wanted to sail, he sailed. The weather didn't much matter. If rain pelted the water and high winds battered the mast, Bobby made the necessary adjustments: reaching for the rudder and tacking left or right. What was the point in piddling away one's days waiting for the perfect conditions? If you wanted to feel the spray of the ocean, then you had to leave the safety of the shore.

On the morning of October 28, 1959, Bobby stood in his Hyannis Port home with its clear view of the chilly Atlantic. He knew that water well, having sailed upon it for the past thirty years since his father, Kennedy patriarch Joseph Sr., had first claimed Hyannis Port as the family's summer destination. The property's three homes and six sprawling acres were the perfect getaway from the public gaze that had long hounded the Kennedys, most of all Bobby's forty-two-year-old brother, Massachusetts senator John F. Kennedy.

Indeed, Jack Kennedy was the reason sixteen people were gathered around Bobby's living room that morning. Among them were political advisers (including the ever-loyal Kenny O'Donnell and Larry O'Brien, who were members of Kennedy's inner circle known as the "Irish Mafia"), lawyers, senatorial aides, and an ex-governor. Rounding out the group were Bobby Kennedy, twenty-seven-year-old Ted Kennedy, seventy-one-year-old Joe Kennedy Sr., and Jack himself.

The Kennedy men had recruited this group for a singular purpose: to devise a unifying strategy to propel Jack to the White House. Though his official presidential announcement wouldn't occur for another two months, Jack's candidacy seemed a foregone conclusion. It wasn't a matter of whether he would run; it was a matter of how.

Despite Jack Kennedy's rising political profile, the leap from junior senator to Democratic presidential candidate was a daunting proposition. Bobby knew it, Joe Sr. knew it, and Jack knew it most of all. But the Kennedys weren't the type of people to give up when the deck seemed stacked against them. Instead, they simply restacked the deck.

Sure, they had other possible candidates to contend with: two-time presidential loser Adlai Stevenson II; the southern-drawling Speaker of the House Lyndon B. Johnson; the out-of-touch Stuart Symington of Missouri; and that chatterbox Hubert Humphrey from Minnesota. But all these men could be bested, Bobby believed, with the proper plan.

While everyone in Bobby's living room loved Jack Kennedy, they were hardly naive about his weaknesses as a candidate: most notably, his age and his religion. If he won, Jack would be the youngest person, as well as the first Catholic, ever elected president. This latter liability, Bobby feared, could haunt his brother well beyond the primary. Only once had a Catholic made it to the top of the national ticket—New York governor Al Smith back in '28—and who could forget how terribly that had turned out? Smith had lost one of the most lopsided elections in United States history. And to Herbert Hoover! Such a blowout was precisely what the Kennedys were hoping to avoid.

While Jack's age and religion were liabilities, there was good news, too. Particularly the sharp contrast between Jack and his likely general election opponent, the all-but-anointed Republican candidate, Vice President Richard Milhouse Nixon. Though Jack Kennedy and Richard Nixon had both been elected to the House of Representatives as freshmen congressmen in 1946, that's where their similarities ended. One was an East Coast Catholic born into great wealth and power; the other a West Coast Quaker born into poverty. In the scripted version, Jack Kennedy might have made the better villain—the gilded, silver-spooned, cradle-to-grave politician who, according to his critics, would do almost anything (from kickbacks to vote-buying to conspiring with the mob) to secure the highest office in the land. But instead, the role of villain would eventually fall to Nixon, the unshaven, shoulder-slumped, future "I-am-not-a-crook" crook.

Neither assessment captured the full measure of these men. But "full measures" are irrelevant in American politics. Most voters required little more than some version of truth that seemed to align with their own opinions. If you could manage that much—and look good while doing it—the battle was all but won.

When people saw Jack Kennedy, they saw a boyish war hero with a smile slightly brighter than the sun. When people saw Richard Nixon, they saw a man whose frumpish appearance and groveling disposition might've landed him in a close race for dog catcher. Nevertheless, by October 1959, "Tricky Dick" Nixon (a nickname he'd earned thanks to his less-than-aboveboard campaign tactics in his 1950 Senate race) was still the man to beat. That was fine with Bobby. With the Republican candidate all but locked in, the only nomination race worth watching belonged to the Democrats. Luckily, Jack knew how to hold a spotlight.

For the next three hours, Jack demonstrated just that to the small crowd of people seated in Bobby's living room. To the astonishment of some ("How does he do that?" marveled Pierre Salinger, a journalist and future press secretary who had joined Kennedy's team just months before), Jack stood with his back to the fireplace and offered a clinic on his encyclopedic political knowledge. He provided a detailed analysis, moving from east to west across the country. His lecture was not meant to impress; it was just who he was. Bobby—all too familiar with his brother's exhaustive knowledge of history and politics—listened as Jack talked through the challenges that lay ahead. Much of it boiled down to a single conclusion: if Jack had any hope of winning the Democratic nomination, the surest path required winning a series of state primaries.

It was, to be sure, an unconventional strategy. Until as late as 1972, candidates routinely skipped state primaries, often dismissing them as "beauty contests" for the limited role they played in delivering the presidential nomination. Instead, most candidates sought to gain the favor of state party leaders whose votes, as delegates to the national party convention, would determine the nominee. Of the fifty states in the union in 1959 (Alaska and Hawaii had just been admitted earlier that year), merely fifteen states plus the District of Columbia would be holding primaries for the 1960 presidential election. And only some of those states bound any of their delegates to the winning candidate, leaving most of the nation's delegates open to dealmaking and negotiations at the convention. For Jack Kennedy, securing bound delegates was only one of his campaign's early goals. He also needed to persuade skeptical Democratic party bosses that he could win despite his age and religion, to prove his national electability going into the convention. The Kennedy team hoped to offer that proof by way of a series of primary wins.

The problem, however, was that the team hadn't reached a consensus on which primaries Jack should enter. The sixteen options spanned the country: New Hampshire was first on March 8, followed by Wisconsin on April 5; then came Illinois, New Jersey, Massachusetts, Pennsylvania, the District of Columbia, Indiana, Ohio, Nebraska, West Virginia, Maryland, Oregon, Florida, and, closing out the primary calendar on June 7, California and South Dakota.

One question was figuring out which of these states offered Jack the best chance to reach a wider audience. Primaries require that candidates cater to each state's unique interests while simultaneously finding ways to speak to the country at large—a balancing act that could prove difficult. For example, while Kennedy's cosponsorship of a dairy bill could play well in the Midwest, it might not be viewed as all that impressive nationwide.

As they considered the primary map, Kennedy's team also had to contend with something called the "favorite son" strategy, in which party leaders would back a nonviable candidate to win a state primary, in order to use their pledged delegates to gain bargaining power with major presidential candidates at the national convention. This disadvantaged out-of-state candidates by limiting their opportunities to amass an early delegate lead, while also momentarily empowering those state leaders who lacked national appeal.

These were just some of the many unknowns that Bobby and the team had to consider as they plotted the clearest path forward. Adlai Stevenson's home state of Illinois was eventually ruled out (though Kennedy would go on to win Illinois as a write-in candidate); and Ohio, Florida, and California were less appealing thanks to "favorite son" candidates Michael DiSalle, George Smathers, and Edward G. "Pat" Brown. Of the rest, one state garnered Bobby's strongest hesitation. From the beginning, and at odds with others in the room, Bobby wanted Jack to avoid Wisconsin.

Bobby Kennedy, pictured here on January 28, 1964, had serious misgivings about his brother running in the Wisconsin presidential primary. He would go on to serve as US Attorney General from 1961 to 1964. LBJ LIBRARY PHOTO BY YOICHI R. OKAMOTO

The one point upon which the whole room could agree was this: while the primary season was shaping up to be a marathon, they'd have to run it like a sprint. The physical toll would be enormous, the financial cost quite high, and at the end of it all, the primary fight could be all for nothing if the powerbrokers at the Democratic National Convention chose to shift their unbound delegates elsewhere.

Following a lunch of roast turkey at Joe Sr. and Rose's home next door, the team reassembled, this time with Bobby at the helm. This was his moment. The chance to prove to his father and older brother that, as his brother's campaign manager, he could oversee the important work ahead. The work began that afternoon, as he divvied up the nation among those in the room. Bobby pointed from one person to another, assigning each person a territory and a mission: lay the groundwork for the barnstorming soon to come. While most in the room that day were focused on helping Jack win the primaries, Ted Kennedy was given the task of winning over delegates in eleven western states. Though most of those states didn't hold primaries, they did hold state conventions at which local party leaders would choose the delegates for the national convention.

In addition to proving to skeptical convention delegates that Jack was ready for the national election, Bobby knew the primaries offered one final advantage. By enduring the primary gauntlet, Jack would emerge better prepared for the general election against Nixon. Every whistle-stop was the equivalent of a political push-up: the more you did, the stronger you became. What Bobby didn't know (what, in fact, no one knew) was that when it came to such training, no state would prove more arduous, more exhausting, or more crucial to winning the presidency than Wisconsin. Unquestionably, the West Virginia primary in May 1960, a month after Wisconsin's, would deliver the knockout blow to Humphrey's presidential run. But it was in Wisconsin—where Kennedy's initial reception could be as frosty as the weather—that he learned the necessary skills for everything to come.

Though much of Jack's success would be credited to the sixteen people in Bobby's living room that day, plenty of lesser-known people beyond those walls would go on to play vital roles, helping a future president chart the course to victory and changing the course of history in the process.

It was now or never. It was boom or bust. It was time for the Kennedy brothers to leave the safety of the shore.

PART I

Before

JULY 1948—NOVEMBER 1959

"When the going gets tough, the tough get going."
—Knute Rockne, Notre Dame Football Coach,
oft-quoted by John F. Kennedy

Dispatches from the Cranberry Bog

Philleo Nash
July 14, 1948

Eleven years, eight months, and twenty-two days
before the Wisconsin primary

As darkness fell on Wisconsin Rapids, Philleo Nash, special assistant to President Truman, reached toward his car's radio dial. Though Philleo remained hopeful that he could find reception this deep into bog country, there was no guarantee. He fiddled with the dial as one garbled voice gave way to another until at last the static turned clear.

Philleo—along with sixty million other radio listeners—was tuning in to hear the speeches from the 1948 Democratic National Convention, broadcasting live from the Philadelphia Convention Hall. The man speaking was a newcomer to the national political scene—the thirty-seven-year-old two-term mayor of Minneapolis who was making a bid for the US Senate, a folksy fellow with a receding hairline by the name of Hubert Horatio Humphrey.

As a Wisconsin native, thirty-eight-year-old Philleo was familiar with Humphrey's rising star, even though Humphrey was relatively unknown outside of the Midwest. In his first term as mayor, Humphrey had distinguished himself by his successful crackdown on crime throughout Minneapolis, a move that earned him reelection in 1947 with a staggering 66 percent of the vote.

It had been a heck of a win for the relatively new Democratic-Farmer-Labor Party, an affiliate of Minnesota's Democratic Party that Humphrey had helped form. And prospects were looking good for Humphrey himself, as he attempted to parlay his mayoral success into what would become a successful run for the US Senate that November.

Philleo would've liked to have known Humphrey better. But in 1942, Philleo left Wisconsin for Washington, DC, to serve as President Roosevelt's special appointee in the Office of War Information. In 1946, Philleo climbed the professional ladder one rung higher, serving as President Truman's Special Assistant and advising the president on matters pertaining to American Indian affairs. A decade earlier, Philleo had struck out to the Pacific Northwest to study the Klamath Indians' ghost dances, a project that earned him a PhD in anthropology from the University of Chicago. Upon his return, he began to see how policy could shape equity. And President Truman took an interest in his expertise.

Who would have dreamed that a guitar-strumming anthropologist from small-town Wisconsin Rapids would be advising presidents? And, equally unlikely, that during the 1948 Democratic

Wisconsin cranberry farmer Philleo Nash, pictured here in 1951, worked as special assistant to President Harry S. Truman from 1946 to 1952. WHI IMAGE ID 48085

convention—when Truman surely needed him—he'd be stuck tuning in from some bog far from the action.

Philleo listened as Humphrey's voice flittered through the cricket-filled night. There was no question of Truman's renomination (the president had sewn that up the previous night). Still, Philleo was missing out on the greatest three nights of Democratic Party hoopla in years. Had he been near a television set, he could've at least watched the convention live, as both the Republican and Democratic conventions were televised that year for the first time. Instead, he was alone. In a bog. Keeping an eye out for cold weather.

Since his father's death two years prior, Philleo had overseen the family's cranberry business, returning to Wisconsin when his White House duties allowed. Philleo had decided to spend much of the summer of 1948 in the bogs, even if it cost him a front-row seat to history-making nights like this one.

Philleo Nash strums a folk song on his guitar for President Truman (in the sunglasses) and others during a vacation at the Little White House in Key West in December 1951. A few weeks later, in January 1952, Wisconsin senator Joseph R. McCarthy would target Nash with unfounded accusations of communism. WHI IMAGE ID 48064

The convention's main drama had shifted from the nominee's selection to the passage of a controversial plank in the party's platform that affirmed support for racial integration. It was high time, northern Democrats argued, for the party to more fully embrace civil rights. The problem, strategically speaking, was how to adopt such a measure without alienating white southerners.

Both voting blocs were necessary for President Truman to defeat the Republican candidate, New York governor Thomas Dewey, in the fall. Would the delegation approve the civil rights plank, or would the issue tear the party apart? Pragmatically speaking, party unity was vital to governing, though philosophically, what good was a party if it refused to stand on the right side of history?

The Democrats' Platform Committee had defeated the resolution to add the civil rights plank the previous night, but Humphrey refused to yield. "My friends," Humphrey bellowed now, his voice unwavering, "to those who say that we are rushing this issue of civil rights, I say to them we are 172 years late."

Philleo leaned in closer to the radio. He knew a thing or two about being late to an issue. He had spent the preceding months working with NAACP lawyer Thurgood Marshall to support an executive order to desegregate the US armed forces, a move that should have happened years before. Truman eventually would make good on the order two weeks after the convention. But he couldn't do so until after securing the renomination, which spoke volumes about the party's disunity on the subject.

"My good friends," Humphrey continued passionately, "I ask my party, I ask the Democratic Party, to march down the high road of progressive democracy. I ask this convention to say in unmistakable terms that we proudly hail, and we courageously support, our president and leader Harry Truman in his great fight for civil rights in America!"

Nothing like putting the president on the spot. Yet Humphrey's phrasing was less caustic than congratulatory, optimistically foretelling Truman's "great fight for civil rights" rather than raking him over the coals for his slow start.

This was the most important speech the Minneapolis mayor had ever given. While some had doubted that Humphrey was up for the task, the mayor put those doubts to rest. Humphrey had been outspoken on civil rights issues for years, not for political favor, but from a place of deep conviction. Such moral clarity would lay the groundwork for Humphrey's future role as lead author of the 1964 Civil Rights Act. So what if he had a reputation for being longwinded? At least he dedicated every breath to pushing the party forward.

But moments after Humphrey finished speaking, near-chaos ensued. For eight minutes, delegates from various states engaged in a shouting match, with white southerners from Alabama and Mississippi most staunchly opposed. But "no" votes also came from Arizona and Kentucky, narrowing the plank's path to victory. In the end, thirty-five delegates from Alabama and Mississippi left the convention hall in protest.

Philleo listened as the drama unfolded. Had he been present in the hall that night, he could have helped Humphrey's cause among the delegates. Instead, those duties were left to Truman's other aides—those who weren't trapped in a bog.

This was not the way things were supposed to go.

Once the dust settled in the convention hall, the delegates voted 651½ to 582½ to adopt Humphrey's civil rights plank. Even sweeter for Philleo, Wisconsin delegates cast the deciding votes.

He'd done it. Humphrey had actually done it.

Yet because he had, party unity crumbled. Within days, the plank's most staunch opponents formed the States' Rights Democratic Party, whose members were commonly known as Dixiecrats, and nominated South Carolina governor Strom Thurmond for president. While Thurmond would, indeed, siphon votes from Truman, he would ultimately fall short of toppling the incumbent. That night at the Democratic convention, however, no one could fully predict the electoral impact of the plank's passage.

The car engine purred as Philleo started the slow drive through the bog and back toward his house. Though he was one thousand miles away from the action in Philadelphia, the signal could not have been clearer.

That night in the bog, Philleo heard the future.

Its name was Hubert Humphrey.

LOCKING HORNS AT THE STOCK YARD INN

Pat Lucey
July 25, 1952

Seven Years, Eight Months, and Eleven Days
before the Wisconsin primary

Pat Lucey stepped outside of Chicago's International Amphitheatre at the end of another long, nail-biting day at the 1952 Democratic National Convention. At thirty-four years old, Pat was the director of Wisconsin's newly formed Democratic Organizing Committee. He retreated from the crowded convention hall to have a drink at the nearby Stock Yard Inn.

The Tudor-style restaurant had a reputation as one of Chicago's finest steak houses. And, located within walking distance of the stockyards, it had the freshest meat in town. Though on this day, "fresh meat" also applied to politicians.

Peering across the room, a bespectacled Pat spied the congressman from Massachusetts's eleventh district. His name was Jack Kennedy, Pat knew, and while the boyish thirty-five-year-old Kennedy had yet to distinguish himself legislatively, Pat had high hopes for the young congressman. The two men had several things in common: both were Catholic Democrats with Irish heritage and a background in military service (Pat had served as deputy quartermaster in Puerto Rico while Jack was stationed in the Solomon Islands during World War II). And though they represented slightly different ideological branches within the party—Pat leaned left, while Jack held center—Pat liked the idea of a fellow Catholic rising through the ranks.

At the moment, though, Kennedy's political future was of little concern to Pat. More pressing was the contested convention that was leaving both men weary. Throughout the convention, jockeying for the top of the ticket—a choice between Illinois governor Adlai Stevenson II or Tennessee senator Estes Kefauver—had left Democrats frustrated and embittered. Kefauver had handily won the first two rounds of votes, but now President Truman was busily trying to persuade the "undecided, the hesitant, or the merely cautious" to support Stevenson. It was personal for President Truman; the previous year, when the Twenty-Second Amendment created presidential term limits, Truman had been exempted, allowing him to seek another term. But Truman had lost the New Hampshire primary to Kefauver—effectively ending his reelection bid. It didn't matter that Kefauver had won twelve of the fifteen primaries that year; President Truman and party bosses were maneuvering to spoil his chances at the nomination.

Kennedy strongly supported Stevenson. Privately, Pat preferred Stevenson, too; but because he loathed Truman's tactics to fix the nomination, Pat was publicly—if not enthusiastically—backing Kefauver instead.

Selecting the party's nominee was shaping up to be far more contentious than it had been in '48 when Truman had won on the first ballot. After the fallout over Humphrey's civil rights speech, the party had managed to stitch itself back together in time to pull off a win against Dewey in the general election. What remained to be seen was whether Democrats could pull it off again in '52. Pat was hardly banking on that outcome if Stevenson clinched the nomination.

Pat decided it was time to meet this Kennedy fellow. While there was much they might've discussed, Pat strode across the bar with a single topic in mind: the convention's selection of a vice-presidential candidate.

"I understand that you Stevenson people are even willing to accept a southerner for vice-president in order to nail down the nomination," Pat told Kennedy accusingly.

It was true. Amid the political horse trading, there was a growing consensus that if Stevenson won the nomination, a southerner would be selected as running mate to balance the ticket—most likely Senator John

Sparkman of Alabama, an outspoken segregationist. Propelling a man like Sparkman to such prominence was an affront to the party's civil rights platform for northern delegates like Pat.

If Kennedy was taken aback by Pat's candor, he didn't show it. Instead, he returned fire.

"Well," Kennedy said, "if you northern liberals are going to sit on your hands and not come around to support our man, the people who participate in putting together the votes to nominate him are obviously going to have a voice in selecting his running mate."

Pat seethed. Who did this elitist New Englander think he was? He bit his tongue, but privately, he was made livid by Kennedy's reference to *"you northern liberals."* How exactly did the Democratic congressman from Massachusetts envision himself? Stalking off, Pat thought of Kennedy's November Senate race against Henry Cabot Lodge Jr. Had Pat lived in Massachusetts, he imagined he'd be voting for Lodge in the next election.

A few hours later, in the early morning hours of July 26, Senator Kefauver cast Tennessee's twenty-eight votes to Stevenson, clinching the nomination for the governor from Illinois.

It's unclear whether Kennedy remembered their first meeting at the Stock Yard Inn. However, by 1959, as he eyed the presidency, he knew enough to reach out to Pat Lucey for help. Over the past decade, Pat had reignited Wisconsin's Democratic Party, rebuilding it from the ground up and infusing it with a life it hadn't seen in decades. From 1919 to 1933, the Democrats had held fewer seats in the state legislature than the Socialists for every year but two. Then, in 1948, as the party continued to struggle, Pat took matters into his own hands. That May, Pat met with several statewide Democratic leaders at the Retlaw Hotel in Fond du Lac. They'd grown weary of the party's failures as well as its state chairman, Charles Greene, who refused to leave his post despite the party's wishes. To be competitive—and to rid themselves of Greene—the party needed a fresh start.

The Progressive Party of the La Follette era had recently disbanded, leaving many of its followers at a crossroads. Did they really want to follow Bob La Follette Jr. back to the Republican Party? What they needed was a more progressive Democratic Party. Something closer to Minnesota's Democratic-Farmer-Labor Party, thriving in the state next door.

By the meeting's end, Pat and the others had begun laying the groundwork for what would become known as the Democratic Organizing Committee (DOC)—a new state Democratic organization built for winning. That fall, Pat himself was elected to the state assembly, proof that progressive candidates could win.

By 1950, the DOC had overtaken the old Wisconsin Democratic Party, solidifying itself as the state party's primary political broker. Pat was hired as director, and for the next several years, he used his position to restore the party's prominence, using the same strategy he had used during his successful campaign for a state assembly seat in 1948: grassroots politicking. For the next several years, Pat burned through shoe leather and tire treads to shift the state's political fortunes. Driving from one town to the next, he'd meet with local politicians and political aspirants, dispensing advice as best as he could. The party hardly rebuilt itself overnight, but Pat made steady progress. And it was paying off at the polls.

A car-top sign promoting Pat Lucey's 1950 congressional bid. WHI IMAGE ID 143819

After crossing paths with Kennedy at the Stock Yard Inn in 1952, Pat continued his organizing efforts. By 1959, following a decade's work, Pat and his circle of supporters had taken the state's Democratic Party off life support and returned it to good health, mainly by recruiting and running viable candidates in greater numbers than ever before.

Between 1954 and 1959, Democrats dramatically improved their odds of returning to power, running for positions both locally and statewide. Pat empowered candidates, utilizing a grassroots approach to recruit those whose values aligned with the Democratic Party. Then, he threw his support behind them, using the state's newly revamped Democratic Party to ensure competitive races.

His success, both as an organizer and recruiter, caught the attention of Jack Kennedy.

On November 13, 1959, Senator Kennedy endured blizzard-like conditions in Wisconsin (including a car-pushing incident along Kenosha's snow-slicked streets) to deliver the keynote at Wisconsin's Mid-West Conference of the Democratic Party in Milwaukee. At the convention banquet, Senator Kennedy railed again against the failure of President Dwight Eisenhower's administration to keep the United States competitive with the Soviets, referring to the previous seven years as the "years the locusts have eaten." He continued,

> I think we can close the gaps and pull ahead. It will take everyone's help, as this record makes clear—officeholders, farmers, teachers, businessmen, miners, taxpayers, workers and bankers. But together we can build a better nation—and a better, happier, more peaceful world, where life is good and men are free—and freedom never falters.

The following night, Senator Humphrey took his turn and received his own warm reception. In his remarks—which seemed particularly aimed at Kennedy—Humphrey lamented how the nation had "fallen for a kind of 'pitch' in our national life that substitutes nonsense for reality, public relations for public service, and showmanship for leadership." Humphrey went on,

This has happened to us not only in the world of TV entertainment
but in politics and government as well. We have been lured away from
the good old American values of truth and reality and not trying to
be anybody but ourselves. Let's get back to reality. Let's forget the
make-up men and go ahead and let the blemishes show.

As Humphrey's words lingered in the air, Pat was approached by Kennedy's longtime aide Ted Sorensen. Thirty-one-year-old Sorensen cornered Pat and asked him if he would be willing to support Senator Kennedy for president.

Pat remained noncommittal at first. As chair of the state's Democratic Party, he wanted to give the appearance of neutrality throughout the primary season. Privately, he thought Jack would make a great candidate—the man was smart and likable. But he had his concerns, among them the senator's less-than-sterling record as a progressive. It was the same concern he'd felt all those years before at the Stock Yard Inn when the Stevensonian wing—Kennedy among them—seemed all too willing to put a conservative segregationist on the ticket.

Perhaps Pat's hesitancy was heightened by having witnessed, just moments before, yet another rousing speech delivered by the more reliably progressive senator from the state next door, Hubert Humphrey.

Sorensen argued that the party wouldn't be able to elect anyone more liberal than Kennedy.

Pat knew Sorensen was right; Humphrey was unlikely to be a viable national candidate. He knew, too, that politicians had room to shift, and with the proper guidance, perhaps Kennedy could shift a little more in Pat's direction.

Sorensen excused himself so Pat could think on the matter. It was a heady proposition: Kennedy wanted him. Needed him, in fact, to win the Wisconsin primary.

As the Democrats in the crowded conference hall made small talk with one another, Pat felt a hint of pride. A decade ago, the room wouldn't have been half as full.

None of it had been easy, but all of it had been worth it. Every mile. Though, indeed, there were still plenty of miles to go.

Pat scanned the room, pondering the future.

He had to admit that "President Kennedy" sure had a nice ring to it.

A POLITICIAN RISES

Ivan Nestingen
August 16, 1956

Three Years, Seven Months, and Twenty Days
before the Wisconsin primary

Sitting in his living room, thirty-four-year-old Ivan Nestingen, the recently elected mayor of Madison, Wisconsin, tilted his ear toward the
radio as sounds from Chicago's 1956 Democratic National Convention
filtered into his home.

They're going to do it, Ivan thought, running a hand through his hair.
They're going to nominate Stevenson. Again.

It seemed like an all-but-done deal as he listened from one hundred
and fifty miles away. After all, Adlai Stevenson II had continued to distinguish himself since his first presidential defeat four years earlier. Following his landslide loss to Dwight Eisenhower in 1952, Stevenson had licked
his wounds by way of a world tour, meeting with dignitaries around the
globe to increase his standing as a world leader.

The intellectual wing of the party liked Stevenson well enough, Ivan
knew, but were there enough of them to get him elected? Not to mention
the other inconvenient truth facing Democrats: Stevenson had already
lost to Eisenhower four years prior. What made anyone think he'd fare
better in a rematch?

Not that the Democrats were overrun with alternatives. Their top
contenders were all longshots: New York governor W. Averell Harriman,
Senate Majority Leader Lyndon B. Johnson of Texas, and Missouri senator

19

Stuart Symington—each of whom Stevenson would best on the first ballot later that night.

What remained unclear was how Jack Kennedy—the junior senator from Massachusetts—would perform in his nominating speech for Stevenson. The last two conventions had made for some memorable moments: first, Humphrey's 1948 blistering defense of the civil rights plank, followed four years later by Stevenson's grandiose acceptance speech.

"The ordeal of the twentieth century, the bloodiest, most turbulent era of the whole Christian age, is far from over," Stevenson had said. "Sacrifice, patience, understanding, and implacable purpose may be our lot for years to come. Let's face it. Let's talk sense to the American people."

Which sounded well and good, except such a message would be better received if the messenger hadn't been raised in such an insulated political dynasty. Stevenson's great-grandfather had served as Abraham Lincoln's senate campaign manager, his grandfather had served as Grover Cleveland's vice president, and his father had been appointed Illinois secretary of state. Stevenson's political pedigree seemed to all but ensure his success, but it also raised the question: what did he know about the plight of the American people?

Similarly, Jack Kennedy had enjoyed his own privileged upbringing in Brookline, Massachusetts, bouncing from one preparatory school to the next and leaving trouble in his wake. Childish pranks marked Kennedy's high school years at the Choate School; most notoriously, a strategically placed firecracker in a toilet bowl. When Jack's boisterous behavior wasn't on display, it was often because he was confined to a hospital bed. As a child, Jack had been stricken with a mystery illness, which in 1934 was diagnosed as colitis—a digestive disease that explained his abdominal pains and weight loss (he would be diagnosed with Addison's disease about a decade later). Yet Jack's ailments did little to slow him. He graduated from Choate in 1935, and, despite middling grades, he was nonetheless named "most likely to succeed" in the yearbook.

Ivan, by contrast, spent his boyhood far removed from wealth and privilege. Born in Sparta, Wisconsin, in 1921, he worked from a young age alongside his father and four brothers in Nestingen's Quality Grocery on West Oak Street. Ivan had no deep political connections. What he had was a Norwegian father who instilled in him the importance of a hard day's work.

Ivan's high school career was far more subdued and studious than Jack Kennedy's, as well. There were no exploding toilets or medical mysteries. Instead, he studied, managed the Sparta High School basketball team, and acted in the senior class play. In his senior photo, eighteen-year-old Ivan is clean-cut, with arching eyebrows, a broad nose, and the hint of an impish smile with pronounced dimples. The humble boy from Sparta would grow up to become the youngest mayor to date in Madison's history, winning reelection twice, each time with a growing margin.

Suddenly, a Bostonian accent drifted over the airwaves, closing the distance between the International Amphitheatre and Ivan's living room.

"We have come here today," Senator Jack Kennedy began, "not merely to nominate a Democratic candidate, but to nominate a president of the United States." He continued,

> Sometimes in the heat of a political convention, we forget the grave responsibilities which we as delegates possess. For we here today are selecting a man who must be something more than a good candidate, something more than a good speaker, more than a good politician, a good liberal, or a good conservative. We are selecting the head of the most powerful nation on earth, the man who literally will hold in his hands the powers of survival or destruction, of freedom or slavery, of success or failure for us all.

That the man in question was not himself, but Stevenson, was but a minor setback. Though Kennedy knew he had no chance at the top of the ticket, what he wouldn't know until the following day was that he'd come short of securing the vice president spot by as few as thirty eight votes. Once Stevenson was formally nominated, he made a surprise move, announcing that the convention's delegates would decide his running mate. After a moment's hesitation, Kennedy quickly gauged his support and then threw himself fully into the nomination process—despite Joe Sr.'s strong reservations. If Stevenson sank like an anchor, who but Kennedy would be pulled down with him? In the end, delegates chose Estes Kefauver of Tennessee to fill the bottom half of the ticket. Bobby Kennedy later blamed Jack's failure on the Kennedy team's lack of organization. Had they better understood the needs of the state's various delegates, they might've pulled it off.

Yet in losing to Kefauver, Kennedy had inadvertently spared his political future, much to Joe Sr.'s relief. Months later, when Stevenson lost to Eisenhower by an even more considerable margin than in '52, Kennedy found himself well positioned for a run in the next presidential cycle.

On August 16, the night of Stevenson's nomination, that future remained unknown. But most everyone knew that Jack Kennedy was a man to watch. He'd been dispatched to rally fellow Democrats in support of Stevenson, and he'd done so while also directing attention back toward himself.

"These are problems that cry out for solution—they cry out for leadership—they cry out for a man equal to the times," Kennedy called, his voice reaching its crescendo. "And the Democratic Party can say to the nation today—we have such a man!"

Had Ivan been watching the speech on television, he'd have seen how Kennedy leaned firmly against the rostrum and transfixed the crowd. Kennedy didn't just sound like a leader, he looked like one—a ready-made president pulled straight from central casting.

Kennedy talked the talk, walked the walk, and had the war record to boot. Everyone who subscribed to the *New Yorker*, *Reader's Digest*, or the *Saturday Evening Post* had read about Jack's heroics in the Solomon Islands during World War II. In the aftermath of PT-109's collision with the Japanese destroyer, Jack—just twenty-six years old in 1943—had led his surviving crewmates on a three-and-a-half-mile swim to a nearby islet. Clamping a belt between his teeth, Kennedy had towed an injured crewmate for much of that distance. Such heroics would have been enough to make headlines, but what solidified Jack's status as a war hero was what happened next: how he continued his swim in search of assistance—growing hungrier and more desperate—until, days later, when he approached a pair of friendly islanders, scratched an SOS message on a coconut husk, and got himself and his crew rescued the following day.

Ivan's own military service, though distinguished, garnered fewer headlines. He enlisted in the army in March 1943, a sleek-framed, 138-pound, twenty-two-year-old soon to be shipped off to the Philippines, where, after receiving the rank of first lieutenant, he oversaw a prison work camp. For Ivan, there were no belts clamped between teeth, no messages scrawled on coconut husks. He followed orders, fulfilled his duty, and rarely spoke of his war years later. Ivan's greatest battle occurred not in the Pacific, but on the home front long after the war.

In 1954, as a thirty-three-year-old alderman on the Madison Common Council, Ivan brought the battle to Joseph McCarthy—the Republican senator from Wisconsin who for four years had tapped into the zeitgeist of the age by preying on the country's paranoia surrounding Communist infiltrators at the Department of State and beyond. Since 1950, McCarthy had indiscriminately targeted government officials and civil servants by claiming they had Communist ties. McCarthy's spurious accusations against government officials made him untouchable for a time. Anyone who dared challenge him risked finding themselves on McCarthy's list of Communists.

Wisconsin senator Joseph R. McCarthy accuses Democratic presidential candidate Adlai Stevenson II of having ties to left-wing extremists during a nationally televised speech in October 1952. WHI IMAGE ID 47424

Ivan refused to let McCarthy's fearmongering go unchecked. In March 1954, Ivan joined Sauk City newspaper editor Leroy Gore's effort to recall McCarthy and remove him from office. On March 18, Gore published an editorial in the *Sauk Prairie Star*, baldly stating, "The Senator Joseph McCarthy of March 1954 is NOT the man the people of Wisconsin elected to the United States Senate in 1952." Gore's fiery argument followed, inspiring anti-McCarthyites statewide to gather in Sauk City to formally organize the "Joe Must Go" Club. Ivan became the organization's secretary. With eight hundred members and chapters across the state, the grassroots campaign flourished. And while the recall effort ultimately fell short of ousting McCarthy, the club collectively gathered some four hundred thousand signatures, the most signatures on a notarized petition in US history to date.

For a little-known alderman to take on a US senator was a bold proposition. Yet Ivan's head-on collision course with Senator McCarthy ultimately served him well, elevating his reputation within progressive circles and playing a role in his assembly seat win in November 1954 and Madison's mayorship in 1956.

More foreseeable had been Jack Kennedy's political rise, which—like Stevenson's—seemed just shy of a birthright.

Union members from United Packinghouse Workers Local 40 sign the "Joe Must Go" petition to recall Senator McCarthy. WHI IMAGE ID 67434

But it was not without its setbacks.

On December 2, 1954, in a bipartisan vote, sixty-seven senators voted to censure Senator McCarthy for the "dishonor and disrepute" he'd brought to their hallowed chamber. Kennedy was the only Democrat whose vote remained suspiciously uncast. Of course, he'd concocted a cover story—he had been recovering from back surgery on the day of the vote, which was technically true but hardly an excuse to remain silent. Had he wanted to, Jack easily could have released a public statement to be read on the Senate floor. Instead, he'd stayed mum.

His silence was motivated by the Kennedy family's friendship with McCarthy. Not only had McCarthy dated a couple of Jack's sisters but he'd also helped Bobby Kennedy land a job on the Permanent Subcommittee on Investigations. McCarthy had even vacationed with the Kennedy family, and Joe Sr. gave generously to McCarthy's reelections. As if that were not enough, Jack Kennedy had attended McCarthy's wedding, and McCarthy himself served as the godfather for Bobby's first child. For personal reasons, it would've been an excruciatingly tough vote for Jack. But this was politics; tough votes happened all the time.

Despite their differences, and even as it remained to be seen whether Wisconsinites would forgive Kennedy for his cowardice on the McCarthy censure, Ivan and Jack were politically well aligned. Idealists, they both dreamed the same dream of a "new frontier," vastly different than Senator McCarthy's nightmarish alternative.

Throughout Jack's three days at the 1956 convention, he'd exceeded all expectations. To great acclaim, he'd narrated the convention's opening night film, delivered an inspiring nominating speech, and parlayed losing the vice president spot into a personal win.

"He had made such a very outstanding appearance in defeat," Ivan later remarked. "And subsequently it was quite well indicated that one way or another that he was interested in being on the national ticket in 1960."

Rising from his chair after Kennedy's speech, Ivan started the walk toward bed, careful not to wake his wife or young daughters.

He didn't yet know it, but his life was about to change forever.

Soon, Senator Jack Kennedy would come calling.

And Ivan would answer.

Kennedy for Proxmire

Philleo Nash, Jerry Bruno, and Vel Phillips
August 22, 1957

Two years, seven months, and fourteen days
before the Wisconsin primary

On a cool August morning in 1957, Senator Jack Kennedy's plane cut through the predawn clouds over the Milwaukee airport and prepared to land. Wisconsin's Democratic candidate for Senate, William Proxmire, was in trouble. And Proxmire's team hoped Kennedy was the man to help.

On the ground, Philleo Nash peered up at the sky, waiting to welcome Kennedy and whisk him away for a grueling eighteen hours of campaigning.

Philleo's presence that day was mostly one of duty. After his time in the Truman administration, Philleo had returned to Wisconsin full time to run the family's cranberry business and was now chair of the Wisconsin Democratic Party. As state party chair, it was his job to help Democrats win back the Senate seat, even though Proxmire wasn't necessarily Philleo's favorite candidate.

For Proxmire's aide Jerry Bruno, however, meeting Kennedy that morning would end up feeling more like fate.

Four years earlier, on an evening in 1953, twenty-eight-year-old Jerry Bruno had finished his shift as a forklift driver at Kenosha's American

Motors factory and joined a buddy at Pete's Bar, a local watering hole where the pair occasionally met for a beer. They hadn't been there long before Jerry's friend mentioned he'd overheard something about a political meeting taking place one floor up.

Curious, Jerry started up the stairs. There, on the second floor of the Kenosha bar, he met the man who would change his life forever: thirty-eight-year-old former state assemblyman William Proxmire, a failed gubernatorial candidate in 1952 with plans to run again in '54. No sooner had Proxmire introduced himself than Jerry took to him, not only because of Proxmire's progressive politics but because the man knew how to listen. Jerry peppered him with questions about his campaign and platform, and Proxmire answered each question patiently and thoughtfully, treating Jerry like an equal. Jerry later recalled,

> This guy Proxmire was somebody I'd never met and never really heard of. But he looked like he cared about what I was asking. He took the time to explain something to me, and he finished by asking me to help him run for governor in any little way I could. That meant a hell of a lot. Nobody had ever asked me what I thought of anything before. I couldn't imagine how anybody running for governor could need my help, but Proxmire had taken the trouble to *ask*—and that was enough for me.

Jerry was no stranger to hard work. As a child, he and his siblings had joined their parents—emigrants from Cosenza, Italy—in picking onions in the fields around Kenosha. When Jerry was in ninth grade, the Depression struck, and he dropped out of school to find work to help support his family. From 1945 to 1947, Jerry served in the navy, returning to Kenosha in 1952 to work for American Motors. In many ways, Jerry's life had been defined by work. Why not do a little more for this Proxmire fellow?

Shortly after meeting Proxmire in the bar, Jerry volunteered to serve as secretary of the Kenosha County Proxmire for Governor Club. During Proxmire's third gubernatorial run in 1956, Jerry took on the statewide role of chairman of the Proxmire for a Better Wisconsin Club—taking a leave of absence from his American Motors job to hand out leaflets, organize rallies, and sell political buttons. In his early years campaigning for

Proxmire, Jerry didn't know much about politics, but he knew plenty about organizing, thanks to his affiliation with United Auto Workers Local 72.

In the spring of 1954, when union members at the Kohler Company went on strike to improve their wages and other portions of their contract, Jerry and his compatriots from UAW Local 72 began picketing and protesting in solidarity. If the nation's second-largest plumbing supply company was unwilling to negotiate with employees, then the employees refused to work. For a time, Jerry dedicated his Sunday nights to the strike, putting himself at physical risk for a cause he believed in. The strike eventually led to hundreds of arrests, though an undeterred Jerry returned to the picket line week after week. In 1960, the National Labor Relations Board ruled against the Kohler Company, effectively ending what many consider the longest major strike in US history.

For Jerry, the strike was about more than the outcome. It was the training ground where he'd learned to organize, publicize, and bring out a crowd—all skills that would prove helpful to Proxmire in statewide elections. When it came to campaign logistics, Jerry possessed a sixth sense. He could look at a room and see the best way to jam the most folks into it. Where some saw a street, Jerry saw a parade route. He put these talents to use for Proxmire, and despite Proxmire's unsuccessful bids for the governorship in 1954 and 1956, Jerry remained loyal. Proxmire's time would come.

And it did, in May 1957, when the red-baiting Senator Joseph McCarthy died at age forty-eight of alcohol-related liver failure (although officially his cause of death was listed as "hepatitis, acute, cause unknown").

McCarthy's death finally achieved what the "Joe Must Go" movement and Boston lawyer Joseph Welch couldn't. In June 1954, in what became known as the Army–McCarthy hearings, Welch defended the US Army from some of McCarthy's more scathing charges against it. The hearings were televised, and the entire nation was able to watch as Welch delivered a line that would become famous. After McCarthy lobbed an unfounded allegation that one of Welch's attorneys had ties to a Communist organization, Welch retorted, "Until this moment, Senator, I think I never really gauged your cruelty or your recklessness."

McCarthy attempted a rebuttal, but he was quickly silenced as Welch kept going.

"Let us not assassinate this lad further, Senator," Welch said angrily. "You have done enough. Have you no sense of decency, sir, at long last?"

Those words broke McCarthy's spell. His national following all but disappeared, his party abandoned him, and he soon faced censure from his colleagues in the Senate. Though McCarthy was never officially pried from his post, the final three years of his career were ruined.

Now, there was the matter of filling the late senator's seat—a seat, with Jerry's help, that Proxmire hoped to fill.

Proxmire had a problem. His first marriage to Elsie Rockefeller had recently ended in divorce, and he'd married Ellen Sawall. Unfortunately, Proxmire's divorce weakened his support in the Catholic-heavy districts

William Proxmire and his wife, Ellen (to Proxmire's right), with supporters of Proxmire's campaign to fill the Senate seat left vacant by the death of Senator McCarthy.
WHI IMAGE ID 30142

around Green Bay and Milwaukee. It was support he couldn't afford to lose if he wanted to beat his special election opponent, Republican Walter Kohler Jr., especially as he'd already lost to Kohler in gubernatorial races twice before.

If Proxmire wanted to win, he needed Kennedy's help securing the Catholic vote—even though Proxmire himself was lukewarm about the prospect of Kennedy's visit. The divorce issue wasn't going away, but it could be downplayed if Kennedy spoke on Proxmire's behalf. But Kennedy risked being a liability, too, since he'd done nearly nothing to halt McCarthy's reign of terror. It was a choice that continued to haunt him— especially in Wisconsin, where Kennedy's silence had been unforgivable.

Nationally, the stakes could not have been higher. The winners of two special elections in Wisconsin and Texas would determine control of the US Senate. This is why the Catholic congressman from Massachusetts had been recruited to give Proxmire a lift.

Of course, for Jack Kennedy, his first visit to Wisconsin was about more than Proxmire. Ever since Jack's 1956 nominating speech for Stevenson, Democrats had begun taking a keen interest in their rising star. Kennedy's visit was a chance for the unannounced presidential hopeful to see how well he might be welcomed in a key midwestern state—information that he and the Democratic National Committee were anxious to receive.

Jerry had never met Jack Kennedy, but shortly after Kennedy stepped from the plane, Jerry felt an immediate kinship. "I think I had the same feeling about John Kennedy that I'd had about Proxmire the first time I'd met him," Jerry later said, "a sense of disbelief that this wealthy, glamorous man who was thinking about running for president actually gave a damn about what I thought of anything."

Kennedy was a hard fellow not to like. To keep track of acquaintances, he assiduously recorded names and personal details on index cards. He wrote thank-you notes. He smiled. When summoned to Wisconsin to mend a fence, he mended it. Or tried to, at least.

Minutes after landing, Kennedy, Philleo, Jerry, and the rest of the entourage headed for the first stop of the morning: Kosciuszko Park on Milwaukee's Southside. There, Kennedy and Wisconsin congressman Clement Zablocki laid a wreath on the Tadeusz Kosciuszko Memorial, honoring the Polish Lithuanian statesman and war hero while giving a nod to Wisconsin's Polish Catholic population. The ceremony would have made a fine photo, if only the staffer whose job it was to snap the picture had remembered to load the film. Suddenly the easy-going, self-assured man with whom Jerry had felt an immediate kinship was replaced by a visibly irritated Jack Kennedy.

"I laid this wreath," Jack said frostily to Jerry.

Meaning: what good was going to the trouble of traveling to the park and laying the wreath if Wisconsin's Catholic community never saw the photo? Without a picture in the papers, it was as if the event never happened. One of the first rules of politics was to spread one's message widely. Which required loading the film.

It was the kind of misstep for which Jack Kennedy had no patience. He demanded planning and precision, and already the trip had failed on both fronts.

Still, they had a schedule to attend to. Their next stop: a nearby Catholic church, where the situation continued to deteriorate.

At the church, Jack was informed that Proxmire (a "real loner" Jerry later remarked, who "never wanted to have anybody involved in his campaigns") had tried to duck out on the appearance altogether.

Jack seethed. He'd woken early, flown eight hundred miles, laid a wreath in an empty park, and steeled himself for a nonstop day of campaigning. And for what? To be ditched by a chronically losing former state assemblyman who didn't want to be seen with him?

Though the day was scheduled to conclude later that night with a dinner in Green Bay, Jack had second thoughts. If this was how Proxmire was going to behave, then why not scrap Green Bay altogether?

Jerry, who'd been working with Proxmire for a couple of years by then, decided it was best to backchannel the problem with Proxmire's wife, Ellen. Maybe she could talk some sense into him.

"You know, the senator is not going to go to Green Bay," Jerry told Ellen. "He's really ticked off at Prox because he doesn't want to stay with him."

Ellen was having none of it.

"Get on the plane," Ellen ordered her husband, "go to Green Bay with him, and be seen with Kennedy. He's going to help you with the Catholic vote."

Begrudgingly, Proxmire agreed.

As Jerry worked to manage Proxmire, Philleo accompanied Jack to the office of the *Milwaukee Journal* for an off-the-record conversation with the newspaper's editorial board. For Proxmire's campaign staff, the meeting's objective was clear: prevent the paper from formally endorsing Proxmire's opponent, Walter Kohler. Following McCarthy's death, the *Journal* had endorsed Kohler in the Republican primary, making it likely that their endorsement would carry into the special election against Proxmire, as well. Philleo knew the *Journal* likely wouldn't endorse Proxmire, for whom the paper had shown little affection. But if the *Journal* remained neutral in the race, its silence would serve Proxmire.

Though the specifics of the conversation that day are lost, the effects of Jack's performance before the editorial board are not. Despite Proxmire's less-than-warm welcome, the senator nonetheless got the job done. He mustered the magic that was required of him, ultimately persuading the paper to express no preference in the race. It was the best-case scenario for Proxmire. Philleo later remarked,

> But something else was accomplished [in that meeting], and that is that Jack Kennedy showed what he really was made of with that editorial conference in the extent of his information, which was very full and detailed; of his coolness under close questioning; of his terseness in reply, and in presentation.

It was, Philleo said, "one of the most impressive ad lib performances that I've ever seen anywhere, and he made a lot of friends for himself on that conference board that morning, including yours truly."

To Jerry's relief, the day improved following the morning's missteps. Jack's strong performance with the editorial board served as a perfect spring-board for his next stop: a luncheon in downtown Milwaukee at the Pfister Hotel. In his remarks, Jack reminded attendees of the importance of two-party representation in the Senate. Republican Alexander Wiley currently held Wisconsin's other Senate seat, and a Democrat like Proxmire could restore the balance, rather than shut out Wisconsin Democrats altogether.

"The party that is in [power] doesn't care too much what it does," Jack said. "I don't think you could strike a stronger blow for the advancement of that interest in this state then to elect a Democrat as a senator."

The man who had been slighted by Proxmire for most of the morning was now fighting tooth and nail on the candidate's behalf. Rather than grumble, Jack smiled. Rather than critique the candidate, he praised the man instead.

Kennedy wasn't the only one holding his tongue. Seated at Kennedy's table was thirty-three-year-old Vel Phillips, who, the previous year, had become the first woman and first Black person elected to Milwaukee's Common Council. A loyal supporter of Proxmire, Vel had been reluctant to attend the luncheon because of her mixed feelings toward Senator Kennedy. She liked him generally and was disappointed when he failed to win the second spot on the Stevenson ticket back in '56. But at the same time, Vel believed Kennedy had fallen short when he voted no on the 1957 Civil Rights Act's Jury Trial Amendment, which guaranteed jury trials in civil contempt cases and standardized how federal juries were selected. Both

Vel Phillips, during a 1961 sit-in at the Wisconsin State Capitol in support of fair-housing legislation. WHI IMAGE ID 28114

provisions were meant to ensure that white juries couldn't simply acquit white perpetrators of voter suppression. Why on earth would Kennedy vote against such a thing?

As a result, Vel had initially declined the luncheon invitation, but she agreed to attend after further coaxing from a friend.

Vel politely listened to Kennedy throughout the luncheon, though when the senator introduced himself and asked for her support, Vel felt compelled to tell him the truth. "You know, I have been a great fan of yours," she began, "but I might as well tell you frankly, I was very disappointed at your vote on the Jury Trial Amendment. I just couldn't understand it; I didn't like it."

"Well, Mrs. Phillips," Kennedy said, "if you have a moment I'd like to explain that to you."

Kennedy and Vel slipped away from the room and spoke privately for fifteen minutes. Kennedy admitted that, given his lack of experience with what he called the "minority problem," he'd grown reliant on advisers to direct him. In this instance, he conceded, perhaps those advisers had led him astray. He would try harder, he told Vel, to reach his own conclusions rather than rely too much on others.

Vel was taken by the sincerity of his explanation, which allowed him to accept responsibility, acknowledge room for growth, and commit himself to do better.

She thought: *Well, what can you say when someone is that forthright?*

Jack's charm won the day, even though the day was cut short. While Jerry could never be sure whether sour grapes, a scheduling snafu, or exhaustion prompted Jack to leave Green Bay earlier than expected, the result remained the same. Citing the following day's commitments and a need to make a plane connection, Kennedy cut short his planned remarks.

Shortly before ten o'clock, Jerry thanked the senator for coming, apologized for the mishaps, and hoped their paths might cross again.

Late that night, Philleo accompanied Jack, adviser Ted Sorensen, and Congressman Zablocki on the puddle-jump plane ride from Milwaukee to Chicago. Peering down at the shadowy heartland far below, Sorensen broached the topic that had surely been weighing on Jack's mind throughout the day: how might Wisconsin voters respond to a Jack Kennedy presidential primary run?

Sorensen shrouded his question as a hypothetical, but Philleo heard the real meaning. Though Philleo was loyal to Humphrey, he couldn't deny that Jack Kennedy had made a strong first impression in Wisconsin. Kennedy's performance before the editorial board had been remarkable, though no more so than his interactions at the luncheon and dinner. Kennedy was a man who could as easily speak to a roomful of suits as a crowded legion hall, a man who could quickly home in on the parts of the Proxmire campaign that needed support and then do his part to support them.

Jubilant supporters dance in the streets of Milwaukee to celebrate Proxmire's win.
WHI IMAGE ID 30197

If Kennedy's visit to Wisconsin was meant to serve as an electability test, Philleo believed he had passed it.

"And that ended one of the most interesting days that I've ever spent in my life," Philleo reflected later, "and my first intimate contact with Jack Kennedy."

Five days later, when William Proxmire defeated Walter Kohler Jr. by more than one hundred thousand votes, the political world was paying close attention. Not only was Proxmire the first Democratic senator elected in Wisconsin since 1932, but he'd won against a popular, two-time Republican governor with statewide name recognition. Across the nation, Republican operatives worried that Kohler's defeat in Wisconsin served as a harbinger for the 1958 midterms. They were right to worry.

While Republicans were wringing their hands, Democrats like Jerry celebrated—not just for Proxmire's win, but for the fact Proxmire had won the seat once held by the state's disgraced senator.

Gone were the days of Tailgunner Joe, hopefully once and for all.

The blue wave was coming.

Back in Washington, Jack Kennedy took note.

THE UNANNOUNCED CAMPAIGN BEGINS

Ira Kapenstein
April 9–11, 1959

Eleven months and twenty-seven days
before the Wisconsin primary

I ra Kapenstein, the twenty-three-year-old Washington correspondent for the *Milwaukee Journal*, wove his way toward the back of the Crystal Ballroom in Milwaukee's Schroeder Hotel.

The date: Thursday, April 9, 1959.

The assignment: The Gridiron Dinner.

While Ira was one of the younger people in the room, his youth was not to be confused with inexperience. Since 1953, Ira had taken on any assignment that crossed his desk, first as a student writer for the State University of Iowa's *Daily Iowan* and later as a reporter for the *Milwaukee Journal* covering an array of beats, from obituaries to sports. Only recently had he landed the political beat, and it suited him. Gone were the fluff pieces of the past; suddenly, Ira's words took on new importance. Not only for the thousands of newspaper readers in Wisconsin but also for the politicians who read the ink.

Ira enjoyed his proximity to power, but the feeling wasn't always mutual. Few things could sink a politician faster than a news story. The wrong headline above the fold in a weekend edition could be a career ender. Out of necessity, a cold peace generally existed between politicians and the reporters who covered them. Politicians were polite, the press was professional, and social engagements between the two groups were few and far between.

This was precisely what made the Milwaukee Press Club's annual Grid-iron Dinner so much fun. It was that rare, let-down-your-hair gathering that was absent of hard questions and headlines. Well, mostly absent of headlines. Someone still had to cover the event, and since Ira was the newspaper's junior reporter, that duty fell to him.

Ira didn't mind. Especially given the dinner's keynote speaker: Massachusetts senator Jack Kennedy. This would be Ira's first chance to cover the senator closely. Kennedy had been well received during his past visits to Wisconsin, Ira knew, especially while campaigning for Proxmire back in '57. But this trip was different because Jack Kennedy was sticking around.

It was officially billed as a "speaking tour," but Kennedy insiders knew it was a fact-finding mission. It was the same fact-finding mission that began in 1957 and would take Kennedy to forty-seven states. How would the senator be received? What chance did he have to win a primary, or, perhaps, the various states' electoral votes in a general election?

For three days Kennedy would crisscross Wisconsin, beginning in Milwaukee. And through it all, Ira would be there. Stay close, that was the rule—you never knew when a story might develop. Not that Ira was out to embarrass Kennedy; he was simply doing his job. A job made all the easier when politicians enjoyed their attention from the press. And Kennedy did. Rather than keep the press at arm's length, he welcomed them heartily.

Kennedy viewed the press as a tool to be used to his advantage. When a politician knew how to engage with the press, the copy wrote itself.

What remained to be seen, however, was whether this particular politician knew how to connect with the wider population of Wisconsin voters. Though on the surface Kennedy didn't appear to have much in common with the average Wisconsinite—in terms of wealth, religion, or geography—the man knew how to hold a room.

That became abundantly clear to Ira moments later when, following some lengthy remarks by Wisconsin governor Gaylord Nelson, Senator Kennedy made his way to the mic. Ira flipped to a fresh page in his notepad and prepared himself for the notetaking to come. Beyond the question of how Kennedy would be received tonight was the more important question of how he might be received a year later, on April 5, 1960—the night of the Wisconsin primary.

That is, if he decided to make a run for the White House by way of Wisconsin.

Murmurs in the press pool had centered around that question, as well as whether Kennedy might use this three-day trip across the state as a springboard for a future presidential run. Oh, how every reporter yearned for some on-the-record comment on the matter. Even a noncommittal commitment would do—which they knew was about all they could expect from Jack Kennedy.

For years, Kennedy's cat-and-mouse game with the press was part of what drew them in. Theirs was a grand flirtation, a coy will-he-or-won't-he that kept newspaper readers and writers on the edge of their seats. Kennedy loved rebuffing rumors of his presidential candidacy. The advantage of revealing nothing was that a nonanswer always ensured a follow-up question. A few more lines of press. A bit more chatter. Sometimes making the news, Kennedy knew, meant withholding it.

Just hours into his trip, the game had begun.

Already, Kennedy had informed the press that as far as primaries went, Wisconsin was "an extremely important state in a key geographic area of the country." He added, too, that given the likelihood of so many Democratic presidential hopefuls, the Wisconsin primary might "look like a campus telephone booth next year."

But all joking aside, Kennedy's interest in the state was undeniable. What was it the Kennedy aide had said earlier that day? That Wisconsin was "fraught with interest" for the senator?

Fraught with interest? What were they to make of that?

In some ways it was the perfect response: evasive enough to reveal nothing, but enticing enough to make the papers.

Mindful of the uncertainty he had stoked, a straight-faced Kennedy stood at the rostrum at the front of the ballroom and appeared to address the elephant in the room.

"I have chosen this forum at this time to make a very important announcement," Kennedy began.

Ira readied his pencil. Was this the moment they'd been waiting for?

Kennedy continued. "I will not, under any conditions or circumstances, be a candidate in 1960—"

Gasp!

"—of the Milwaukee Press Club."

The crowd erupted in laughter, and Ira grinned.

If ever a politician knew how to make good use of the pause before the punchline, surely it was Kennedy.

As the crowd quieted, Kennedy's remarks turned serious:

> We have been speaking lightly here tonight about our political differences and disagreements. We have left no doubt that our parties and our politicians and our newspapers are not always in agreement with each other. There are some who would conceal these divisions—there are many who deplore them. For unity has become a popular goal of our times. . . . But it would be a tragedy, it seems to me, if in our quest for unity we chose the lowest common denominator of agreement in preference to a program of high enterprise in noble causes. For we in this country have always placed our trust and respect in the people. We believe in proving our credentials and our principles in the open competition of ideas. We prefer sturdy dissent to timorous unity. So let the debate go on—and may the best ideas prevail.

Ira's pencil scratched his notepad. While Kennedy was ostensibly speaking about press relations, Ira couldn't help but hear the early rumblings of a presidential stump speech. Placing "our trust and respect in the people?" An "open competition of ideas?" The subtext was clear: this was a precampaign campaign speech.

"For what we need now in this nation, more than atomic power, or air power, or financial, industrial or even manpower, is brainpower," Kennedy said. "The dinosaur was bigger and stronger than anyone else . . . but he was also dumber. And look what happened to him."

Another chuckle rippled through the ballroom.

Kennedy focused much of the remainder of his speech on international issues, with references as geographically wide ranging as Germany, Algeria, and the Soviet Union and an emphasis on the need for bold leaders with bold ideas ready for the world stage.

Perhaps, Jack Kennedy implied, a bold leader like him.

Ira flipped to a fresh page in his notebook. The campaign coverage had begun.

The following afternoon—after a morning at the University of Wisconsin–Milwaukee and a luncheon at Sheboygan's Foeste Hotel—Kennedy, Ira, and the rest of the entourage arrived in Beloit. A railroad town with riverfront property, Beloit was home to Beloit College—a liberal arts school whose student body leaned conservative. Kennedy, who liked a good challenge, strode toward the campus's Eaton Chapel unfazed.

Designed in the Romanesque style, the nineteenth-century chapel was the campus's crown jewel: a bats-in-the-belfry, weatherworn structure, complete with rounded arches and ornate carvings etched into stone.

As Kennedy entered to find a crowd of five hundred students, Ira stayed just a few steps behind, part of a press pool that included local and national journalists and even a student reporter from the college's newspaper.

For much of the afternoon, the students peppered the senator with questions. One student asked how Kennedy would have handled the Little Rock school integration crisis, to which Kennedy replied, "It is the basic responsibility of the executive to enforce the laws . . . and if challenged the executive must bring power to bear." (Though in an attempt to soften the stance, he noted, too, the "adverse effect" of arming paratroopers with bayonets and dispatching them to the south.)

But the question that rankled Kennedy the most was the one he would continue to field for some time: what chance did a Catholic have of becoming president?

"It has not been a hindrance to my political career to date," Kennedy coolly replied. He conceded the answer would be determined at the polls, and he hoped that Americans had the good sense to cast their votes "on the basis of personal competency rather than church affiliation."

Ira knew a thing or two about the isolating effects of religion. As a Brooklyn-born Jew studying journalism in Iowa City, Ira had found himself in the minority among Catholics, Methodists, and Lutherans. As a journalist, Ira had the good fortune of not having to answer for his religion daily. Kennedy, however, was not so lucky. For the next year and a half, Kennedy would be regularly confronted with the Catholic question. Throughout that time, he would try out an array of answers, at last hitting all the right notes in September 1960, less than a month before the general election.

"Contrary to common newspaper usage, I am not the Catholic candidate for president," he would say that day to the Greater Houston Ministerial Association, with a hint of indignance in his voice.

> I am the Democratic Party's candidate for president who happens also to be a Catholic. . . . But if this election is decided on the basis that forty million Americans lost their chance of being president on the day they were baptized, then it is the whole nation that will be the loser, in the eyes of Catholics and non-Catholics around the world, in the eyes of history, and in the eyes of our own people.

Had Kennedy produced that answer during his stop in Beloit, he might've dispensed with the Catholic question once and for all.

In the meantime, there was another question worth squirming about, and Ira was dumbfounded that no one was asking it. After Kennedy's speech at Eaton Chapel, as reporters casually waited outside, Ira wondered aloud why no one was curious about Kennedy's dodge of the McCarthy censure back in '54. So far, no journalist had been bold enough to bring up the McCarthy controversy. Why had Kennedy avoided the vote?

"If somebody doesn't ask about it pretty soon," Ira said offhandedly, "I will."

The comment caught the attention of a man who happened to be standing nearby—Dave Powers, Kennedy's longtime friend and a key figure in the senator's so-called Irish Mafia. Powers's loyalty to Kennedy ran deep, and though he hadn't intended to infiltrate the press pool that day, his close proximity to Ira allowed him to overhear the comment all the same.

Powers slipped back to Kennedy, new information in tow: they ought to keep an eye on this Ira fellow.

The following night—after a breakfast in Madison, followed by visits to Janesville and Green Bay—Kennedy wrapped up his tour in a church basement in Appleton. More than a little weary after three days of whirlwind travel, Ira paused to catch his breath. Almost as exhausting as running for office, it seemed, was reporting on it.

As Kennedy concluded his final speech, a flurry of hands lifted high in the air.

A reporter from Appleton, Wisconsin, finally asked the question: How does the senator respond to Eleanor Roosevelt's quote that Kennedy ought to have shown "less profile and more courage" when it came to Joe McCarthy's censure vote?

The jab, of course, was a perfect play on Kennedy's Pulitzer Prize–winning book, *Profiles in Courage*. Though the quote had been well reported, the criticism still stung. For the first time all visit, Kennedy was flummoxed. Not even the Catholic question had caught him so off guard. All conviviality deserted him. Though he must have known the question was coming, there was simply no answer to satisfy the Wisconsinites sitting before him in the church basement.

Eleanor Roosevelt had long been a vocal critic of the Kennedy family. Her frustrations had started with Joseph Kennedy Sr., for his appeasement of Hitler while serving as ambassador to Great Britain in the leadup to World War II. Yet her criticism of the Kennedys hardly stopped there. In 1956, she had flatly refused to support Jack Kennedy's bid for the vice presidency, in no small part because of his dodgy refusal to vote on McCarthy's censure.

While Franklin D. Roosevelt Jr. would be Kennedy's avid supporter and surrogate throughout the primary and beyond, Eleanor often provided a neutralizing effect—throwing cold water on Kennedy's effort to win over one of the most revered members of his party.

Finally, Kennedy informed his audience that he welcomed criticism from Mrs. Roosevelt, or anyone else, on the matter.

Ira scribbled the response in his notepad.

Though Kennedy's nonanswer might not have seemed newsworthy, the fact that the question has been asked at all—and that McCarthy's ghost had been resurrected at close range—was proof that Wisconsin voters hadn't forgotten the trespass.

Though his story had already been filed, Ira raced to the nearest phone to call in this last-minute addition. Much to his surprise, the detail made it into the final copy in Sunday's late edition.

Days later, Ira received a telegram from Senator Kennedy thanking him for his coverage of his Wisconsin visit. "The one regret I have in connection with your being with us was occasioned by something beyond my control," Kennedy wrote. "The deadline which your paper fixes and the untimeliness of your [McCarthy] questioner were responsible for your inability to file the story you waited for so long."

Ira realized that the senator had read the early edition of the paper and not the later one, which, in fact, *had* included the quote about McCarthy.

But even more shocking to Ira was that the senator had known of his interest in the McCarthy question to begin with.

How? Ira wondered.

Later, the pieces came together—how his lip-flapping near Eaton Chapel had been overheard by Powers, who had passed it along to Kennedy.

Taking to his typewriter, Ira thanked the senator for his kind note and assured him that the quote had, in fact, made the late edition of the paper. No need for "regret" after all.

As a peace offering of sorts, Ira also sent along a more favorable article he'd written about the visit, for which Kennedy thanked him in a more sincere follow-up letter.

As Ira held the senator's letters in his hands, one fact was clear: Senator Jack Kennedy now knew the name Ira Kapenstein.

He wouldn't soon forget it.

Breakfast at Kennedy's

Jerry Bruno
June 1959

Approximately ten months before the Wisconsin primary

By 1959, after a brief stint running Senator William Proxmire's home office in Milwaukee, Jerry Bruno had moved to Washington, DC, to serve as Proxmire's "Wisconsin secretary," handling much of the senator's constituency casework. One day, while riding the private subway between the Senate office building and the Capitol, Jerry heard a familiar voice: "Hey Jerry, how's Wisconsin? How's Proxmire doing? Is he still anti-everybody?"

Jerry glanced over to find Senator Jack Kennedy seated directly alongside him.

Jerry turned flush, remembering all too well Jack's near-disastrous Wisconsin trip back in 1957.

Proxmire? Anti-everybody? That didn't seem quite right. But anti-*some* people, on *some* days, during a heated election? That he could agree with.

"Listen," Jack said, changing the subject, "I may run for president. What do you think of my chances in the Wisconsin primary?"

What do I think? Jerry wondered.

It was the kind of question he didn't get asked every day, certainly not from anyone who stood a real shot. Jerry paused before responding.

"Well, Humphrey's very viable," Jerry finally said. "He's like our third senator. He's always been around for labor. He's going to be a tough guy to beat."

Jack nodded. He'd come to the same conclusion.

But Jerry hadn't said that Kennedy ought not to run, or that he didn't stand a chance against Humphrey. Which, to Kennedy, sounded a lot like a starting pistol.

There was something about Jerry—his boldness, his bravado, his get-the-job-done-at-all-costs mentality—that Kennedy liked. At five foot five, it wasn't uncommon for Jerry to be the shortest person in the room, but he was never overlooked. Jerry was the small dog with the big bite. Mr. Fix It. A one-man clean-up crew. But most of all, Jerry was Jerry: unflinching, unwavering, rock steady. The scrappy fighter who always had your back.

Which was just what Kennedy needed.

That June, Jerry happened to run into Kennedy again, this time in the corridor outside the senator's office. Jack ushered Jerry inside, but they were quickly interrupted by a phone call.

"I'm not going to be able to talk," Jack told Jerry, covering the receiver with his hand. "Why don't you come and have breakfast with me tomorrow morning? My secretary will give you the directions."

Dumbfounded by this sudden attention, Jerry agreed.

At eight thirty the following morning, Jerry parked outside the Kennedys' private Georgetown residence, half an hour early. The last thing he wanted was to keep them waiting, but equally embarrassing would be arriving too soon. What if he woke baby Caroline? Or Jackie? Or the senator himself? He sat in his car as the minutes ticked by, wondering what on earth Kennedy wanted with him.

At the appointed time, Jerry straightened his suitcoat and made his way to 3307 N Street, a lean, Federal-style rowhouse with a black front door and matching shutters. Jerry recognized the front door from the news—it was often the backdrop for Kennedy's press conferences—but he never dreamed he'd be walking through it.

Jerry took a deep breath, checked his tie, and then knocked.

Jack welcomed him in, though the greeting did little to ease Jerry's nerves. He couldn't help but remember how perturbed the senator had been during the wreath-laying ceremony in Milwaukee two years prior.

How the staffer had forgotten to load the film and the fallout that had resulted. Not to mention Proxmire's refusal to be seen with the guy.

Hell hath no fury like a slighted senator, Jerry knew.

If Jack remembered their rocky start, he didn't mention it. Instead, he directed Jerry to a seat at the lavish breakfast table and, as the sun streamed through the tall windows and a wide-awake eighteen-month-old Caroline raced toward the kitchen, Jack picked up the conversation where they'd left off the previous day.

Jack asked Jerry questions about Wisconsin politics, Humphrey's strength as a potential primary opponent, and the allegiances of the state's major players. Jerry answered as best as he could, though within minutes, it became clear to them both that the senator was as knowledgeable as Jerry was. No doubt about it, Jack had done his homework on Wisconsin's political scene. Jerry's lifetime in the state still hadn't leveled the playing field.

"I'd had experience in Wisconsin working in a Senate race," Jerry later recalled, "but talking about the presidency, that was something else."

Jerry worried he'd failed to impress the senator, but Jack Kennedy felt differently. Jerry was a little rough around the edges, sure, but that's what Jack needed. After all, Jack was already neck deep in tweed-jacketed Ivy Leaguers. Plus, Jerry was a navy vet, which Jack liked, and he rivaled Ivan Nestingen and Pat Lucey in his knowledge of Wisconsin politics. If Jack hoped to win support from the Proxmire wing of the Wisconsin Democratic Party—not to mention the labor vote—then he needed Jerry to lobby on his behalf. Siphoning votes from Humphrey wouldn't be easy, Jack knew, but if anyone could do it, it was the man from Kenosha seated across the table.

Over breakfast (which for Jack generally consisted of orange juice, toast with jelly, a pair of soft-boiled eggs, broiled bacon, and coffee), the senator laid out his primary path for winning the nomination. His team was still debating whether that path should include Wisconsin, but Jack wanted to begin laying the necessary groundwork just in case. Of course, he'd need the right person to oversee the work. Thankfully, the right person was seated across from him at the breakfast table.

"Why don't you go back and organize it?" Jack asked.

Jerry sat in silence as the offer sank in.

Had Senator Jack Kennedy just offered him a job organizing his Wisconsin primary race?

The previous month, Ivan Nestingen had taken the role of president of the newly formed Kennedy for President Club. And Pat Lucey, who remained publicly neutral because of his role as chair of the state's Democratic Party, had become a great behind-the-scenes ally, as well.

"Go to work for [Ivan and Pat]," Jack said. "I'll put you on my payroll."

Flattered and flummoxed, Jerry was disinclined at first to make such a risky career move.

It would mean "taking a real gamble," Jerry said, expressing his concerns to the senator. "If you lose, I don't know if Proxmire will take me back."

And if Proxmire didn't—and if Jack lost—then where would he be? After years working in politics, Jerry had little interest in driving forklifts at American Motors. Was he willing to trade in everything he'd built with Proxmire to take a chance on Kennedy? A man he barely knew, outside of a rough day of campaigning and a couple of brief chats?

Jack understood what he was asking of Jerry, but he'd asked it of other men, too. Dropping everything to work for him wasn't meant to doom one's career; it was an invitation to forge the new frontier alongside him. The risks were high, but so were the rewards. It wasn't for everyone.

Jack said the only thing left to say, confiding in Jerry, "I've got a pretty good chance."

Jerry knew it was true. Still, it was a long way from a guarantee. Everything that had come before—his fights on behalf of big labor, the picket lines, the protests, his chance meeting with Proxmire in the bar—all of it seemed to have led him to Jack Kennedy's table.

Was he willing to walk away now?

It was clear Jack wanted a quick answer, but Jerry couldn't give him one. Instead, before he left, Jerry promised to think about it and get back to Jack in the coming days.

Walking toward his car, Jerry felt the world shift beneath his feet.

The truth was, Jerry liked Jack a lot. From the moment his plane touched down in Milwaukee in August of '57, Jack had proven himself to be a good sport, despite the day's many mishaps. Sure, Jack had shown his frustration over the whole "forgetting to load the film" fiasco, but Jerry liked a politician with fire.

Of course, Jerry liked Proxmire, too—and he owed the man a great debt. Without Proxmire, he'd still be working the loading docks back in

Kenosha. But was loyalty reason enough to stay? If this was Jerry's one chance to make history, *big* history, didn't he owe it to himself to try?

Jerry tied himself in knots for days before the answer became clear to him. "You know, what the hell have I got to lose?" he told himself. "A year ago, I was a factory worker, and today the guy who thinks he's going to be president wants to hire me."

In late June, Jerry informed Proxmire of his decision. At first, Proxmire took the news relatively well. But after two days of near-constant press on Jerry's decision to leave Proxmire for the Kennedy campaign, Proxmire angrily cut all ties with Jerry.

"Bruno is on his own," Proxmire said.

Despite their history, Proxmire—who was publicly neutral but privately pro-Humphrey—could no longer be associated with Jerry, who was now closely linked with Jack.

From here on out, there was no safe harbor for Jerry should Kennedy lose. Which left Jerry with one option: ensure that Kennedy won.

Jerry packed his bags and headed home to Wisconsin.

The battle had begun.

Jerry Bruno (the man on the left), and presidential assistant John J. McNally (wearing glasses) are greeted at the Honolulu International Airport, June 8, 1963. ROBERT KNUDSEN, WHITE HOUSE PHOTOGRAPHS, JOHN F. KENNEDY PRESIDENTIAL LIBRARY AND MUSEUM, BOSTON

THE UPHILL BATTLE

Ivan Nestingen, Pete Dugal, and Philleo Nash
November 13, 1959

Four months and twenty-three days
before the Wisconsin primary

I van Nestingen, the mayor of Madison, gripped his steering wheel tightly as he tried to navigate the thick snow falling over Kenosha's slick streets. This was not how Ivan had imagined the day would go. But Wisconsin winters were as unpredictable as the state's politics. Just when you thought you had a read on things, the wind shifted.

Politically speaking, Wisconsin was due for a change. The progressive days of "Fighting Bob" La Follette—and his meteoric rise from congressman to governor to United States senator—now seemed like ancient history. In recent years, La Follette's populist legacy had been shunted aside, replaced by a conservative takeover of Wisconsin politics. By 1948, Republicans had won the governorship and both houses of the state legislature and dispatched Republican senators and congressmen to Washington. This trend had held true in 1956, as well, when Wisconsin voters overwhelmingly cast their ballots to reelect President Dwight D. Eisenhower.

Something needed to change at both the state and national levels, Ivan knew, and it would take the right man to do it.

Thankfully, that man was seated beside him in the car.

Massachusetts senator Jack Kennedy stared forlornly out the window as the snow continued to fall. In good weather, the forty-mile jaunt from

Kenosha to Milwaukee took no more than fifty minutes, but on this day, the treacherous road conditions slowed them down considerably.

It was the kind of Wisconsin welcome Kennedy had come to expect—less a red carpet than a white one. Throughout the day, the weather had increasingly jeopardized Kennedy's appearance at the Kenosha Union Club, and, even worse, the one that followed: the kick-off keynote address for the Wisconsin Democratic Convention in Milwaukee.

At least Kennedy could take comfort in knowing that Vice President Richard M. Nixon, who was also in the state that day, would be just as inconvenienced by the weather. For the past two days, Kennedy and Nixon had been engaged in a shadow campaign. Neither man admitted that their simultaneous trips to Wisconsin had anything to do with a future presidential run, but it was hard to ignore the campaign-style events that dominated their visits.

Kennedy's tour across Wisconsin so far had taken him to River Falls, Eau Claire, Marshfield, Portage, and Watertown. The previous day, after speaking at Wisconsin State College–River Falls, Kennedy had accepted a ride to a noon event at the Eau Claire Elks Club from a thirty-one-year-old man named Pete Dugal, who ran a small oil company in the nearby village of Cadott. As chairman of Chippewa County's Democratic Party, Pete was thrilled to get an hour of uninterrupted facetime with the senator. At some point during their drive, Pete mentioned to Kennedy that he hoped to be elected as a district chairman at the state convention two days later. It wouldn't make him a major power player, Pete knew, but he wanted Kennedy to know he had at least some support in western Wisconsin's Humphrey-leaning ninth district.

In fact, Pete and Jack were destined for many future drives together—some of them legendary—throughout northwestern Wisconsin. But neither man knew that when they parted ways in Eau Claire an hour or so later.

In a series of dueling events that day, Kennedy and Nixon each tried their best to cast themselves as presidential material, making lofty speeches about the role of the United States on the world stage. However, the story dominating Wisconsin headlines that November involved a more pressing regional matter: cranberries. Arthur Flemming, secretary of the US Department of Health, Education and Welfare, had just issued a statement warning that a batch of cranberries from the Pacific Northwest had been contaminated by aminotriazole, a dangerous weed killer believed to cause cancer in rats, and alerting the public not to buy cranberries if they couldn't confirm the origin.

Flemming's timing could not have been worse—especially for Wisconsin, the nation's leading cranberry producer. With Thanksgiving just weeks away, the fifty-million-dollar cranberry industry was in peril. At peak buying season, cranberries were being yanked from store shelves and restaurants just before the biggest meal of the year. Cities were destroying shipments of cranberries no matter their origins—Chicago health authorities, for example, seized twenty tons of cranberries from Wisconsin Rapids. Suddenly one of the state's most vital industries appeared headed toward freefall.

Both Kennedy and Nixon took full advantage of the opportunity to cater to the state's worried voters.

On November 12, Kennedy and Nixon spoke at separate events in the same county—Kennedy at the Hotel Charles in Marshfield and Nixon thirty miles down the road in Wisconsin Rapids, in the heart of cranberry country. The toastmaster for Kennedy's event happened to be the state's most influential cranberry farmer—Philleo Nash, President Truman's former staffer, who by 1959 had become Wisconsin's lieutenant governor. Philleo had been a Humphrey man since that fateful night in the cranberry bog in 1948, when he'd heard the Minneapolis mayor's impassioned civil rights speech. Over the next decade, their relationship strengthened as Humphrey regularly visited Wisconsin to assist in rebuilding the state's Democratic Party. Despite some ideological differences, Philleo had worked hard with Pat Lucey to put the state's Democratic party first. But when Pat and Ivan had organized the Kennedy for President Club, Philleo had been conspicuously not invited. The truth was, Philleo had liked Kennedy ever since their day of campaigning for William Proxmire back in '57. But the Kennedy people seemed to like Philleo a little less.

Complicating Philleo's allegiance was the fact that he and Humphrey shared a political base, and Philleo had his own reelection to consider. If he turned his back on Humphrey now, he would risk alienating his most

During the 1957 State Democratic Party Convention at Madison's Hotel Loraine, Pat Lucey (left) challenged incumbent Philleo Nash (right) in the race for state party chairman. Lucey defeated Nash by a margin of five votes. WHI IMAGE ID 138934

loyal supporters in the leadup to the 1960 lieutenant governor's race. All of this would be hashed out later, of course. What mattered most at the moment was cranberries.

Philleo strongly suspected that Nixon would be making a public display of his newfound love of cranberries. So, before the event in Marshfield, Philleo made certain that cranberry juice would be readily available for Senator Kennedy, too.

As Nash predicted, Nixon indulged in four large helpings of cranberry sauce that night in Wisconsin Rapids, offering a pandering *mmm, mmm, good* assessment to a room full of onlookers. "I see no reason for hysteria over cranberries on any consumer's part," Nixon told reporters. "I am certain the Department of Health, Education, and Welfare is working rapidly to separate those comparatively few contaminated cranberries, and I, like other Americans, expect to eat traditional cranberries with my family on Thanksgiving Day."

Meanwhile in Marshfield, Kennedy enjoyed a glass of cranberry juice in front of a standing-room only crowd of fifteen hundred people. Jerry Bruno, now working with Ivan Nestingen on Wisconsin's Kennedy for

Senator Kennedy and Philleo Nash pour Ocean Spray cranberry juice.

President Club, had spent weeks ensuring the hall would be at full capacity. Yet in the photograph commemorating the event, the crowd isn't even in the frame. Instead, Philleo and Jack each place a hand on the glass gallon jug, smiling widely as cranberry juice flows into a small paper cup. (When a photographer encouraged Kennedy to sling the jug over his shoulder and take a sip, Kennedy drew the line. He'd drink the juice, but he wasn't about to look like some backwoods yokel while doing it.)

Later that evening, a reporter asked how he was feeling. "Well, [Nixon and I] have both eaten them, and I feel fine," Kennedy said. "But if we both pass away, I feel I shall have performed a great public service by taking the vice president with me."

Neither berries nor blizzards weighed heavily on Kennedy's mind the next day, as Ivan steered them through the snow. Hubert Humphrey—who was scheduled to close the Wisconsin Democratic convention the following evening—was Kennedy's real worry. That Humphrey would win Wisconsin seemed, to many people, a foregone conclusion. From his early years as Minneapolis mayor to his decade in the Senate, the affable, farmer-friendly Humphrey had claimed Wisconsin as a second home. Humphrey was particularly popular in the Protestant-leaning agricultural districts of western Wisconsin, leaving even less room for Kennedy to make inroads.

Then, on Kenosha's Washington Street hill, the tires of Ivan's Chevrolet suddenly struggled to gain traction. Ivan planted his foot on the accelerator, hopeful that the tires might catch. The engine hummed, then roared, to no avail.

As the tires spun, Kennedy—who was far better disposed to Palm Beach sunshine than Kenosha snow—opened the door and quickly climbed out of the vehicle. Ivan turned just in time to see the senator heading toward the back of his car.

Ivan watched in his rearview mirror as a tan-faced Jack Kennedy heaved his full weight against the bumper. This was no Addison's disease–ravaged Jack, but the man who'd spent his youth running for touchdowns in Hyannis Port and who, sixteen years earlier, had saved his PT-109 crewmates after surviving a Japanese destroyer attack.

As Jack pushed hard against the back of the car, streetlights splashed light all around him. Not a spotlight, not yet, but close. The slush-filled streets slipped beneath him, but Jack held firm, one foot in front of the other, inching the car upward. A separate car had been traveling behind Ivan and Jack, carrying Irish Mafia members Kenny O'Donnell and Dave Powers, two of Kennedy's most loyal allies. Within moments, Kenny and Dave were at Jack's side. Together, the trio managed to ease the car up the snowy hill until at last the tires caught. From his place a few cars back, *Milwaukee Journal* reporter Ira Kapenstein watched the scene unfold.

No image could more fully foretell the primary fight to come: a Kennedy versus Humphrey royal rumble which, for the former, would prove quite an uphill battle, indeed.

How, after all, could an elitist, East Coast Catholic ever compete with a beloved, salt-of-the-Earth midwestern Protestant? The answer: with help from those who believed in him.

The political climb would be steep.

But Kennedy was all fight, all grit, all vigor.

Ivan needed only to glance in the rearview mirror to see it.

PART II

DURING

JANUARY 1960—APRIL 1960

"Jack Kennedy, the Democratic frontrunner, and Hubert Humphrey, his most dogged pursuer, were plunged in all-out campaigns to win the state's presidential primary on April 5. A victory for either candidate might unlock a boxful of delegates from other states. A defeat could prove disastrous."
—FROM *LIFE* MAGAZINE'S "STRATEGIC WARPATH IN WISCONSIN,"
MARCH 28, 1960

Making It Official

Pat Lucey and Vel Phillips
January 21, 1960

Two months and fifteen days before the Wisconsin primary

B ack in October 1959, during the planning meeting in Bobby Kennedy's
Hyannis Port living room, Bobby had opposed Jack's entrance into
the Wisconsin primary. It was an opinion shared by many others in the
room that day.

According to one journalist, "Wisconsin was uppermost in the minds
of all at the moment, . . . but Wisconsin was dangerous."

Though Wisconsin had been the first state in the nation to mandate
primary elections, its primary rules could lead to unpredictable outcomes.
Case in point: Wisconsin opted for open primaries, which meant any voter
from any party could vote in any primary. As a result, voters from one party
could influence another party's primary outcome by casting their votes
across party lines. In addition, Wisconsin elected many of its delegates by
congressional district; this meant a candidate could win the popular vote
but still fail to secure delegates in the less populated districts she or he lost.

Wisconsin was dangerous for Kennedy for another reason, too. If
Kennedy lost in Wisconsin, any hope of clinching the nomination at the
convention would be all but out of reach. Kennedy needed the win in Wisconsin to prove to the political bosses that his appeal reached beyond the
East Coast. Not only that, Kennedy needed the win to stop Humphrey,
whose low poll numbers nationwide made him a better spoiler for Kennedy
than a serious national contender. Simply put, Kenny O'Donnell and Dave

Powers later reasoned, if he lost in Wisconsin, "Kennedy would have been finished as a presidential candidate, and Humphrey himself would have been no better off politically."

In Joe Kennedy Sr.'s estimation, Wisconsin was "the crisis of the campaign." If they didn't do well in Wisconsin, he said, "we should get out of the fight."

Jack Kennedy agreed. "If I am beaten [in Wisconsin]," he said, "I am out."

For two months, the campaign vacillated on whether to enter the Wisconsin primary at all. The question was made even more complicated by uncertainty in Ohio. Kennedy couldn't afford to lose delegates from either state, but he also couldn't afford to run in both. At the behest of Harry Truman and Senator Stuart Symington of Missouri, Ohio's Democratic governor Michael DiSalle had been recruited to run as a "favorite son" candidate in the Ohio primary, a move that was designed to allow DiSalle to give the state's sixty-four pledged delegates to Symington, or perhaps Majority Leader Lyndon B. Johnson, at the convention.

Kennedy was having none of it. Shortly before his official announcement that he would run for president, Jack and Bobby Kennedy, along with Connecticut Democratic chair John M. Bailey, met DiSalle in a motel near the Pittsburgh airport. Reports differ on how "cloak and dagger" their meeting was, but according to some accounts, they used false names in an attempt at discretion. Not one to parse words, Bobby made it clear to DiSalle that if he hoped to avoid a potentially ruinous primary fight in Ohio, he had to pledge his delegates to Kennedy. Much to the Kennedys' pleasure, DiSalle agreed, making the decision to enter the Wisconsin primary far easier.

Ultimately, though, what gave Jack the confidence to officially enter the Wisconsin primary was the internal polling data from the number-crunching whiz kid Lou Harris, whose groundbreaking polling techniques would influence politicians for decades. After polling twenty-three-thousand Wisconsin voters—the most extensive polling ever done in a single state up to that point—Harris concluded that Kennedy could carry the state with 63 percent of the primary vote, potentially winning eight or more of the state's ten districts.

Yet, on January 2, 1960, when Jack formally announced his candidacy for the presidency, he remained suspiciously quiet about Wisconsin. While he made clear his intention to run in at least some of the state primaries ("I believe that any Democratic aspirant to this important nomination should be willing to submit to the voters his views, record, and competence in a series of primary contests"), he noted only his intention to file for the uncontested New Hampshire primary on March 8. As for Wisconsin's primary on April 5, Kennedy declined to commit.

Finally, after months of debate and indecision, the day had arrived.

Pat Lucey, the forty-one-year-old chairperson of the Wisconsin Democratic Party, was thrilled. Any minute now, Jack and Jackie Kennedy would touch down at Milwaukee's Mitchell Field and then be escorted to the nearby Pfister Hotel, where Jack would finally make it official: he was entering the Wisconsin primary.

Usually such an announcement would hardly register with the public. But Pat understood that this was different. If Jack Kennedy was destined for the White House, the road began here.

Unfortunately, the state Democratic Party lacked any consensus on a presidential nominee. Some candidates, like Humphrey and Oregon senator Wayne Morse, jumped into the primary fray alongside Kennedy. Others—including Johnson, Symington, former Illinois governor Adlai Stevenson, and New Jersey governor Robert B. Meyner—preferred to bypass the primaries in the hopes of a convention win. Everyone had a horse in the race, and the Democrat's stable was feeling quite cramped.

Wisconsin governor Gaylord Nelson privately favored Humphrey; former state party chair Jim Doyle Sr. backed Stevenson; and then there were those like Pat, who hoped Kennedy could overcome his outsider status to topple the senator from the state next door. Humphrey's charm was undeniable, his service to Wisconsin's farmers was well known, and the prospect of anyone snagging the primary out from under him had long seemed like a longshot—though Kennedy's internal polling suggested that was beginning to change.

Pat's biggest concern was a question that couldn't yet be answered: were American voters ready for a Catholic president?

They certainly hadn't been in 1928, when a ten-year-old Pat took his first crack at political activism on behalf of the Democrat's presidential nominee, Al Smith. Pat had laced his shoes, thrown on his jacket, and gamely canvassed door-to-door throughout his hometown of Bagley, Wisconsin. Even as a young boy, Pat had loved the idea of a Catholic president. But when Smith was soundly defeated at the hands of Herbert Hoover, Pat learned a valuable lesson: like it or not, religion mattered.

Now, thirty-two years later, Pat couldn't help but wonder if such narrow-mindedness might also plague Jack Kennedy.

The state's religious makeup had, indeed, been a factor in Kennedy's decision to enter the Wisconsin primary, as 32 percent of the state's population identified as Catholic—more than any other primary state to the west. If a few of Wisconsin's predominantly Catholic districts in the eastern part of the state went to Jack, perhaps they might offset the Protestant-leaning districts in the west.

Pat watched as the twin-engine, forty-seat Convair CV-240—dubbed the *Caroline* for Jack and Jackie's two-year-old daughter—descended through the clouds and kissed the runway, taxiing for a moment before it reached the tarmac. Joe Sr. had purchased the plane the previous September, leasing it to the campaign to ensure that his son could cover the most ground by taking to the air.

The plane door opened, and out stepped Jackie, who reached for her coat collar to keep out the chill. By contrast, Jack was coatless, hatless, and smiling widely, refusing to acknowledge the winter weather. Pat greeted them both warmly, then joined them in the waiting car that would transport them to the Pfister. Pat knew this was how it was going to be for the next three months: a flurry of airport pick-ups and drop-offs, with countless tire-burning miles in between.

For the Kennedys, winning was everything, and the surest way to do so was to build the best team money could buy. For the past year or so, Jack and Bobby had done just that. There was the inner circle, of course—advisers Kenny O'Donnell and Dave Powers, as well as strategist Larry O'Brien and the rest of the East Coast team. But thanks to Pat and Ivan, Wisconsin would field its own team. Ivan would serve as the public-facing chairman of the Kennedy for President Club of Wisconsin, while Jerry Bruno would oversee the club's daily behind-the-scenes operations as director.

As chairperson of the state Democratic Party, Pat technically needed to remain neutral, though his presence alongside Kennedy at the Pfister telegraphed his preference. There were other early supporters, too, like Wisconsin attorney general John Reynolds, whose February 1960 endorsement further confirmed that high-profile statewide Democrats believed in Kennedy's electability. And Vel Phillips, a key ally in Milwaukee's Black community. And Congressman Clement Zablocki, representing the state's fourth congressional district. And Democratic Party treasurer David Rabinovitz. And Toni McBride, vice chairwoman of the state party. And Robert Moses, broadcaster for Farmers Union on the Air. And Marvin Brickman, executive secretary of the Madison Federation of Labor.

And who could forget those local volunteers organizing Kennedy clubs in each congressional district? Collectively, they were an indefatigable army, taking on every on-the-ground effort imaginable, from door knocking to phone calls to coordinating campaign stops. While Jerry ran the command center from the state headquarters in Milwaukee, the district offices were on the front lines. The trick to a successful campaign, Bobby Kennedy insisted, was to give a role to everyone who wanted one—to create a personal connection between the individual and the wider campaign. This was not Jack Kennedy's campaign, or Jerry Bruno's campaign for Jack. This campaign belonged to Bill who licked the envelopes, and Betty who worked the phones. It belonged to the high school and college kids who knocked on the doors, just as Pat had done all those years before.

If they carried out their plan just like that—personalizing the political landscape in each city, village, and town in every district—then they'd find themselves smiling on April 5. But any misstep could spell disaster. And the biggest mistake they could make, Pat figured, was to underestimate Humphrey's strength.

On the way to the Pfister that morning, Kennedy's car passed the ice-encrusted Milwaukee Bay. The bay served as a symbol of sorts: a seemingly endless sea of bone-chilling cold that, though pretty to look at, was best left untouched—certainly in mid-January.

To win the Wisconsin primary, you couldn't admire the place from afar. You had to go to the places that made you uncomfortable, enduring near-frostbite conditions for days on end, shaking countless hands outside of factory gates, hoping that your own hands didn't numb.

Democratic phone bank volunteers from the United Packinghouse Workers Locals 88 and 21. From left to right: Ruby Espionga, Gayle Hill, Beatrice Holland, and Ann Wilson. WHI IMAGE ID 67273

Was Jack up for all that? Was anyone?

Upon arriving at the Pfister, Jack and Jackie were escorted to a table overflowing with microphones. An eager press awaited them, including Ira Kapenstein, seated to the left of the candidate. Madison mayor Ivan Nestingen positioned himself directly behind Jack, telegraphing his support. Dressed in suit and tie, Jack looked the part of a presidential candidate, while Jackie—resplendent in a bright red dress—appeared more suited for the red carpet. It was precisely this mashup of dashing public servants and glamorous movie stars that made the Kennedys such an irresistible couple. In Jack and Jackie, people glimpsed their hopes manifested in human form. People weren't sure whether to envy them or emulate them.

As the cameras clicked, Jack made his intentions clear. "I shall run in the Wisconsin presidential primary," he said. "I am fully aware of the difficulties that course involves. No other candidate, real or unannounced, has indicated a willingness to enter any primary adjoining the home state of another contender—including New Hampshire, which is next to my own state of Massachusetts."

This was a direct challenge to Humphrey, which the Minnesota senator was smart enough not to accept. New Hampshire's primary on March 8 was the first of the sixteen primaries that year, and it offered Humphrey certain defeat. (Jack would end up running more or less unopposed there, clearing 85 percent of the vote.)

A reporter asked Kennedy whether he considered himself the underdog in Wisconsin.

"Well, there are several polls," Jack said, cherry-picking the one that best served his purpose. "There's a poll I saw yesterday that was taken last fall by a magazine here which showed me running behind. I've seen some polls that I would say we're quite close, is my guess."

"Your own polls show you ahead," the reporter piped in.

"No," Jack insisted, "in fact they show me very close."

"The Harris poll—" tried another reporter, but Jack interrupted, dodging the question.

"I never attempt to put myself in any category," Jack said. "I would say it's a very tough fight for the obvious reason I've given. In the same way I would consider Senator Humphrey having a very tough fight if he were to come into New Hampshire. I am going into a state which is adjoining Minnesota."

Had he been pressed further on the Harris poll, Jack's claims of underdog status would have been put into doubt. And being viewed as such was essential for Jack. It was better to look like a loser and come out a winner rather than the other way around. And being the alleged underdog gave the Kennedy campaign more firepower when enlisting the support of donors and volunteers. Frontrunners risked growing complacent; underdogs didn't.

Vel Phillips arrived at the Pfister Hotel shortly after Kennedy's announcement. Duties at city hall had kept her from coming earlier, which was just as well, as some of her colleagues were beginning to accuse her of being too partisan. But this was politics, was it not? Didn't siding with your preferred candidates come with the territory?

FACING: Vel Phillips and John F. Kennedy, date unknown. PHILLIPS FAMILY ARCHIVE

Vel eyed the room to see that most of the fanfare had ended. The room had been bustling with reporters and well-wishers just minutes before, but now only a few folks remained, including the newest presidential candidate, who strolled her way from his place across the lobby.

"Vel, it is so good to see you," Kennedy smiled. "I'm so glad you were able to come."

"Well, I'm sorry I couldn't have been here sooner," Vel said.

"I want you to know how very much I appreciate what you've done in coming out and endorsing my candidacy," Kennedy said. "I know you have done so under a great deal of pressure and strain, and Pat [Lucey] has told me some of the things, personally, that you have had to go through. And I want you to know how much I appreciate it."

Kennedy was right. Vel had paid a personal price for publicly supporting him. Humphrey's longstanding fight for civil rights was well known throughout the Black community. Vel's endorsement of Kennedy had hindered Humphrey's candidacy and imperiled her relationship with Humphrey, a man she considered a friend. Her decision alienated closer friends, too, including Frank Wallick, who had been a key advocate in advancing

Vel's role as a national committeewoman at the 1958 convention. Unfortunately, Wallick was also Humphrey's presidential campaign manager. In December 1959, Vel and Wallick crossed paths at a bookstore, and Wallick refused to speak to her. Worse still, Vel's own mother was a Humphrey fan. Once Humphrey received Jackie Robinson's endorsement ("[M]y mother puts Jackie Robinson just about next to God," Vel remarked), the pressure was all but unbearable.

Yet she'd given her support to Kennedy because she believed in him. In selecting her candidate, she wanted someone who could win the White House. Much as she valued Humphrey, he lacked the "Kennedy flavor."

But when Kennedy acknowledged the pressure Vel was under, she brushed it aside. "Think nothing of it," she said. "I know you're going to do all that we all know you can do."

Senator Kennedy smiled, then suggested Vel head up to the hotel suite where Jackie and Jean Lucey were engaged in what Kennedy described as "girl talk."

"All right," Vel agreed, though she didn't know Jackie well.

The previous November, as Jack and Vel had posed for a news photographer during a visit in Milwaukee, Jack had paused to compliment Vel's black and white suit. "You know," he said, "Jackie has one just like that."

Vel had been skeptical. Though the purchase had been a bit of a splurge, Vel doubted that she shared a suit with a woman who'd quickly become a worldwide fashion icon.

"Oh, really?" she said politely.

"Exactly like that," Kennedy continued, "with the same black whatever-you-call-that around there."

"Well, thank you very much," Vel said, hardly convinced. "I hope she enjoys it."

Vel was no stranger to pandering politicians, and she had quickly chalked up the senator's remark as little more than that.

Now, on that late January day months later, Vel made her way up to the hotel suite to meet Jackie and Jean. "I understand that we have a suit alike," Jackie said warmly.

Vel was surprised that the senator's comment had made it back to Jackie. "Yes, [but] I didn't really believe," she said, her words trailing off.

"You know, I had a feeling you wouldn't," Jackie said, walking toward the hotel closet, "so therefore I brought mine."

Vel was stunned as Jackie pulled out a black and white suit. It was, indeed, the exact same one.

From that moment on, she knew Jack Kennedy was a man of his word.

Shortly after the press conference, Jack and Jackie were whisked back to the airport to catch an afternoon flight to Omaha, where, to much less fanfare, he would announce his uncontested primary run in Nebraska.

By the end of the primary season, Jack would officially enter seven state primaries (New Hampshire, Wisconsin, Indiana, Nebraska, West Virginia, Maryland, and Oregon) and be a write-in candidate in three others (Illinois, Massachusetts, and Pennsylvania). By contrast, Humphrey would officially enter five (Wisconsin, West Virginia, Washington, DC, Oregon, and South Dakota) and be a write-in candidate in four more (Illinois, Massachusetts, Pennsylvania, and Nebraska). While some of these contests would feature other write-in candidates (mostly Stevenson, Symington, Johnson, and the occasional favorite son), the primary field would remain relatively clear for Kennedy if he could dispatch Humphrey early in the primaries—preferably in Wisconsin. Then the campaign could focus on the dark horse candidates, Stevenson and Johnson most of all.

Kennedy's approach to the primaries risked spreading himself too thin, but to win a lot of ground, you had to cover a lot of ground. Moreover, Kennedy prided himself in entering every presidential primary "which binds its delegates for one or more ballots, where no legitimate favorite son candidate is running" (in addition to entering several nonbinding primaries, too). But first, there was Wisconsin to contend with, and Pat was ready.

Pat accompanied the Kennedys to the airport, a mix of nerves and excitement. Though Pat was convinced that Jack's entry into the Wisconsin primary was the right choice, years later he would reflect on what he called his "rather provincial view." He did not understand the national political scene as well as the Kennedys did. Yet he made up for it with his regional knowledge. Pat's superpower was dependent on his self-described provincialism. He may not have known which way the wards swung half a country away, but he knew how they'd swing in Wisconsin. For the time, that was all that mattered.

After more than a decade of rebuilding Wisconsin's Democratic Party, all that shoe leather and tire tread was paying off. Now, what remained to be seen was whether Jack Kennedy could manage a primary win. And not just a squeaker, but a blowout. If they could crush Humphrey next to his home turf, there'd be no reason for Humphrey to limp along to West Virginia. It was best, Pat knew, to settle things here in Wisconsin.

Jack felt similarly, though he may have privately doubted such a fortuitous outcome. Sure, the Harris poll looked good, but who believed a poll this far out?

Standing alongside Pat in the airport that day, Jack made his reservations clear.

"Well," Jack said wryly, "now that you've conned me into this thing, how do you feel about it?"

Flummoxed, Pat searched for words.

"Well," Pat managed, "that I would feel pretty terrible if you lost."

Jack smiled.

"Well, don't feel that way about it," Jack said. "As of today, my chances of getting the nomination are a lot less than fifty-fifty. If I win the Wisconsin primary, they'll be slightly better than fifty-fifty. So, if you look at it that way, I'm not gambling very much."

Though "slightly better than fifty-fifty" were hardly the odds the Kennedy team desired, it was the best they could hope for under the circumstances. The only point everyone could agree on was that what happened in Wisconsin on April 5 would fundamentally change the election. Would Jack flatten Humphrey, be flattened by Humphrey, or meet somewhere in the purgatorial middle?

As Jack boarded the plane to Nebraska, Pat began to feel the full weight of the work ahead of him. Rather than buckle, he braced himself. With the right team, they could get it done.

At least he hoped.

A Stroll through the Snow

Bobby Kennedy and Chuck Spalding
Late January 1960

Approximately two months before the Wisconsin primary

If there was one thing Bobby Kennedy couldn't stand, it was stagnancy. A sailboat left to bob in the water. A train stopped dead on the tracks.

This proved a problem one winter afternoon in January 1960, when a train from Milwaukee to Eau Claire screeched to a halt several miles before reaching its destination. Among the many passengers on that train were thirty-four-year-old Bobby and forty-one-year-old Chuck Spalding, a political adviser and longtime Kennedy friend. For the past few hours, Bobby and Chuck had watched with growing dread as a snowstorm pummeled their train window. Eventually that snow turned to ice, and that ice glossed the tracks, and the conductor—who knew full well the dangers of such a wintery mix—had no choice but to hit the brake.

Outside their window stretched a tundra—a mostly blank landscape aside from the fallow fields brushed with snow. There were trees, of course, and the tracks themselves, but otherwise few landmarks to point to.

Chuck later guessed they had stopped about five miles outside of Eau Claire. But to Bobby, the distance was irrelevant. After all, they were here to set up a campaign headquarters in Eau Claire, and he wasn't going to let a little snowstorm get in the way.

Tightening his jacket, Bobby started toward the train door.

No, Chuck may have thought. *Is he serious?*

But Chuck didn't need to ask, because he already knew the answer. For years, Chuck had regularly joined Bobby and their friends on weeklong sailing trips along the coast of Maine. For Chuck, those trips revealed something about Bobby, not a fatal flaw so much as a personality trait: Bobby refused to give in or give up when something was in his way. When Bobby had a plan, he stuck to it—come hell or high water or both. He was known to sail his boat into harm's way; when other sailors would've steered clear of inclement weather, Bobby did the opposite.

Over the next several hours, Bobby and Chuck walked the rails into the heart of the state's ninth congressional district. Chuck, with his gangly six-foot-four-inch frame, trailed after Bobby—a man who, within a year, would become the youngest attorney general in history and one of the most powerful men in the country. Yet here they were, ruining their loafers to make an eight o'clock meeting in Eau Claire. What words the men shared during their long walk toward the city are lost to history. But one can imagine Bobby strategizing each step of the way, informing Chuck—a relative newcomer to political campaigns—what it might take for Jack to pull off a win. It was a task that would be especially hard in Wisconsin's western districts, where Humphrey remained incredibly popular for his support of agriculture and labor. How in the world could Jack compete with that? How could they persuade salt-of-the-earth farmers and factory workers that the silver-spooned Kennedy understood their lives, hopes, and needs?

If Chuck wondered what he'd gotten himself into, he partially had himself to blame. He had signed up to help Jack by any means possible. Such were the consequences of their friendship.

Chuck first met Jack Kennedy in the summer of 1940, when Chuck was visiting his roommate's family at their summer home across the bay from Hyannis Port. Chuck and his roommate had just finished a round of golf when his roommate suggested they stop by the Kennedy compound to say hello to his buddy Jack.

It was on the first floor of Joe Sr.'s sprawling home where a twenty-two-year-old Chuck first laid eyes upon Jack, who, in that moment, sure seemed a long way from the presidency. A jovial twenty-three-year-old

Harvard grad, Jack was half buried beneath letters from dignitaries and copies of his recently published thesis-turned-book, *While England Slept*. "It was just a wonderful disarray of papers," Chuck later remembered.

Chuck and Jack hit it off immediately. Not only because they were both writers (Chuck's debut cowritten novel would be published three years later), or because of their shared interest in military service (they were both destined for the navy), but also because of the ease they felt around one other. Jack was an intellectual but a raconteur, too.

"[H]e was the most engaging person that I've ever known," Chuck later said. "I was lucky and knew a lot of people myself. But I've never seen any company in which he wasn't the brightest and most entertaining."

The pair remained connected for years to come—from California to Cape Cod, from Palm Beach to Boston. In 1945, following separate stints in the navy, Chuck moved to California to write screenplays, while a twenty-eight-year-old Jack worked as a foreign correspondent, with reporting assignments that included the Potsdam Conference, where Soviet Leader Joseph Stalin, Prime Minister Winston Churchill, and President Harry Truman negotiated the end of World War II.

Jack Kennedy, Chuck Spalding, and an unidentified man sail aboard the *Victura* off the coast of Hyannis Port.
CECIL STOUGHTON, WHITE HOUSE PHOTOGRAPHS, JOHN F. KENNEDY PRESIDENTIAL LIBRARY AND MUSEUM, BOSTON

In late June 1945, Jack had arrived in San Francisco to cover the drafting of the United Nations charter for Hearst Newspapers. Chuck was with him as he waited for a cab one day.

"You know," Jack lamented to Chuck as they stood at the street corner, "I just can't do what other people can do. The back bothers me and I'm sure now that Joe is dead that I'm going to go into politics."

This was the first Chuck had heard Jack speak about running for office. The previous summer, the Kennedy family had been devastated when Jack's older brother, Joe Kennedy Jr., was killed in an explosion during a navy mission in World War II. Joe Jr. had planned to return after the war and run for Congress—part of a grand plan to eventually reach the White House.

"One politician was enough in the family," Kennedy reflected, "and my brother Joe was obviously going to be that politician."

Yet following Joe's death, that eventuality could no longer be true.

Upon learning of his friend's interest in running for office, Chuck said, "That would be wonderful." Who could be a better politician than Jack?

From left to right: Chuck Spalding; Jackie Kennedy's brother-in-law, Prince Stanislaus Radziwill of Poland; First Lady Jacqueline Kennedy; and President John F. Kennedy, in Hyannis Port on July 28, 1963. CECIL STOUGHTON, WHITE HOUSE PHOTOGRAPHS, JOHN F. KENNEDY PRESIDENTIAL LIBRARY AND MUSEUM, BOSTON

The following year, when Jack won the congressional seat for Massachusetts's eleventh district, Chuck's confidence was confirmed. Six years later, when Jack won a US Senate seat, it seemed there was no stopping him.

Chuck's work on the West Coast had kept him from actively participating in Jack's earlier campaigns. But by January 1960, when it was clear Jack was making a presidential run, Chuck knew it was time to lend a hand. He approached Bobby, Jack's campaign manager. "Listen," Chuck told Bobby, "I'd like to do what I can for the rest of the way. I can get away, and I'd like to throw in."

Bobby knew an ally when he saw one.

"I'm going to Wisconsin on Wednesday," Bobby told him. "So get on the plane, and I'll meet you in Milwaukee."

Waiting to announce his entrance in the Wisconsin primary had been a pragmatic choice, one that bought the campaign a little more time to gauge the public's response to Jack's candidacy, especially the religious question.

For his part, though, Bobby still had his doubts. He still wasn't sure they could win enough voters in enough districts to make the state primary worth it. Bobby especially needed someone he could trust in western Wisconsin. It was precisely because Chuck wasn't from Wisconsin that Bobby wanted him there. Every campaign needed an outside eye to better understand the internal politics of a place.

An heir to the third-largest meatpacking company in the country, Chuck had grown up in Lake Forest, Illinois, the wealthy town that had inspired F. Scott Fitzgerald's *The Great Gatsby*. Eau Claire, by contrast, was a former lumber town, where workhorses were more common than polo ponies. The two cities' origin stories couldn't have been more different: Lake Forest was born from pious Presbyterians with a Puritanical bent, while Eau Claire was rooted in hardscrabble German and Norwegian lumbermen. At its peak in 1884, upwards of 989 million board feet of logs floated down Eau Claire's Chippewa River, glutting its wide waters and making the town's mill owners rich. But like all booms, the lumber industry eventually went bust. The lumbermen had felled the white pines with such fervor that little was left to cut by the early twentieth century.

Eau Claire's second coming was tires. In 1917, the Gillette Tire Plant opened its doors and provided jobs for two hundred and fifty residents. Forty-odd years later, by the time Chuck and Bobby were hiking into town, the US Rubber Company plant—as it was known then—employed close to three thousand people.

This was why Eau Claire was worth the walk. Because long shot as it was to win the ninth district, if Bobby and Chuck could convince the factory workers to vote for Kennedy, then winning the ninth became less of a stretch. Consisting of eleven counties on the western side of the state, the ninth district was firmly Humphrey territory. The people of Eau Claire County had long admired the senator from next door. Humphrey was equally loved by the farmers in the district's less-populous counties, like Buffalo and Trempealeau and Barron. Just north of Chippewa County, the ninth district gave way to the tenth, where fourteen counties—many of them home to farm and dairy families—gave Humphrey the edge as well.

But Chuck hoped to change that.

While Chuck's pedigree didn't exactly shout "workhorse," he was up for the task. Like Jack, he'd enjoyed the privileges of wealth—private schools and an Ivy League education among them. But also like Jack, Chuck had served his country with distinction in the navy, where he had learned to complete the mission at all costs, which was what he was poised to do now.

Chuck was happy to do it, though he might have been happier if he could've avoided Wisconsin weather. Had there been any openings for campaigning in Hyannis Port, for instance, he might've preferred that option. Or even a return to Lake Forest. But Bobby had said Wisconsin, and so Wisconsin it would be.

Walking through the hoar frost, their breath catching in the air, Chuck and Bobby pressed on until at last they saw the lights of Eau Claire. There was the tire factory, the river, and the Hotel Eau Claire—the latter of which would serve as Chuck's home base for the next two months.

Bobby turned to Chuck, a smile frozen on his face.

"Now," Bobby said, "aren't you really glad you came?"

FACING: Tire factory employees in Eau Claire, leaving work at the end of their shift. WHI IMAGE ID 63600

Fuzzy Math

Ivan Nestingen and Pat Lucey
January 30, 1960

Two months and six days before the Wisconsin primary

Joe Kennedy Sr. could throw money at most of his son's problems, but he held no influence in what was quickly becoming the latest front in the primary war: a battle within Wisconsin's Democratic Administrative Committee. If Kennedy had been a weaker candidate, it never would have come to this. But Kennedy had quickly begun outspending, outpolling, and outhustling Humphrey at almost every turn, and the state's Humphrey-leaning Democratic Administrative Committee decided it needed to do something to tilt the playing field.

State election rules dictated how Wisconsin's thirty-one primary delegates were apportioned. Under existing rules, ten delegates went to the candidate who won the state's overall popular vote, and two delegates went to the winner of each of the state's ten congressional districts. (The thirty-first vote would be divided between a national committeeman and committeewoman who were split between the candidates.)

But in January 1960, Sam Rizzo, chairperson of Wisconsin's Humphrey for President organization, sponsored a rule change to fundamentally alter the delegate math to favor Hubert Humphrey. Rizzo's proposal would limit the popular vote winner to five delegates and would divvy the remaining five delegates among the state's ten congressional districts, increasing their votes from two delegates to two and a half. Even if Kennedy won the popular vote, the proposed rule change could give Humphrey enough delegates to stay in the race, thanks to his strong pockets of support, especially in the state's farm- and dairy-leaning southern and western districts.

On a Saturday afternoon at the end of January, committee members met at Milwaukee's Kaiser Knickerbocker Hotel where, after two hours of raucous debate, they passed Rizzo's proposal by a vote of fourteen to twelve. The fix was in for Humphrey. Maybe not the full fix, but enough of one for the Kennedy camp to cry foul.

In Madison, Ivan Nestingen seethed.

Ivan had figured he'd seen it all, but he was wrong. Back when Joe McCarthy was spitting vile, everybody knew where everybody else stood. But these days, the line between friend and foe seemed far less simple.

Ivan had known the Humphrey team would be tough to beat, but he'd underestimated the lengths they'd go to avoid losing. For Ivan, it was a wound that cut deep. Many of the people who'd voted in favor of the rule change were people Ivan had trusted, folks he'd worked with for nearly a decade.

Even some members of the Humphrey campaign were uncomfortable with the behind-the-scenes maneuvering. But what choice did they have? As Kennedy's strength grew, it became increasingly apparent that Humphrey was unlikely to win the popular vote. If Humphrey could eke out a few more delegate votes from the districts, perhaps it would quiet the calls for Humphrey to get out of the race.

If there was a silver lining, it was that this whole charade served as incontrovertible proof that the Humphreyites were scared. They knew a hobbling horse when they saw one, and Kennedy was pulling farther away every passing day. Ivan knew he couldn't blame Rizzo entirely. As much as he hated to admit it, the man likely pulling the strings in Humphrey's favor was Ivan's old friend Gerald Heaney, a Minnesotan on the Democratic National Committee who also happened to be Humphrey's campaign manager.

On February 3, Ivan wrote an angry letter to Heaney, accusing him of masterminding the fix:

> Your leadership in the effort to make this change is well known. You
> actively campaigned for the change on behalf of Senator Humphrey
> and solicited votes from among members of our administrative com-

mittee. Clearly you were seeking an unfair advantage for Senator
Humphrey by changing the rules in midstream to his advantage. . . .
Now you have successfully intervened in our primary to change our
ground rules. We would have appreciated you having left our presidential primary rules as they have been for those many past years.

Two days later, with a conciliatory tone but admitting no wrongdoing,
Heaney replied:

The eyes of the entire United States will soon be on the Wisconsin primary. If we conduct the campaign in a decent, aboveboard manner,
expose the record of the Republican Party and discuss the issues that
are important to the people of Wisconsin, we will be doing a great
service not only to the Democratic Party, but to the nation as a whole.
On the other hand, if we permit the campaign to degenerate into a
personality conflict among people in the various organizations, we
will all be harmed.

Heaney made no effort to deny his support for Humphrey but instead
hinted at future reconciliation, so far as the general election was concerned.

"If as a result of this kind of a debate Hubert Humphrey is victorious
in the State of Wisconsin, we will indeed be happy," he wrote to Ivan. "If
on the other hand, the voters should prefer Senator Kennedy, you can be
sure that we will accept the defeat in good grace."

Regardless of the outcome, Heaney added, "we're all going to want
to work together in the future." Months later, Heaney would make good
on his promise. Come November, Heaney's efforts in Minnesota's eighth
district would help to swing fifty thousand additional votes Kennedy's way,
a substantial number in a state that Kennedy would win by a mere 1.43
percent. In Wisconsin, Heaney and other Humphrey supporters would be
less successful in persuading their constituencies to rally behind Kennedy,
which would contribute to Nixon winning the state.

But in the short term, Heaney's promise of future support did little to
soothe the present problems. For Ivan, the limits of loyalty had been tested
and fallen short. He'd been badly burned by a friend.

Prior to the committee's decision, Senator William Proxmire had optimistically heralded the state's Democratic primary as a chance for the party's greatest leaders to test out new ideas. Yet now there was blood in the water. Any chance for a respectful clash of ideas now seemed impossible.

In the absence of a political record as long and distinguished as Humphrey's, Kennedy relied on public perception to win over voters—any mudslinging would only diminish his image. Better to endure a few blows, Kennedy's advisers had generally agreed, than return fire. Throughout much of the Wisconsin campaign, Jack did just that. But the administrative committee's changes to the delegate math was a trespass too egregious to go unchallenged.

In the days leading up to the committee's vote, Jack expressed his frustration in a private letter to Pat Lucey.

"It is both puzzling and disturbing to find that the supporters of one of the principal contestants suggests this change at this time," Jack vented. "Apparently, it is believed that . . . some advantage would accrue to the candidacy of Senator Humphrey by changing the rules of our primary in the closing months."

Even Wisconsin governor Gaylord Nelson (technically neutral, though a Humphrey supporter through and through) felt the revised delegate formula was improper at such a late date and said so publicly. The committee ignored his concerns.

In a statement given shortly after the committee's vote, Kennedy remarked, "Sen. Humphrey enjoys many advantages in Wisconsin already. . . . I did not think his supporters would attempt to add another advantage."

He might've stopped there, but he didn't.

"I think this matter will be settled by the people of Wisconsin," Kennedy continued, "when they vote in the primary on whether they agree with this manipulation of the Democratic Administrative Committee."

The rule change was so bald-faced that about the only politically minded person who refused to condemn it was the primary beneficiary. "For anyone to accuse the Wisconsin Democratic committee of manipulation is to falsely accuse," Humphrey said. "The decision is theirs, not mine." It made for an odd statement. Was Humphrey defending the committee or simply distancing himself from their decision?

Jack could have publicly hammered Humphrey for playing dirty, but instead he reached toward his better angels, remarking several days later:

> Let me make it completely clear right now that I do not intend to attack my Democratic opponent, to review his record, or to engage in any argument or debates with him. I do intend, when his name is mentioned, to speak well of him. I request, moreover, that everyone working on my behalf in this state abide by the same principles. For this is not a campaign against anyone. This is a campaign for the presidency.

Such a generous statement helped shine Jack in an even more favorable light. It was a little trick he'd picked up after losing the vice-presidential nomination back in '56: when life deals you a lousy hand, make it a better one.

By refusing to throw political punches, Kennedy had effectively safeguarded himself from future attacks by Humphrey. Of course, Humphrey was still welcome to try (and there was no shortage of Kennedy liabilities he might've tried to exploit), but he risked his own image in the process. Down in the polls and with limited fundraising, Humphrey's image was all he had left.

Though Ivan and Pat were ardent Kennedy supporters, they knew Humphrey had a long reputation for being loyal and honest; he knew how to look a voter in the eye. Both Ivan and Pat respected Humphrey a great deal—in some ways, Humphrey's progressive leanings more closely aligned with their own. Nevertheless, both men recognized the power of that Jack Kennedy magic, difficult as it was to define. As Pat remarked later,

> The Kennedy campaign was, for a very large part, just an effective presentation of a celebrity. [Jack Kennedy] spoke with obvious detailed knowledge on various issues when the occasion arose, particularly on labor legislation. But he also spoke knowledgeably about foreign affairs, about atomic energy, and about all these other things. But the appeal, it seemed to me, was something different. And it was a broad appeal. It was an appeal to young people.

No matter the circumstances, Jack Kennedy always seemed to find some way to come out on top. He'd bob and weave his way to the presidency if he had to, smiling every step of the way.

TED TAKES THE LEAP

Ted Kennedy, Jerry Bruno, and Ivan Nestingen
February 14, 1960

One month and twenty-two days before the Wisconsin primary

S tanding at the top of Tomahawk Ridge in Middleton, Wisconsin, twenty-eight-year-old Ted Kennedy took a deep breath, then fit his borrowed skis into the icy tracks of the ski jump. This was the Black Hawk Ski Club's annual ski jump competition—an event that was expected to draw nearly ten thousand spectators, or, as Jerry Bruno saw it, ten thousand potential voters from Wisconsin's second district. As such, Jerry had dispatched Ted Kennedy and Ivan Nestingen to shake hands and woo the crowd.

If Ted had wondered what kind of people fling themselves from steep, wood-framed ramps to determine who can fly the farthest through the frigid air, the answer was now clear: Wisconsinites. This was a far cry from what Ted had meant when he'd told Jerry that he liked to ski. He'd meant slopes, not jumps. But that shouldn't have mattered—they were supposed to be here working the event, not competing in it.

Earlier that morning, after picking up Ted from the airport, Ivan had suggested that Ted change into ski clothes—complete with a pair of jumping skis borrowed from one of Ivan's friends. Not because Ted had to ski, Ivan had assured, but simply so he'd "look like part of the crowd."

Ted was happy to do it. What better way to win over votes than to prove he was one of them? After suiting up and arriving at the jump, he even took a leisurely run down the hill.

"Why don't you go over to the practice jump and take a look at it?" Ivan next suggested. "But don't bother going off unless you want to."

Unless he wanted to? Ted didn't mind a downhill run on soft snow, but the odds of him voluntarily launching himself one hundred and ninety feet through air were slim. Still, he agreed to have a look.

But as soon as Ted and four fellow skiers had marched to the top of the jump—ostensibly to "take a look"—the Marine Band down below suddenly began to play "The Star-Spangled Banner," a signal that the competition was about to start. Ted turned back toward the steps from which he'd come, checking to see how easy it might be to slip back down undetected.

Unfortunately, his plans were interrupted by the announcer's voice booming over the loudspeaker: "Now at the top of the jump, Edward Kennedy, the brother of Senator John F. Kennedy! Edward has never jumped before, but maybe if we give him a big hand, he will try it!"

Somewhere far below, Ted figured, Ivan was probably having the laugh of his life. Later, Ted would find the humor in it, too. But not right now.

Ted inched forward on his skis, craning his neck to get a better look at the slick tracks just ahead of him. With his very pregnant wife, Joan, at home, now wasn't the best time to risk breaking his neck.

Of course, he'd do almost anything for Jack, and he had already proven himself an asset to his brother's political life by managing Jack's successful 1958 bid for Senate. But organizing and canvassing was one thing; flinging himself down an icy ramp was another.

"Here he comes, ladies and gentlemen!" the announcer continued. "What a true sport he is! I am sure the senator would be proud of him!"

Far below, the Marine Band began a drumroll as the crowd shouted and whistled its enthusiasm.

Now or never.

If not now, Ted knew there would be hell to pay. "It was either jump," Ted recounted later, "or if my father found out, I'd have to go back to Hyannis Port and lick stamps for the rest of the campaign." Gritting his teeth, Ted peered past the crowd and the cars and pointed his ski tips down the track, then let gravity do the rest. He tried to slow down but with every passing foot, he picked up speed. Then it happened: he was sailing through the air.

It was over in seconds.

Ted collapsed into a thick pile of snow, dusted himself off, and slowly stood.

The crowd roared in appreciation.

It had all happened so fast: one minute he was safe at the top of the jump, the next he was airborne, and now he was regaining his bearings on solid ground and, adrenaline pumping, walking over to the broadcast booth.

The announcer handed Ted the mic. He could've come up with a few choice words for Ivan—and likely Jerry, too—who'd gotten him into this mess. But he chose, instead, to use the platform wisely.

"Did anyone see Hubert Humphrey at the top of that jump?" Ted shouted breathlessly into the mic. "Then support my brother, John. I'm here to help my brother."

It was Ted's finest moment in Wisconsin. Not only because of what he'd said, but because of what he'd done. Quite by accident, it earned him folk hero status. And Wisconsinites would long remember his grit.

Ted's wife, Joan, would remember it, too. In a letter that April, Joan Kennedy would thank Ivan's wife, Geraldine Nestingen, for the thoughtful baby gift of Wisconsin booties for young Kara, which Joan described as "a perfect memento and reminder of [Ted's] busy days there around the time of her birth."

"Someday," Joan continued, "Ted will tell his daughter all about his first (and last!) ski jump."

Long before Kara Kennedy was old enough to learn of her father's flight, Ted would share the story with Wisconsin's primary voters.

That March, when Ted was dispatched to a dinner in Wisconsin Rapids to fill in for his brother, he put his newfound popularity to work. To a crowd four hundred people strong, Ted grinned, waved, and worked the Kennedy charm. "It is a great deal more pleasant to be here today," he said, "than at the top of a ski jump."

Once more, the crowd went wild.

Jackie Steals the Show

Jerry Bruno and Jackie Kennedy
February 16, 1960

One month and twenty days before the Wisconsin primary

Already they were well behind schedule, but there was little to be done. If Jerry Bruno had learned anything over the past nine months as the state director for Jack Kennedy's presidential campaign, it was that Jack was never one to be whisked away from adoring crowds, nor were the crowds willing to give him up. Not even the Humphrey-friendly AFL-CIO crowd in Kenosha, which was currently mobbing the man. But not far away, twelve hundred supporters were milling around Kenosha's American Legion Hall, eager to meet the candidate. And cheap beer wasn't going to keep them waiting there forever.

Thankfully, Jerry had a secret weapon to keep them happy. Her name was Jackie.

As Jack hobnobbed with labor leaders at the AFL-CIO, Jackie Kennedy smiled brightly from a makeshift stage across town. Kenosha's American Legion Hall was a far cry from Southampton, and Poughkeepsie, and New York, and Boston, and DC, and Hyannis Port (and all the other places Jackie knew well). Still, she did her best to fit in. But it wasn't easy.

Later, Jackie would admit that Wisconsin had been her least favorite of the primary states. On the campaign trail she often found the people to be cold and "suspicious of anyone sort of gregarious." Some days she and Jack would enter a general store to find no more than three people clustered near the back. Persuading them to shake hands proved even more difficult.

"In Wisconsin, those people would stare at you like sort of animals," she said later, adding, too, that she never met a single Wisconsinite she liked, "except for the people who were working for Jack."

Had the day been hers, she'd have been far from Wisconsin. Or, if she had to be stuck here in Kenosha, then she'd be back in her hotel room reading Tolstoy's *War and Peace*, which she'd brought along for a little less-than-light reading, or Kerouac's *The Dharma Bums*, also in the rotation that spring. But the day was Jack's, as was true of most days on the campaign. And stalling before a Wisconsin crowd was a small price to pay if it might help her husband win the presidency.

Once they were done here, she knew they'd have to start all over in another state. Then there was the general election, if they made it that far, which would tack on another six months.

But she also knew this was what she'd signed up for. When she had first met Jack in May 1952, he had still been a congressman from Massachusetts, and it was clear to her even then that he wouldn't be in that role for much longer. Within months, Jack would beat Henry Cabot Lodge Jr. for a Senate seat, and what was left after that? Jack defied gravity, at least when politics were concerned. Though that was not to say he hadn't had his share of professional setbacks, or that the couple hadn't endured more than their share of personal ones.

In 1955, two years after their wedding, Jackie's first pregnancy had ended in a miscarriage. Tragically, that grief was compounded on August 23, 1956, when Jackie gave birth to the couple's stillborn daughter, Arabella. Jackie was devastated. And she was alone. Jack, meanwhile, was yachting with friends in the Mediterranean and had to be convinced to return. With him on the yacht was Florida senator George Smathers, who told Jack, "You better haul your ass back to your wife if you ever want to run for president."

Only then did Jack fly home to Jackie's side.

Up on that Kenosha stage, Jackie's smile held firm. Right now, all that mattered was how long she'd be able to hold the crowd. She hoped she could last as long as was required of her.

To the surprise of some in Jack's inner circle, and despite her private misgivings about the state, Jackie proved to be a huge asset in Wisconsin. Some had feared her designer dresses and expensive tastes would be off-putting to the more modest midwesterners. But, as it turned out, Wisconsinites were generally taken by her, even if the feeling wasn't entirely mutual.

One day, during a small-town campaign stop, Jackie had worked one side of the street while Jack worked the other. This divide-and-conquer approach had served them well in the past, providing a more personalized experience for each prospective voter. Jack could've shaken hands all day had there been enough hands to shake, but there weren't. Glancing Jackie's way, however, he noticed she had a different problem.

Jackie Kennedy works the campaign trail with her husband, Senator John F. Kennedy, Madison Mayor Ivan Nestingen (second from right), and others. WHI IMAGE ID 58661

"Jackie's drawing more people than I am, as usual," Jack grumbled to his aides.

For many people in Wisconsin, Jackie was a rarity. Stylish, worldly, and as regal as a queen, she was nonetheless willing to pose with a prized ham in a Wisconsin diner, or chat with the patrons, or—as she'd proven earlier that afternoon in Kenosha—go to even more extraordinary lengths to get her husband elected.

Shortly before she arrived at the American Legion Hall, Jackie had stopped inside a local Kenosha supermarket. As she watched the shoppers meander the aisles, she was suddenly struck by an idea. She had a captive audience, she realized, so why not make the most of it?

Strolling toward the microphone for the store's loudspeaker system, Jackie asked the manager if she might say a few words to the shoppers. The manager, who'd surely never received such a request, handed over the mic without question. Jackie thanked him, smiled, cleared her throat, and began.

"Just keep on with your shopping," Jackie said, her voice echoing throughout the store, "while I tell you about my husband, John F. Kennedy."

What happened next would remain legendary for years to come. Decades later, shoppers in the store that day would tell their grandchildren how, on Tuesday, February 16, 1960, while picking up produce, or canned yams, or Ovaltine, they heard the voice of Jackie Kennedy drifting down upon them like a gentle breeze. How, underneath the store's fluorescent lights, they'd halted their carts in their tracks and tilted their ears toward the loudspeakers. No one could quite remember her exact words, though everyone seemed to agree that she'd spoken to them in a language they could understand. They listened carefully as Jackie Kennedy—*the* Jackie Kennedy—spoke plainly and earnestly about her husband's navy service, his public service, and his commitment to the country at large. There was something to be admired, too, in how this woman—so far removed from the world she knew best—had come to them humbly with a single message.

"Please," she said, "vote for him."

Now, at the Kenosha American Legion Hall, Jackie shared the stage alongside several others: her sister-in-law, Eunice Shriver; Kenosha's mayor, Eugene Hammond; and, possibly an even bigger draw than Jackie, twenty-six-year-old Alan Ameche, a UW–Madison Heisman Trophy winner, fullback for the Baltimore Colts, and Kenosha's hometown hero. At six feet tall and two hundred pounds, his boxy frame barely able to fit into his suitcoat, Ameche made for an odd pairing next to Jackie, as stately as ever in her dark dress and pearls.

Before them, a packed crowd stood shoulder to shoulder as another two hundred people waited outside. Ameche bravely approached the mic, putting his hometown hero status to good use. Apparently, Jackie thought, the proceedings would begin with or without her husband. Which was just as well. These people had waited long enough.

Ameche waved and grinned and launched into a speech, and the crowd reveled in every second. Ameche said all the right things, though, in truth, he could have said just about anything and received uproarious applause. But he said the words that would most help Jack Kennedy, that it was his firm belief that Kennedy would be the country's next president.

The crowd cheered.

Next, still trying to buy Jack time, Mayor Hammond took his turn at the mic. He described how he'd met Kennedy on three occasions and how his admiration grew with each subsequent visit. Jack, he said, could talk to people "in a way to make you feel proud to call yourself a fellow American."

The crowd clapped politely.

And then, all eyes turned toward Jackie, who stood slowly and then gamely approached the mic.

"I apologize for my husband's tardiness," she began. "But in the meantime, I'd be glad to take any questions of a nonpolitical nature."

Questions came from all corners of the room.

What does the senator like to eat?

Tell us about Caroline!

Tell us about the Kennedy family!

Once the questions wound down and Jack was still nowhere to be seen, Jackie tried another tack.

"Let's sing a song," she said. "Does anybody here know 'Southie is my Hometown'?"

The crowd's expressions turned blank. What did they know about some song about south Boston?

But there was at least one song they all knew, one that had been sung over and over at rallies throughout the state, a version of Frank Sinatra's "High Hopes."

Jackie and Ameche led the crowd in singing the tune, the lyrics of which the campaign had cheekily altered:

"Everyone is voting for Jack
Cause he's got what all the rest lack
Everyone wants to back—Jack
Jack is on the right track . . ."

Thankfully, that "right track" had finally led Jack to the American Legion Hall. With a bit of coaxing by Jerry, Jack had finally left the AFL-CIO meeting hall and was now making his way into the American Legion.

Jackie sighed in relief. At least she wouldn't have to teach the people of Kenosha the words to "Southie is my Hometown." If she was frustrated by her husband's late arrival, she hid it, taking a moment, instead, to revel in the crowd's frenetic energy. In this moment, as in almost all the moments of their public life, she had no choice but to share Jack with the world. She smiled, clapped, posed, sang songs, and answered questions. It was hard to imagine that this was her life now—and maybe her future, too. It was a small taste of what life might be like as First Lady—both liberated and cloistered, all at once.

The minute Jack took the stage in his suit and dotted floral tie, it was almost as if the rest of them had disappeared. Even Ameche seemed to vanish into the backdrop as all eyes focused squarely on the senator.

With Jackie seated to his right, Jack offered the same pitch he'd been making since his official entrance into the primary a few weeks before. He pledged to visit as much of the state as possible over the next six weeks leading up to the Wisconsin primary, which, he said, was "the most significant in the United States."

The crowd inside the legion hall cheered, while the two hundred or so people outside strained to catch every word relayed over a speaker system.

No sooner had Jack concluded his remarks than he was overrun by supporters, all of whom wanted to shake hands with the next president of the United States. For the next ninety minutes, Jack indulged them, smiling and posing for every camera in his field of vision.

Jackie knew better than to think her husband might call it an early night. There were no early nights with Jack, especially during campaign season. Instead, she watched politely as her husband soaked up the spotlight, maintaining her smile even as the press demanded more.

Only forty-nine days until they'd have their answer in Wisconsin.

And then, only another 217 days after that.

It would all be over in a little under a year, Jackie knew. And if the winds blew in their favor, it would be worth it.

For all their personal trials, Jackie had meant what she'd said in the supermarket. She believed her husband was capable of greatness. But greatness came at a price, and Jack wasn't the only one to pay it.

CHANCE ENCOUNTERS

Karel Yasko and Ivan Nestingen
February 23, 1960

One month and thirteen days before the Wisconsin primary

Forty-eight-year-old Karel Yasko smiled as he listened to the laughter that filled the dining room of Madison's Hotel Loraine. This was the perfect venue for the night's festivities: the Wisconsin chapter of the American Institute of Architects annual convention. To the untrained eye, the ten-story hotel was a brick box on West Washington Avenue, but to Karel—Wisconsin's newly hired state architect—it was a fine example of the Beaux Art tradition, which melded Tudor and Mediterranean styles. Completed in 1924, the Hotel Loraine was just one of the many achievements of Milwaukee-based architect Herbert Tullgren, who was famous for designing schools, hotels, and apartment buildings throughout the state.

As state architect, Karel had become adept at seeing the artistry in places others often overlooked. A different kind of artistry was required in pulling off a night like tonight. So far, everything was going as planned. State chapter members happily filled every white linen–covered table, exuding an air of opulence in their suits, ties, and dresses as the cocktail hour gave way to dinner.

Karel, who preferred a drafting table to a banquet table, nonetheless had agreed to serve as the evening's emcee. Looking around the room, he was pleased to see that everyone was enjoying themselves. Maybe a little too much. But so what if his colleagues indulged a bit? If anything, it would help his jokes land with a bit more zing.

Yet the best joke of the night was the one Karel hadn't prepared for.

Karel was sitting at the front table of the hotel dining room when a fellow architect and chapter committee member approached him. The committee member had learned that Jack Kennedy and his wife, Jackie, were staying just few floors up with their campaign staff, and they were about to head out for a campaign event. Would it be all right, he asked Karel, if he invited the Kennedys to pay a quick visit to the architects?

That sounded wonderful, Karel said. Getting to meet a presidential candidate from either party was something he thought the architects in the room would appreciate.

The committee member went to find Ivan Nestingen, Madison's mayor and chairman of the Kennedy for President Club of Wisconsin, and asked if the Kennedys, on their way out for the evening, might pop their heads into the dining room to say hello. He'd try, Ivan told him. Nothing fancy, though. Just a brief hello, a couple of handshakes, and maybe a few words if time permitted.

All that sounded fine to Karel, who guarded the secret while he waited for the famous couple to arrive.

The elevator doors opened, and a dapper Jack and a dazzling Jackie began their cinematic descent down the balcony stairs. It was a grand entrance that should have silenced the room—two famous and breathtakingly beautiful people dressed in their best, walking down the architectural world's equivalent of the red carpet. But the architects at their tables—absorbed in their discussions and drinks—barely took notice. Except for Karel, who beamed as the Kennedys made their way toward the front of the room.

Later, Karel would wonder if the lack of attention the Kennedys received had something to do with the Republican-leaning crowd. For his own part, Karel welcomed them warmly, grasping Jack's and Jackie's hands and thanking them profusely for taking the time.

"Would you care to say a word or two to the architects of our state?" Karel asked.

Jack, who hadn't even known who was in the room two minutes prior, happily agreed. He proceeded to give, as Karel would later describe it, "an extemporaneous, spontaneous talk on the responsibility of the architect to society. . . . He called it the exploding society, and that made a tremendous impact on those people, and I'm sure unwittingly he gained votes."

Karel listened in awe. "The great regret of my life," he would go on to say, "was that someone forgot to turn on the tape recorder."

But that wasn't his only regret of the evening. Because immediately before Jack's speech, Karel would commit a blunder so memorable that its legend soon surpassed the speech itself.

Reaching for the microphone, Karel quieted the crowd and began his introduction.

"We have with us tonight a candidate for the Democratic nomination for president," Karel said, "and I thought that you would like to see one in the flesh."

The crowd chuckled.

"I introduce you to," Karel began, "Senator Robert Kennedy!"

As Karel turned to pass the mic to Jack, the room erupted in uproarious laughter.

Confused, Karel replayed the introduction in his mind before realizing the terrible truth.

Had he said, Senator Robert Kennedy?

It was an innocent mistake, but it was mortifying.

A good-humored Jack accepted the mic with a grin. "Yesterday I was in Eau Claire," Jack began, "and a nice old lady came up to me and said, 'Mr. Kennedy, I'm so glad that your sons are taking an active part in public life. I think that's wonderful.' So I said, 'Thank you, Madam, but I happen to be one of the sons, you're talking about my father.'"

The laughter grew.

"Just before that I'd been up to Wausau where the skiing was pretty good, and some of the young people got around me and said it was wonderful that I found time to ski up there last weekend, and I had to tell them that was my brother Ted."

Louder still.

"The best of all . . . was over in Sheboygan," Jack continued, "and a very nice pair of ladies came up to me and said, 'It's wonderful that busy people like you can still find time to have a large family of children.' So I just had to sadly tell her that was my brother Robert."

By then, even Karel was laughing.

"And he took me off the hook so beautifully," Karel later reflected.

If this had been Karel's only encounter with Jack Kennedy, it would've made for a good story. But what happened next made for a better one.

Karel's family had stayed behind in Wausau when he'd taken the job in Madison, and every Friday night he flew back to see them. A few weeks after his embarrassing mishap at the Hotel Loraine, Karel was lounging in the all-but-empty Madison airport, waiting for the final flight of the night. Suddenly there was a slight commotion, as people gathered to get a glimpse of a plane that was taxiing toward the gate. Karel looked up. It was the *Caroline*.

No, Karel thought. *Impossible.*

He watched as campaign staff assembled, led by a man with a large cigar who turned out to be Pierre Salinger, Kennedy's future press secretary, along with Ivan Nestingen, whom Karel recognized from the Hotel Loraine, as well as several others.

It was freezing that night, about twenty degrees below zero. When Kennedy appeared moments later, he was hatless, his hands buried deep in the pockets of his thin blue topcoat, his shoulders raised toward his ears. Kennedy took a moment to chat with Ivan before his eyes drifted toward Karel on the opposite side of the room.

Karel tried making himself invisible, to little avail. Though they had only ever seen each other during those few embarrassing moments in the hotel ballroom, the look on Jack's face confirmed he remembered everything.

Grinning, Jack strode in Karel's direction.

Leaning forward, hand outstretched, he said, "Bobby Kennedy's the name."

Karel didn't know whether to burst out laughing or drop dead on the airport floor.

"I'm sorry," Karel said miserably, "for what happened that night."

"You know," Jack smiled, "the big problem is those three stories were true. I didn't make them up, but they just seemed to fit."

Jack excused himself to greet the twenty or so folks who'd gathered to see him ("I'm Jack Kennedy, and I'd appreciate your interest in the upcoming election"), and then—once the hobnobbing was complete—he turned back Karel's way. By then, Karel had taken a seat on a hard bench, resting for the flight ahead. It was a little past ten o'clock, and after a long week, Karel was anxious to get home to his family. He wasn't the only one in need of a rest.

Looking exhausted, Jack sank beside him, stretched out his legs, and said, "If I fall asleep, wake me up before my crew gets here."

Karel promised the senator that he would.

Jack—who'd become adept at catching a few winks wherever he could—was asleep within seconds. Reclined on the bench, it was as if all the pressures of his presidential run suddenly faded. They sat there for some time, completely uninterrupted, as Karel tried to trace the strange circumstances that had led him to this moment. First, a chance run-in at the Hotel Loraine, and, now, a second run-in at the airport. Of all the ways the stars might've aligned, this seemed rather fortuitous. Karel was glad for the chance to brush shoulders with greatness, even if he'd paid the price with a bit of embarrassment along the way.

The minutes passed in silence until Karel spotted his plane taxiing toward the gate. Though he'd never woken a senator before, he figured a bit of humor might do the job.

Tapping the senator, Karel said, "Bob, Bob it's time to go."

Jack woke with his humor intact.

"Yes, Ted," Jack grinned sleepily.

And then they were gone, both "Bob" and "Ted" moving their separate ways.

THE CANDIDATES SQUARE OFF
IN CLINTONVILLE

Hubert Humphrey
March 11, 1960

Twenty-five days before the Wisconsin primary

Hubert Humphrey and Jack Kennedy stood shoulder to shoulder in front of a red barn and farm silo on the outskirts of Clintonville, Wisconsin, posing for a cover shot for *LIFE* magazine.

Hubert smiled as photographer Stan Wayman snapped one photo after another, only stopping long enough to fiddle with the settings.

He'll be wrapping up any minute now, he figured, *just keep smiling.*

But Hubert knew that was mostly wishful thinking. The big city photographers could snap forever. For them, money was no object. They could buy up half the film in the world in pursuit of the perfect shot. Yet, somehow, none of their photos ever seemed to depict Senator Humphrey half as favorably as they showed the man to his left.

Hubert glanced toward Jack Kennedy to catch him sporting the perfect smile and the perfectly coiffed hair that was a far cry from his own receding hairline. All the pundits warned that Kennedy's "youthful inexperience" might be his undoing, though the photos only ever captured the youthful part.

Not that Hubert would trade his substance for Jack's style. Jack may have walked the walk, but Senator Humphrey talked the talk. And then some. His gift for gab was so powerful that even he struggled to control it. His

Minnesota senator Hubert Humphrey speaks to a small crowd in southwestern Wisconsin's Vernon County during one of his many primary campaign trips across the state. In the crowd, near the far left of the photograph, is state party chairman Pat Lucey.
WHI IMAGE ID 45420

words unfurled like an endless ball of yarn. If he got in front of a room full of farmers or union men, it was all over; God bless the poor janitor who'd have to stay late to lock up. Hubert simply loved those leather-handed, blue-collared, salt-of-the-earth folks. They may not know the jib sheet on a sailboat, but they could assemble an engine with their eyes closed.

As Wayman adjusted his camera settings, Hubert took the opportunity to straighten his overcoat. His eyes met Jack's for a moment of awkwardness, but the moment passed. They were professionals, after all, and loyal Democrats. What could be easier than sharing a photographer's frame?

Of course, it could've been a whole lot easier if Kennedy wasn't outspending the Humphrey campaign by such a wide margin. Not only that, but most of the money was coming from out East. It prickled Hubert to no end. Didn't that just prove his central argument, that Jack Kennedy wasn't one of them? Didn't voters want to elect a man of the people? Or did they want someone like Kennedy—some version of themselves they'd never be? For reasons beyond Hubert's understanding, the polls were suggesting a good many Wisconsinites were leaning Kennedy's way. After everything he'd done for them, Hubert thought he deserved better.

At least the backdrop might work to his advantage, he figured. No doubt Wayman had wanted to capture the "essence" of Wisconsin, which was what brought them here in the first place, to this former sawmill town in the vast, agricultural middle of the state. Kennedy, meanwhile, might never have visited a place like Clintonville were it not for the promise of cameras. For him, it was just some place en route to a better place. Wasn't that always the way with the Kennedys? Make everything a steppingstone to something else? Jack had barely even found the Congressional cloakroom before he'd catapulted to the Senate. And here he was, just two years into his second term, and he was already setting his sights on the White House.

To Kennedy, Clintonville might have been just a photo op, but to Hubert Humphrey it was sacred ground. A reminder of his own small-town roots in Doland, South Dakota—a town, like so many other towns, that had endured financial hardships in the years leading to the Great Depression. By 1926, both of the town's banks had closed, leaving local businessmen like Hubert Humphrey Sr.—a pharmacist and merchant—with few options to pay their creditors. Hubert would never forget that terrible day in 1927 when he'd come home from school to find his parents weeping beneath the front yard cottonwood tree, and the way his father had looked him in the eye and explained that selling the family home was the only way to pay the bills.

What did Kennedy know of such struggles? That family could afford anything—even elections. From July 1959 through the Wisconsin primary, Joe Kennedy Sr. would infuse his son's campaign with a million dollars, while the Humphrey campaign would spend $116,500 throughout the Wisconsin primary. Even if Wisconsin swung his way, Kennedy's disproportionate spending would hamstring Humphrey in West Virginia, where he would be saddled with $17,000 in debt upon his arrival.

As Wayman continued to click, Hubert tried to hide his frustration. But it was hard, particularly when he and his staff froze themselves half to death in the steely behemoth that passed for their campaign bus, while Jack and his team soared across the state in the *Caroline*. For the past many weeks, on countless dark and dismal Wisconsin mornings, Senator Humphrey had corralled his team onto their frigid bus, where they bundled up tight against the frosty, predawn chill until the sun rose to thaw them. One dark

The cover of *LIFE* magazine featuring Humbert Humphrey and John F. Kennedy, published March 28, 1960. STAN WAYMAN/THE LIFE PICTURE COLLECTION/SHUTTERSTOCK

morning, as Hubert shivered on his cot in the back of his bus, he'd heard a plane cutting across the sky. Whether it was the *Caroline* or not was irrelevant. In Hubert's mind, every plane belonged to Jack. To the surprise of his campaign aides, he allowed his exasperation to get the better of him. "Come down here, Jack," he'd hollered, "and play fair."

Humphrey's smile and receding hairline wouldn't much matter in the grand scheme. When *LIFE* magazine's nearly seven million readers peered at the cover of the March 28 issue from newsstands across the country, all they'd see was Jack Kennedy anyway. Years later, a humbled Hubert Humphrey would take stock of all the lessons he'd learned that winter and spring in Wisconsin. Among them was that style could be just as important as substance.

"I think I saw in the Wisconsin primary the great personal attraction of Kennedy to the young people," Humphrey would reflect. "I also think that I saw where a man's personality, his demeanor, his sense of being gallant, went over beyond the issues because he was close enough to being right on the issues so that you couldn't really get to him."

Humphrey concluded that Jack Kennedy simply possessed a "great personal magnetism." It was a magnetism that caused the press to swoon. While the news-obsessed Jack was known to agonize over bad press, bad press for him was rare.

"To this day it astounds me," Humphrey said. "You could go to the A&P store. You could go to any grocery store. You'd pick up a woman's magazine—there would be a wonderful article, good pictures, nice things, always, everything. From the *Foreign Affairs Quarterly* to the family magazine. It didn't make any difference what it was, it was a good, solid piece."

Humphrey's press was never so flattering.

"I would be interpreted as being brash or talkative or this or that," Humphrey recalled, "and [Kennedy] was always interpreted as being intelligent and delightful and meaningful and so on. And, needless to say, it would bother me."

Humphrey found Kennedy's political strategy self-serving: the man relied too heavily on his image and overlooked policy in the process. While Humphrey labored on the minutiae of his senatorial work, Jack focused on putting himself in positions to improve his political fortunes. But to call him on it would risk further tarnishing Humphrey's own image. As Humphrey learned the hard way, Jack Kennedy was like Teflon—nothing stuck.

Later, Humphrey conceded that he bore much of the responsibility for his loss. Had he simply committed to running earlier, he would have had a chance to build up the necessary campaign infrastructure. Instead, he had hemmed and hawed endlessly, weighing every pro and con while Kennedy put the finishing touches on his campaign.

Throughout 1959, Humphrey's aides regularly tried to intervene. "If you're going to run for president, run for president," they told him. "Quit being a senator. You can't be shuttling back and forth between one speech and another and getting back to the Capitol. Look at John Kennedy. He doesn't worry about that."

His aides were right. By December 1959, it was time to make a choice. It was time, as he put it, "to fish or cut bait."

The problem, though, was that by the time he decided, Kennedy had already caught the biggest fish. As Humphrey hedged, he missed out on recruiting men like Pat Lucey, Ivan Nestingen, and Jerry Bruno—the latter of whom he tried to win over to no avail.

Humphrey may have had more party loyalists in his corner, but their numbers didn't translate into statewide votes. As Humphrey's regional director Harvey Kitzman later remarked,

> I think in Wisconsin one of the drawbacks that Hubert had was that he had very little organization. When I talk about organization, I mean top-notch, qualified men or women to come in and run the various headquarters. This is an important factor in a campaign. I don't care how good the candidate is, if he doesn't have himself sur-rounded with some capable people to carry on . . . he's in trouble. Hubert did not have this.

What Humphrey had, Kitzman recalled, were two major offices in Milwaukee and Madison, along with a handful of poorly run local offices scattered throughout the state. What he needed, Kitzman believed, were political insiders on par with Kennedy's.

Humphrey's lack of political professionals led to a disorganized cam-paign. Nothing better reflected the disarray than the disconnected phones at Humphrey's campaign headquarters. Even if people had wanted to reach the Humphrey office in 1959, there was no good way to do so.

"It was," Humphrey later lamented, "unbelievably bad."

When the press questioned him on his disorderly campaign, Humphrey defended the mess.

"Thank God, thank God," he said. "Beware of these orderly campaigns. They are ordered, bought and paid for. We are not selling corn flakes or some Hollywood production."

His bravado wasn't fooling anyone. And by the time Humphrey was finally getting around to reconnecting his phone lines, Jack Kennedy was finalizing the details of his official announcement to enter the race.

In early December 1959, Jack's campaign informed Humphrey's people of their plan to formally announce Jack's candidacy in early January—as a courtesy, and to ensure they didn't steal one another's airtime.

Humphrey seized the opportunity to strike first and made his own announcement in late December, which immediately got lost amid the holiday season.

"It was a stupid thing," Humphrey admitted later. "But we thought that if we didn't [enter first] it would look like a sort of afterthought following a Kennedy initiative."

The combination of these self-inflicted setbacks had led Senator Humphrey to this moment in front of a snow-covered Clintonville barn, down in the polls against an east coaster with virtually no legislative record to speak of.

Though down, Hubert wasn't counting himself out. Even if some days it seemed for naught. How could his old campaign bus compete with Jack's plane? His wife, Muriel, was passing out copies of her recipe for beef soup, while Jackie was walking around like some runway model. If that wasn't enough, the whole Kennedy clan had decided to move in. One day Ted Kennedy was soaring off a ski jump in the second district, and the next Kennedy's sisters and mother, Rose, were sipping tea in half the households in the state! How big could one family be?

But Hubert refused to give in. After all, he had one thing that Jack lacked: firsthand experience of real people's problems. That had to count for something, didn't it? Who wanted to vote for the world-trotting son of some disgraced ambassador when they could put their money on the midwestern son of a druggist?

If Hubert's smile came less naturally for Wayman's camera, it was only because he had less to smile about. His base was turning its back on him. Time was running out.

What Hubert wanted to say—and what he would say weeks later—was that "the only legitimate kind of politics is politics of the record, not a razzle-dazzle, frizzle-frazzle synthetic type of phony politics." They were electing the president of the United States, not some star for a Hollywood drama.

Personality was all well and good, but policy mattered too. Didn't it? Did a man's record mean nothing?

Wayman took a step forward and snapped a photo, then retreated a step and snapped another. Jack smiled. Hubert smiled.

Or maybe it was a grimace in disguise.

DRIVING SENATOR KENNEDY

Pete Dugal
March 17, 1960

Nineteen days before the Wisconsin primary

Since late January, Jack Kennedy had become a whirlwind campaigner, blurring through Wisconsin's hamlets and cities, his smile blazing, his hand outstretched. The Wisconsin primary was just two and a half weeks away. At six thirty on a Thursday morning—St. Patrick's Day—thirty-one-year-old Pete Dugal, from nearby Cadott, Wisconsin, peered through his windshield to see the silhouette of Jack Kennedy heading toward him through the early morning darkness of Eau Claire.

This was the second day of a five-day blitz across the state's ten congressional districts, and it was shaping up as one of the most ill-fated campaign days to date.

As Chippewa County's Democratic Party chairman, Pete's mission was to make sure Jack could speak at every café, Elks Club, and high school that would have him. Not that all of them were forthcoming with their invitations. Hubert Humphrey was so beloved in the western districts that Pete sometimes struggled to find Kennedy suitable speaking venues. Why listen to some out-of-towner carpetbagger, western Wisconsinites figured, when they could hear Humphrey, who was by Kennedy's own admission the best orator in the Senate.

What Pete's neighbors and friends failed to understand was that Jack Kennedy was somebody special. Not just another gladhanding politician (though he was that, too), but a bridge to the next generation of leaders.

Pete Dugal and Senator Kennedy at a campaign stop in Eau Claire in 1960.
GILBERT TANNER/LAURIE GAPKO COLLECTIONS

Jack represented a new order, serving as a respectful rebuke to the gray-haired "this-is-how-it's-always-been-done" generation. Jack dazzled with possibility. The old guard had been running the show since forever, Pete knew; why not give someone new a try?

Pete's first drive with Jack back in November now seemed like a lifetime ago. Sure, it had been thrilling to transport the senator from River Falls to Eau Claire, but these days such drives were mostly just par for the course. This is not to say that Pete didn't cherish his time driving Jack around northwestern Wisconsin; he did, only now there was a friendly ease to their routine.

"Morning, senator," Pete smiled as Jack entered the car. "You ready?"

Pete was a few inches shorter and a few pounds lighter than the senator seated next to him. But they shared the same blue eyes and the same brown hair—even if Pete kept his trimmed shorter. Though they were both committed to arriving at their many campaign stops on time, they were already a tad behind schedule. Pete picked up the pace, hurrying down the quiet roads on the forty-mile drive to the town of Cornell, population 1,685.

Upon their arrival, Pete brought the car to a halt in front of the N-Joy Cafe, a modest roadside diner indistinguishable from the many others Jack had been frequenting for months. The senator leapt from the car and went inside, only to find that eight people had shown up to meet him.

If the esteemed politician and war hero was bothered by the small turnout, he hid it. Instead, he reached for an elderly woman's hand—the proprietor, no doubt—and gave it a shake. The woman walked him to a nearby table, revealing a green and white cake she'd baked for him in honor of St. Patrick's Day. Kennedy smiled, graciously accepted a slice of cake and a cup of coffee, and made small talk with the handful of people who'd come out. He flashed a smile, posed for a photo, and—for the sake of his own political survival—made himself available to talk to every one of them.

Though internal polling continued to show that Humphrey was poised to wipe the floor with Jack in Wisconsin's northwestern districts, Jack refused to concede any ground. Instead, he forged unapologetically into the heart of Humphrey's territory, siphoning off votes wherever—and however—he could. Pete had to hand it to him: whether Jack was speaking to ten or ten thousand, he always made the moment seem like a good use of his time.

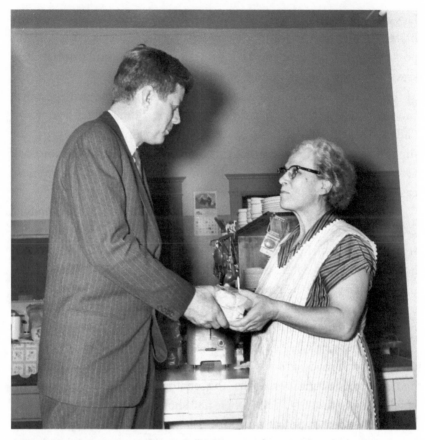

Senator Kennedy receives three pounds of bologna from Rose Hovland of Hovland's Cafe during a campaign stop in Bloomer, Wisconsin. *EAU CLAIRE LEADER-TELEGRAM* (FORMERLY THE *EAU CLAIRE DAILY TELEGRAM*) AND FRED STEFFENS

When it came to planning Jack's trips, Jerry Bruno oversaw most of the details. But Jerry was good about empowering people like Pete—people who knew their districts inside and out—to pick the places that were sure to be winners. Unfortunately, and as a harbinger for the rest of the day, Cornell hadn't exactly been the showstopper Pete had hoped for. Nevertheless, he knew that if the eight folks at the N-Joy each talked Kennedy up to another eight people, then they'd be getting somewhere. There were no shortcuts in the rural districts: you had to win one voter at a time.

Kennedy would have preferred otherwise. Despite enduring the one-on-one handshakes and how-do-you-dos, Jack was no fan of personal politicking, even though he excelled at it. What he liked was a quick reception, followed by brief remarks, then a smooth getaway to the next place. He was a forward momentum machine, and when he came to western Wisconsin, Pete helped to keep that momentum going. Pete was the fuel for Kennedy's jet, but he was more than that, too—part navigator, part pilot, part ground control.

Following their stop in Cornell, Pete and Jack continued twenty miles north toward Ladysmith, population 3,584, a former railroad and lumber town on the banks of the Flambeau River. They were accompanied by a few cars full of campaign staff and members of the press, which contributed to Pete's desire to stick to the schedule. But Jack had other plans.

Glancing out the window, the senator noticed several nuns in full habit awaiting him alongside the road.

"Stop the car," Jack said.

It was the last thing Pete wanted to do, not only because of the schedule but also because of how it might look. This wasn't just another whistle stop to shake hands with the locals. This was a Catholic candidate for president—the first since Al Smith's disastrous run—hobnobbing with nuns. Pete knew better than to question Jack's political instincts, but he had to wonder: did he not understand how this might play in western Wisconsin? Or in the country at large, for that matter? If Jack wanted to minimize the Catholic question, shouldn't he distance himself from the nuns?

No sooner had Pete pulled to the side of the road than Jack exited the car to greet them, even indulging the sisters by paying a brief visit to their nearby convent.

Details differ, and while Pete recalled visiting a handful of nuns, Kennedy aide John Treanor—who also claimed to be in the driver's seat that day—recalled a "mirage" of three hundred or so nuns blocking the road in front of them.

"Did you arrange this [stop], too, John?" Kennedy was said to have asked Treanor.

"I died a thousand deaths," Treanor later remarked.

The optics were terrible. Here was an entire battalion of habit-wearing sisters engulfing the future president, their Mother Superior even attempting to pin a dyed-green boutonniere to Kennedy's jacket. And on St. Patrick's Day, no less! So much for downplaying Kennedy's Irish Catholic faith.

Reporter Ira Kapenstein hopped from a trailing car and began scrib-
bling in his notepad as Jack happily chatted with the nuns. Meanwhile,
campaign adviser Kenny O'Donnell hustled toward Pete.

"Why the hell did you stop?" O'Donnell cried.

"Gee, he told me to," Pete said, "and I couldn't very well go against him."

"That'll be the only press we're going to get out of this trip," O'Donnell
said miserably as the photographers swarmed. "They'll sure as heck have
pictures of it."

By noon, Kennedy had met with a grand total of eight people in Cornell,
a handful of nuns in Ladysmith, and an unknown number of others as
they made brief stops at one small town after the next. All things considered, it was shaping up to be a less-than-successful day. To make matters
worse, when they stopped for lunch, a German priest ("the dirtiest looking
Roman Catholic priest I have ever seen," Treanor later remarked) held
court in what was supposed to be the restaurant's private backroom. In
his soup-stained vest, the priest circled the forty or fifty people who had
gathered for the campaign lunch, Treanor would recall, "shaking hands,
and saying in a very loud, guttural accent about how wonderful it was to
have a Catholic running for president."

Pete, Treanor, and the rest of the Kennedy entourage prayed the priest's
proclamations wouldn't make the papers. The nuns would suffice.

Despite the campaign's attempts to distance Kennedy from his Catholic
supporters, the candidate himself was often unwilling to do so. Turning
his back on some of his most dogged supporters seemed like bad politics.
The trick was to retain his Catholic support while reassuring Protestants,
Evangelicals, Lutherans, and people of other faiths and denominations
that a vote for Kennedy was not a vote for the papacy. For many voters,
anti-Catholic sentiment boiled down to fears of loyalty and policy. Would
Kennedy's allegiance ultimately lie with his fellow countrymen, or with his
faith? And many voters were concerned that Kennedy's religion would af-
fect his policymaking, particularly in relation to birth control. The Roman
Catholic Church was officially opposed to birth control, so did that mean
Kennedy would be, too?

Ultimately, both fears were unfounded. But such prejudices held powerful political consequences. Kennedy knew that his religion could be a cudgel used against him if or when a campaign turned dirty. If Kennedy had his way, religion never would have been a campaign issue. As far as he was concerned, there were far bigger problems to resolve than where, and to whom, Kennedy prayed.

Indeed, Jack could have used some prayers later that afternoon. Upon arriving in the village of Phillips, he was accosted by no nuns, no priests, not even a green and white cake. Instead, his only company was silence.

No one had shown up to greet him, so an undeterred Jack struck out to find a crowd for himself. He quickly learned that it wouldn't be as easy as he expected. He soon looked like a "forlorn and lonesome young man" who was "wandering solitary as a stick through the empty streets of the villages of Wisconsin's far-north Tenth Congressional District," according to Theodore H. White, a bespectacled forty-four-year-old political reporter who'd been trailing the Kennedy and Humphrey campaigns and who was there that day.

Kennedy started at a hardboard factory, where workers, according to White, "grunted and let him pass." He had even less luck at the local newspaper, "which was totally indifferent to the fact that a presidential candidate" had paid them a visit. Next, Jack worked the cafés, where he was met with a cold and skeptical reception. He didn't much look or talk like the people of Phillips. All they knew for sure was that his name wasn't Hubert Humphrey, and therefore they paid him little mind.

"The town," White would write, "was as careless of his presence as of a cold wind passing through."

For most of the afternoon, it was like this in town after town after town.

Pierre Salinger, Kennedy's adviser and future press secretary, would later remember how Kennedy was "hatless, trudging like a trooper through the icy streets of one tiny town after another, his hands plunged into the pockets of his blue cashmere top coat during the few moments when he wasn't shaking hands and greeting the local folks, many of whom were openly startled to see [Kennedy] in the reddening flesh on their own Main Street."

That was certainly true for the people who recognized Kennedy, though plenty of people didn't.

At a tavern that afternoon, Jack approached a man and woman nursing their beers.

"My name is John Kennedy and I'm running for president," he said, delivering his standard opening line.

The man glanced up to consider the stranger with the fancy coat and the East Coast accent.

"President of what?" he asked.

After the bust in Phillips, Pete and Jack, with the rest of team trailing behind them, continued north toward the mining town of Montreal, Wisconsin, where Pete hoped they'd have better luck. Unfortunately, they arrived at the mine at the end of a shift, just as the miners were showering and changing into clean clothes.

"We were trying to pin buttons on these people," Pete would recall, "and half of them were running around there naked so that was a kind of a problem."

To everyone's surprise, Jack's fortunes changed when they rolled into the nearby town of Hurley. Pete glanced toward the senator to see his eyes widen as he took in the crowd of up to eight hundred people who were packed along the small town's streets. Moments before speaking to his supporters, Kennedy, in his eagerness, accidentally stuck himself in the hindquarters with a campaign pin. He let loose a string of curse words, then found his smile just in time to greet the enthusiastic crowd.

Some of that enthusiasm may have come courtesy of the area's miners, who, at the end of their shifts, had a reputation for reserving their more debaucherous behavior for Hurley's bars and strip clubs. One way or another, Jack became privy to Hurley's reputation.

"Are there really a lot of whores in this town?" Jack asked Pete as they left Hurley in the rearview.

"That's what they say," Pete said, pressing his foot down on the accelerator.

By nightfall, Pete had added some two hundred miles to his odometer, driving Jack from Eau Claire to Cornell to Ladysmith to Ingram to Prentice to Phillips to Montreal to Hurley. "What a hell of a way to spend Saint

Patrick's Day," Jack grumbled, shortly before they left for their final stop in Ashland, the small port city on the shores of Lake Superior where they'd be sleeping that night.

When they arrived in Ashland, the exhausted group split up and headed for two of the town's motels. When Pete and another Kennedy adviser attempted to check in to their motel, they were met with an enthusiastic motel owner who, in her zeal to accommodate Kennedy's well-known back problems, had acquired a board for him to sleep on. They had to explain that Kennedy himself wouldn't be sleeping there that night, but was instead staying at the motel's competitor up the road. The owner, perhaps a bit heartbroken, sent Pete and the adviser packing.

By day's end, White estimated that Kennedy had "seen no more than sixteen hundred people, of whom probably twelve hundred were children too young to vote." While Kennedy's doggedness was admirable, White said, the senator's failure that day to win the hearts and minds of rural Wisconsinites seemed to reinforce the preposterousness of his presidential run.

"Except," White added, "that it did not seem preposterous to Kennedy himself."

Nor did it seem preposterous to Pete, whose commitment to Jack Kennedy was unflagging. Rain or shine, day or night, any time he was called upon, Pete would gamely get in the car.

"Morning, Senator," he'd say, pulling the car door wide. "You ready?"

He needn't have asked.

LOST IN THE PASTURE

Bobby Kennedy and Jerry Bruno
Mid-March 1960

Weeks before the Wisconsin primary

Late one night, after another long day on the road, Bobby Kennedy approached a phone booth in a town somewhere in Wisconsin. He inserted the coin and dialed.

Back in Milwaukee, Jerry Bruno reached for the ringing phone.

"Yeah, what's up?" Jerry asked.

"I don't know where I am!" Bobby shouted.

"Well, where are you?"

"I don't know," Bobby said, growing more irritable. "That's why I'm calling you."

Jerry adjusted the phone and searched his desk for the day's schedule. "What's the name of the town?"

"If I knew where the heck I was," Bobby shouted, "I wouldn't be lost!"

Sighing, Jerry risked another earful from Bobby by asking yet another question: "Um, well, describe it, describe the town."

Bobby peered out of the dimly lit phone booth. It looked like the same small town he'd seen the day before. And the day before that. And the day before that. How different did towns even get in Wisconsin?

Bobby tried to remain calm, but it was hard. All he kept thinking about was how he didn't want to be there in the first place. And he wasn't just talking about the phone booth, but the entire state. If any path to the presidency could've avoided Wisconsin and its godforsaken weather, and its loyal Humphrey voters, and its poorly marked roads, Bobby would have taken it in a heartbeat. But no such path existed.

Only five months had passed since that hopeful day in Hyannis Port, when the whole gang had met in his living room for that fateful strategy meeting. But it had begun to feel more like five lifetimes. Bobby had known the primary route would make for a risky journey. But what he hadn't known—at least not fully—was just what a hard nut Wisconsin would be to crack. Who could've guessed that the dairy state would suddenly become the epicenter of the political world? For nearly two months, Bobby had tried to outhustle Humphrey's campaign, speaking to every hamlet and city and glad-handing every farmer and laborer along the way. It felt like being trapped on a carousel: around and around, again and again, and never gaining ground.

Could that be true? Surely, they were gaining some ground, at least if Lou Harris's polling was to be believed. Not that the polls held all the answers. Even when one indicated the campaign was up, it was always best to play like you were down. Bad news kept the volunteers scrappy, after all, and the candidate, too.

Bobby had acquired his win-at-all-costs mentality in the unlikeliest of places: the Harvard football team. At twenty-one, he'd been the team's runt, barely measuring in at five foot nine and 155 pounds. But his small size hardly prevented him from hurling his body directly into his opponents across the line of scrimmage. So what if he broke his leg on the football field? What mattered was that he knew how to play through the pain.

Grit mattered. Determination mattered. Nobody knew that better than Bobby.

By March 1960, he was already well versed in such lessons, both on the gridiron and beyond. His first foray into the political arena was back in '52, when Bobby—just twenty-six—had helped his brother soundly defeat Senator Henry Cabot Lodge. The win had left political insiders scratching their collective heads. In 1952, Democrats were falling like tin soldiers, but not when Bobby was managing the campaign—Eisenhower had trounced Stevenson by eight percentage points nationally, yet in Massachusetts, Kennedy still beat Lodge by three.

Eight years later, as he stood in a phone booth somewhere in Wisconsin, Bobby had no simple solutions for the problems he faced, including the biggest of all: how in the world he was going to beat back Humphrey in Humphrey's own territory? Was it possible that the Minnesota senator could be Jack's spoiler? That after all they'd done—every mailer and phone call, every speech and handshake—they'd still place second in Wisconsin? It was a nightmare scenario, but indeed it was possible. Despite Humphrey's weaknesses, the man was not going down easy.

Bobby couldn't help but feel a little bad for Humphrey, who'd later grumble that running against Jack felt like "an independent merchant competing against a chain store." But that was the whole point. Run the man ragged. Make him think twice before continuing to West Virginia and the other primary states. For Bobby, it all came down to electability. And if the Democrats wanted to spare the world a Nixon presidency, then Jack was the man to do it.

The truth was, there was plenty to like about Humphrey. At Jack's invitation, he'd even spoken at their youngest brother Ted's law school just a few years before. To say that Humphrey had been warmly received was an understatement, as he received "standing ovation after standing ovation."

No doubt about it, Humphrey was smart and kind, with a disposition that transformed most any stranger into a friend. The problem was, he didn't have national appeal. He couldn't possibly be the man for the moment. That was Jack's job.

Much as Bobby would've preferred to avoid this matchup against Humphrey, Humphrey had insisted. Now they were on a collision course, and come April 5, only one would remain on the track.

None of it was easy, nor was it supposed to be. Wasn't this what campaigning was all about? When Jerry had told Bobby to campaign like a Wisconsinite—shaking hands at the factories, the Elks Clubs, the Lions Clubs, at every club with an animal in its name—he'd just done it. Didn't even need to think twice. If it was uncomfortable, so be it. If it was beneath him, who cared? Besides, nothing could be worse than poor Ted hurling himself from the top of that ski jump.

The Kennedy men weren't the only ones making sacrifices. Their mother, Rose Kennedy, and their sisters had fanned out across the state like an invading army, hosting teas and talks with every housewife who'd have them. They were organized, cordial, and kind enough to take the edge off the so-called "ruthlessness" of the Kennedy campaign. Not to mention their star power. These were women who'd been featured in magazines. Women who'd dined with the queen. Who wouldn't want to receive an invitation to an event at which they were present?

Then, of course, there was Jackie—glorious Jackie, who possessed the same irrepressible charm as Jack. She was a novice campaigner, but a natural, too. Bobby had recently dispatched Jackie and Ted to Wisconsin Rapids while Jack dealt with a procedural vote back in Washington. And the duo had done spectacularly. Had Jackie not pointed out that she was giving her first campaign speech, no one would've noticed. She didn't love the spotlight—not the way Jack did—but she'd do anything short of milking a cow to help her husband win Wisconsin.

Bobby hadn't been asked to milk any cows yet, though he had spent the afternoon judging a bull contest, which was what brought him to this part of Wisconsin to begin with.

Peering out from the phone booth, Bobby tried to answer Jerry's question.

What did he see?

For starters, he saw a make-or-break state that, if it didn't kill him, would lead his brother to the political promised land. In Wisconsin, the race was about more than delegates. It was about quieting the opposition's chatter about Jack's electability. It was about moving beyond the religious question as best they could, or at least developing some strategy to contain it. Winning Wisconsin was about testing the loyalty of big labor and the limits of Humphrey's appeal. It was, in short, precisely where the campaign needed to win to prove Jack's fitness for the general election.

If they couldn't finish Humphrey off here, they'd be forced into a rematch in West Virginia, where they'd confront an entirely different demographic on an entirely new battlefield. It was a scenario that grew likelier with every passing day, though Bobby wasn't yet ready to wrap his head around it. For the moment, West Virginia was still some far-off horizon; what mattered most was Wisconsin.

Wherever the hell in Wisconsin he was.

At last, Bobby answered Jerry's question directly.

What did he see?

"Well, I'm looking out the window of a phone booth and I see one bar, another bar, and on my side of the road a huge cow pasture with a bunch of cows staring at me, wondering who the hell is this jerk in the phone booth in the middle of winter, in the middle of Wisconsin!"

Jerry understood Bobby's frustration. As Jerry considered his next words carefully, Bobby kept going: "This is just great. We are going to blow this whole campaign! This whole thing is too disorganized, and we're never going to pull this off!"

Jerry felt those stinging words directed squarely toward him. How could he not? After all, he was the state director. Organization fell to him.

"We shouldn't have even gotten into this thing—we're going to blow it!" Bobby shouted. But then his words steered away from Jerry and perhaps closer toward their intended target.

"I am not going to be able to pull this thing off," Bobby said, "and I am going to blow it for Jack!"

Bobby was on a lonely road, Jerry knew—both literally and figuratively. But then, amid his frustration, a clue emerged.

"What the hell am I doing trying to judge a prize bull contest anyway!" Bobby wondered aloud.

Jerry seized on the detail. "Did you say prize bull contest?"

Bobby confirmed it.

"Watertown, Wisconsin!" Jerry cried. "That's where you are!"

Bobby hung up the phone and headed back toward the car. He started the engine and turned on the lights. It would be a long, dark drive to the hotel, Bobby knew. But at least he knew where he was headed.

At the Gates

Ted Kennedy
March 29, 1960

Seven days before the Wisconsin primary

Ted Kennedy turned his attention away from Eau Claire's US Rubber Company plant and looked toward the rushing river beyond the plant gates. One week and it would all be over. One. More. Week.

The Wisconsin primary was wrapping up, and the long road ahead shimmered like a distant premonition. It seemed foolhardy to predict what might happen next, yet Jack's campaign seemed obsessed with gauging every eventuality, relying on polling, data, and gut instinct to help them find their way. For the Kennedys, winning elections often boiled down to a common denominator: getting the candidate in front of the people who needed to see him most. Today, those people were the first- and second-shift factory workers at the tire plant in Eau Claire.

Ted and Jack waited near the gates, greeting workers at the shift change. "Shake hands with the senator, shake hands with the senator," Ted called.

"Happy to meet you," Jack said, extending his hand. "Glad to see you."

Sometimes the workers stopped to chat; other times, they pushed briskly past with their lunch pails. These were men who had work to do or who'd already spent the day doing it. Men who wore ball caps or didn't, had crew cuts or didn't, and who smelled like rubber—always. They wore winter coats and rolled jeans. These were working-class, meat-and-potatoes people. People who, on the surface at least, might not seem to have much in common with someone like Jack.

Some factory workers were barely eighteen, while others were old enough to be their fathers (and in some cases were). Some had graduated from high school, while others had bypassed diplomas for a good-paying job at the plant. The plant employed thirty-two hundred employees— nearly a tenth of the city—and could churn out thirty thousand tires a day.

It was a hell of an operation, Ted knew. And if Jack could win these men over and prove to the hardworking, blue-collar factory workers of western Wisconsin that he was their candidate, then it was lights out for Humphrey.

"I'm John Kennedy," Jack continued, "candidate for president . . ."

Ted stood to his brother's right, his beige suitcoat in contrast to Jack's long, dark overcoat.

"How you doing?" Ted smiled. "Here. Take some literature about Senator Kennedy . . ."

A slow afternoon drizzle was slapping the pavement around the plant, misting the notepads of the dozen or so journalists who'd joined the Kennedy campaign during one of the final swings through the state.

It was only three o'clock, but already Jack had covered about one hundred and thirty miles that day. They'd started early with a morning press conference in Minneapolis. Then off to a high school in Hudson, Wisconsin, then New Richmond and Ellsworth and several other small towns, and finally, the tire factory in Eau Claire. All things considered, it had been a pretty good day. During lunch, Jack had spoken to an enthusiastic crowd in a Methodist Church basement, followed by an impromptu street corner speech from atop a car. This deep into the primary, most of the speeches were beginning to sound the same. But Jack always made it seem as if he were saying the words for the first time, as if those gathered to listen were hearing something new. That was the trick: make everyone feel like an insider. Take the personal approach to campaigning, and let it ripple out.

Campaigning wasn't rocket science, though some of Jack's pollsters might've preferred that it be viewed in a more scientific light. Polling helped, of course, most notably by helping the campaign press the issues that mattered most to the people who needed to hear them. Such polling had lured them back to the ninth district, standing outside the tire factory in the rain.

To win Wisconsin—and the United States at large—they needed to build a coalition much like Roosevelt had built back in the 1930s: one that included the blue-collar vote, the white-collar vote, the urban vote, the rural vote, the minority vote, organized labor, conservative Catholics—hell, anyone they could get. If they got their crack at Nixon in the general, then every demographic was necessary, vital even, as history would soon prove.

Senator Kennedy, with Jackie Kennedy seated to his right, speaks to diners at Skogmo Cafe in Chippewa Falls, February 26, 1960. *EAU CLAIRE LEADER-TELEGRAM* (FORMERLY THE *EAU CLAIRE DAILY TELEGRAM*) AND FRED STEFFENS

The Kennedys weren't the only ones calling in their coalition-building reinforcements. In this final week of the primary, Humphrey was sending his own surrogates scurrying throughout the state. Folks like Senator Eugene McCarthy (no relation to Joseph McCarthy), whom Wisconsinites adored, and Minnesota governor Orville Freeman, who was as congenial as they came.

For the Kennedy campaign, the key was to outwork them. To schedule more events with more people and create more opportunities for Wisconsin's voters to get their ten seconds of facetime. Ideally with Jack, but

Senator Kennedy shakes hands with well-wishers in Lancaster, Wisconsin, March 25, 1960. *DUBUQUE TELEGRAPH HERALD*

anyone was better than no one. That the Kennedy brothers bore a striking enough resemblance to confuse a portion of the electorate worked in Jack's favor. The Kennedy men came in triplicate: some days you got Jack, other days Bobby or Ted. If you shook hands fast enough, sometimes the voters didn't even know the difference.

The new issue of *LIFE* magazine had just reached newsstands, and there on the cover were Hubert Humphrey and Jack Kennedy posing before a barn. Jack's smile radiated. Ted had seen it all his life and had witnessed Jack's magnetism from close range. Jack had a way of smiling with his mouth and his eyes, in a way that seemed to amplify his charisma. He exuded stoicism and optimism in equal measure. He looked like the type of man who could lead a country through a crisis, while also looking like the man who would steer clear of that crisis before it began.

Standing just a few inches taller than Humphrey, Jack appeared cut from the same cloth as the Greek heroes. He wasn't quite Adonis, but voters didn't want Adonis. They wanted Odysseus, someone as clever as he was capable. Heroic and humble both. Someone who made the hard, right choice to set his compass back toward the people he loved.

Either that, or Jack was Achilles, and if that was true, then his heel might be revealed right here in Wisconsin. Was he too young, too inexperienced, too Catholic? There were plenty of heels from which to choose. Photos within the magazine reminded Ted of his own sacrifices. The first showed Ted decked out in his ice fishing gear somewhere in Wisconsin. But the other was the more dramatic of the two: a shot of him soaring off the ski jump the previous month. Ted could chuckle about it now, though there had been no laughter as he sailed through the air that day. Just the teeth-gritting hope that he wouldn't bust up his body so badly that he'd have to stop campaigning.

Still, it was a small sacrifice in the grand scheme. And everyone was making them. Not just family members, but friends, too. None more so than Dave Powers of Boston, who'd been Jack's right-hand man for years.

Dave, who'd accompanied Jack throughout the primary, had the unenviable job of waking the candidate most mornings. Some nights they didn't finish campaigning until well after midnight, only to start things up again at five thirty in the morning. Poor Dave had to slink into Jack's room, break the news that morning had come, and hope he didn't get harangued. The godforsaken hour was matched only by the godforsaken temperatures, generally in the single digits or close to it throughout most of those February mornings in Wisconsin. But what choice did he have?

On some predawn hour on February 16, when they had fifteen hundred hands to shake at a meatpacking plant, Dave and Kenny O'Donnell had debated letting Kennedy sleep in past his scheduled five thirty wake-up time. After all, the senator hadn't even gotten to bed until two o'clock.

"God, Dave, I don't have the guts to wake him at that hour," Kenny said.

"Well, fifteen hundred people are hard to get in this damned part of Wisconsin. If we let him sleep until nine, he'll be mad at us for letting him miss a crowd like that."

And so, at the appointed time, Dave entered the senator's chilly bedroom, peering out the window at the negative fifteen-degree morning just beyond.

"Who's that?" Jack asked, woken by the sound of footsteps.

"It's Dave Powers, senator. It's five thirty."

"What the hell are you doing in here at five thirty, Dave?" Jack snapped.

Dave reminded him of the meat-packing plant, of the fifteen hundred hands to shake.

Rolling from the bed, Jack reached for his long johns. It wasn't his usual attire, but the extra layer had proven necessary in such an inhospitable terrain. Next came the undershirt, the button-up, his suit coat, and pants. And finally, the finishing touch of the candidate's uniform: a single fur-lined glove for his left hand, while his right hand remained exposed. It was perfect for handshaking. After all, no need for both of his hands to freeze.

Jack stood outside the meatpacking plant that morning, shaking hands with every worker who passed. Dave stood right there, just as he always did, handing out the buttons and the pamphlets and encouraging workers to consider a vote for Kennedy.

But of course, no one said it better than Jack, or as often.

"I'm John Kennedy, candidate for president, and I'd like to have your vote in the primary. . . . I'm John Kennedy, candidate for president . . ."

At one point that morning, Dave had turned to Kenny and whispered,

Students from Hillsboro High School, in Hillsboro, Wisconsin, surround Senator Kennedy after a campaign speech. WHI IMAGE ID 106754

"God, if I had his money, I'd be down there on the patio at Palm Beach."

Instead, Jack shook hands until his own hand bled. He needed to prove to the plant workers that he didn't mind rising at dawn, braving the cold, and putting in a long day's work.

Once the last of the workers had passed, Dave, Kenny, Jack, and the others took shelter in a nearby café, ordering coffees in tall paper cups—perfect for warming their hands. Dave peered toward his buddy Jack as the steam rose from their cups.

What did he see?

Courage, no doubt, but resilience, too. Jack hadn't renounced his privilege, but at least he hadn't retired to Palm Beach. Instead, he used his father's wealth as a crucible for change. Money was fine, but power was better—especially if you wanted to do something big. That's what Jack Kennedy wanted. To do something big, not only for himself, but for his country. To rededicate these United States to justice, service, and peace. Which were just some of the causes that drew him to all those factory gates. Some days it was a meatpacking plant, other days it was all tires.

No matter the product, the factory visits were essential: a chance for Jack to appeal directly to the people, sharing his optimistic brand of populism one handshake at a time.

On the rainy afternoon in Eau Claire, with only seven days to go, Jack held out his hand to another rubber worker. "Happy to meet you," Jack said.

"Happy to meet you," the rubber worker said, leaning in for the shake. "But I like Humphrey, too," he confided. "The primary's going to be a rough fight."

That worker vanished, and Jack held out his hand to the next man in line. Then the next. Then the next.

"Glad to meet you, happy to meet you, I'm John Kennedy, candidate for president."

It made for a beautiful display of democracy. Here was the potential future leader of the free world smiling and nodding and shaking hand after hand at some river town factory in western Wisconsin. To win over American voters, you had to show them that you were just like them, or at least not opposed to learning what it was like to be them. Though Jack hadn't worked in a factory a day in his life, that didn't mean he was incapable of understanding the work. Or the dignity that came with it.

"Meet the senator!" Ted called, "Meet the senator!"

The workers streamed from the factory, many extending their hands. Jack smiled. Ted smiled.

One week. One. More. Week.

Primary Day

Philleo Nash and Ivan Nestingen
April 5, 1960

Wisconsin primary day

P hilleo Nash walked through the door of Milwaukee's Kaiser Knickerbocker Hotel to find Hubert Humphrey and a few of his longtime
friends enjoying dinner at the hotel's restaurant. Philleo braced for the
small talk soon to come, though he had no time for it. The returns would
be rolling in any minute now, and all their work—every door knock, every
mailer, every event—was all coming down to this.

How his candidate could manage to stomach a square meal was beyond Philleo, who was already tied in knots. He'd endured plenty of his
own elections, of course—winning and losing along the way—but this was
different. Over the next few hours, the trajectory of US history would lean
one way or another. Was the country ready to put forth one of the most
progressive candidates in history, or would they side with that fellow from
the East Coast?

Philleo approached the table and dutifully exchanged greetings, a
warm smile spreading across his face as he shook hands with Humphrey's
guests. Small talk ensued, and Philleo did his best to exude an air of hope-
fulness, even if, in recent days, such feelings had become hard to come
by. The polls had tightened and the winds at last appeared to be blowing
in Humphrey's favor, but those winds had come awfully late in the game.
Privately, the best Philleo could hope for was a five-five district split. A
break-even scenario would give Humphrey a psychological victory, if

nothing else. As for the popular vote, Philleo had pessimistically predicted a Kennedy blowout, perhaps as high as 65 to 35 percent. Not that he ever would have whispered a word of such an outcome to the people seated around the table that night.

Minutes later, Philleo pried himself away from Humphrey and the others, then strode dutifully to the press room downstairs. Surprisingly, the early returns from the teletype machine showed Humphrey outperforming two-to-one in a few of the state's rural districts. Philleo glanced at his watch—6:10 p.m. They still had time before they'd know anything definitively. But that didn't keep people from asking.

"Well, what do you think?" a voice called from behind.

Philleo turned to spot Theodore White, the political reporter who'd been following both campaigns for months. "Well," Philleo conceded, "I did not expect these returns to be this good."

The northern districts always reported first, Philleo knew, which served as a somewhat accurate bellwether for what was coming. Philleo watched as 10 percent of the votes were reported, then 20 percent, then 30, and still Humphrey was holding tight. But by 1960, Philleo had endured enough election nights to know better than to put too much stock in early returns. The truth was anything could happen. No one knew whether the state's open primary rule would skew the results, or how much the Democratic Administrative Committee's vote to change the delegate math would end up helping Humphrey. Philleo wanted Humphrey to win as much as the next supporter, but he also wanted Humphrey's win to go unquestioned.

As the early returns trickled in, Philleo couldn't help but indulge his dream scenario. If Humphrey could hold the western ninth and tenth districts as expected, as well as Dane County in the second and La Crosse in the third, followed by an upset in the state's central counties in the seventh, then they'd have the five-five split to keep Humphrey competitive.

For Humphrey, the second district was essential. The district's Dane County—home to the University of Wisconsin's flagship campus in Madison—was arguably the state's intellectual epicenter. If faculty and students were looking for an alternative to Stevenson, Humphrey hoped to be their man. The district's rural outlying areas were vital, too, but the heavily populated Dane County was a must-win; as Dane County goes, many believed, so goes the second district. Working in Humphrey's favor there was what the Kennedy campaign perceived as negative press that had long plagued them from Madison's *Capital Times*. Fed up with the coverage, Kennedy had once marched up to the paper's editor with a folder's worth of clippings and announced, "If I were to form an image of myself based on these clippings, even I wouldn't vote for me."

Humphrey's strength in the second district came from an unexpected source: Jim Doyle Sr., executive director of the Stevenson for President Committee. While Stevenson himself was not a candidate on the Wisconsin ballot, Doyle and his supporters backed Humphrey in the Wisconsin primary in the hopes of preventing Kennedy from winning the nomination on the first round of balloting at the convention.

All of this worked to Humphrey's advantage. And at this stage in the game, Humphrey needed every advantage he could get.

For the next hour or so, Philleo and Teddy White watched the returns together. In all, there were 3,440 precincts to report, and by seven thirty, the returns were picking up. "Well, what do you think?" Teddy asked Philleo again and again. Philleo remained tight-lipped, refusing to predict anything close to a Humphrey victory.

One fact remained clear, though, throughout the first hour or so of returns: Kennedy would not be enjoying the popular vote landslide that Philleo had worried about. Teddy took notes as Philleo kept his eyes on Milwaukee County. Given the county's sizeable Catholic population, Kennedy would likely win there, but the margin would make a difference. And what if Humphrey did somehow pull off a win there? What if the pollsters were wrong? What if Joe Kennedy's money didn't matter? What if the independent merchant beat the chain store for a change?

As the returns continued, Philleo listened with the same growing excitement he had felt the first time he'd heard Humphrey's voice blasting from the truck radio in the cranberry bog. July 14, 1948. Just shy of a lifetime ago. Philleo had listened from his place in the bog as the Minneapolis mayor spoke from the convention hall in Philadelphia. In eight minutes of fiery rhetoric, Humphrey had relit the torch for the progressives. Twelve years later, Humphrey was still the progressive's torchbearer. But would the Democratic Party allow him to serve as their nominee?

Excusing himself from Teddy and the rest of the press, Philleo approached the hotel suites where Humphrey, Minnesota governor Orville

Freeman, and the others had gathered. When Philleo entered the room, everyone began asking for his assessment. Philleo admitted that he liked what he was seeing. But as they all knew, the true picture wouldn't develop until the Milwaukee returns.

Philleo lingered alongside Humphrey, hopeful that proximity alone might comfort the old brawler. He knew Humphrey's entire political life had led him to this crucial moment. From his early days as Minneapolis mayor, then onto the Senate, it all came down to this. Hubert and Muriel sat side by side on the hotel couch, maintaining joviality as best they could.

At the start of the evening, it was all smiles and laughter.

But then the winds changed direction yet again.

Less than a mile away, Jack Kennedy sipped soup on the third floor of the Pfister Hotel.

The suite was crowded with Kennedy's inner circle: Jackie, of course, and Jack's sisters Jean and Eunice, but also Dave Powers, Kenny O'Donnell, and Madison mayor Ivan Nestingen, who was peering out the window at the city far below. Lake Michigan was all but invisible in the dark, but Ivan knew it was out there somewhere, the waves crashing relentlessly against the shoreline.

The phone kept ringing with some new detail to be analyzed. What did the high turnout mean? How many precincts remained? What on earth was taking so long in Milwaukee? They monitored the information as best they could, but in the end, all that mattered was the final tally.

It is easy to think that important history is made only in important places, like the halls of Congress or on battlefields. Yet sometimes history is made in more modest places, too: a third-floor hotel suite, for instance, in Milwaukee. A documentary film crew, led by director Robert Drew, had set up shop in the hotel suite to capture the moment. Drew's camera was positioned across the room, recording every whispered word and expression. Ivan did his best to avoid the camera, though it was hard to steer clear of its frame.

Ivan watched as the director kept his focus mainly on Kennedy. Jack managed to ignore Drew's camera and hold its attention all at once. If

State Democratic leaders greet Senator Kennedy at the Madison airport in October 1960. From left to right: Madison mayor Ivan Nestingen; Marvin Brickson, head of the Madison Federation of Labor; Senator Kennedy; Governor Gaylord Nelson; and state party chairman Pat Lucey. WHI IMAGE ID 45434

tonight went as planned, Robert Drew would capture a new front in the battle for the White House—the first glimpse of a newly emboldened Democratic frontrunner.

Ivan couldn't help but feel partially responsible for whatever happened next. He had initially been hesitant about encouraging Jack to run in the Wisconsin primary, but after seeing the man in action during the Proxmire campaign, Ivan knew Jack had a chance. The longer Ivan followed Kennedy's career, the more he felt the senator owed it to the country to run. Sure, Kennedy was young and privileged, but those problems could be overcome with the right ground game. That was where Jerry Bruno had come in: fighting like some rabid dog to nail down every vote. Jerry, Pat, and Ivan himself—when coupled with Kennedy's team—had created the conditions for success.

But could they pull it off?

God love Hubert Humphrey, but this was not Humphrey's time. The party needed a national figure with national appeal, someone whose popularity extended beyond the Midwest. Put Hubert in a room full of midwestern farmers or laborers, and he'd knock the socks off Kennedy every time. But the general electorate was not limited to midwestern farmers or laborers. To some people, Humphrey's perceived provincialism was his strength, but to others, he was an out-of-touch country bumpkin. Teddy White characterized Humphrey best, describing his "romantic, almost quaint faith in ordinary people." Humphrey's "quaint faith" was what made him so appealing to "ordinary people." But would those ordinary people return their faith in kind?

Radio reports began to crackle through the room; Ivan glanced toward Jack, who was listening without an expression: "Humphrey . . . may carry five districts," the broadcaster reported. "It's now clear that the chances of a Kennedy sweep have all but slipped away . . . it could be a long night for newspaper and radio men covering the election, [as] one of the most elaborate and intense campaigns in the state's history could all mean nothing."

Kennedy maintained his poker face, though his constantly tapping knee served as his tell.

Late that evening, the Milwaukee returns rolled in, and, finally, the outcome was clear: likely to win six of Wisconsin's ten districts, along with the overall popular vote, Jack Kennedy was going to squeak out a victory.

In winning by such a small margin, as least as far as districts were concerned, Kennedy paved the way for a rematch against Humphrey in the West Virginia primary the following month. Ivan tried to read Kenny's and Dave's expressions, though now they were the ones with the poker faces.

"What does it mean?" asked Jack's sister Eunice.

"It means," Jack said, "that we have to do it all over again."

It was a solid showing, though hardly the decisive victory the campaign had wanted. Despite their best efforts, the western districts had refused to budge; the same was true of Dane County in the second district and La Crosse in the third. Humphrey had won all of them, and he'd nearly picked off the seventh, too, which Jack had clung to by a mere seven thousand votes.

As it stood now, Kennedy claimed twenty delegates to Humphrey's ten, which sounded good on paper, but it didn't amount to a can of beans given the eight hundred or so he'd need to secure the nomination at the national convention in July. What they'd needed in Wisconsin was a knockout punch; what they'd gotten was the right to another round in the ring with Humphrey.

Ultimately, the crossover vote in the state's open primary appeared to have at least some impact on the outcome, particularly in the Fox Valley, where a significant number of Republican Catholics voted for Kennedy, boosting his margin of victory in the primary. Twelve thousand more people voted in Wisconsin's Democratic primary than would vote for Kennedy that fall in Wisconsin's general election, which suggests that at least some of those extra primary voters were crossover Republicans. Far less of a factor was the Democratic Administrative Committee's controversial rule change to the delegate math, which ultimately awarded Humphrey two additional delegates (though he would later release all of his delegates before the convention anyway).

The Wisconsin primary had been devoid of wild cards or "April surprises." Kennedy had lost where it was expected he might—in the Protestant-leaning districts of the west, and in the Humphrey-loving second. In the immediate aftermath, it was difficult for the Kennedy campaign to discern just what role religion had played at the ballot box. After all, the Protestant-leaning western districts were also farming country and bordered Humphrey's beloved Minnesota—as such, religion was but one factor of many. As much as Kennedy hoped otherwise, there was no denying the outcome: he'd won with Catholics and lost with Protestants. The "religious question" would continue to haunt him into West Virginia and beyond.

Still, Kennedy would downplay the reality as best he could, noting that associating his district wins with Wisconsin's Catholic voters was akin to arguing he'd excelled "in the beech tree and basswood counties and not so well among the hemlock and pine." It made for a nice analogy, even if the analysis didn't quite hold.

Kennedy and his entourage made their way to the WTMJ-TV newsroom, where a newscaster asked Kennedy how the night's results "shaped up" to his expectations.

"Well, I was hopeful we could take six districts, and I think we have a good chance to do that," Jack said, repressing his frustration as the final tabulation continued. "And we'll have the majority of the popular vote, which will give us a good result."

"Senator, how do you feel after this exhaustive campaign?" the newscaster continued.

"It's been a long campaign, many months," Kennedy agreed, "but I think we were successful by running against a very hardworking, formidable opponent in my colleague and friend Mr. Humphrey. If I could be successful against him, I'd be delighted to take the lead in Wisconsin, which is in the heart of the Midwest and next to Minnesota. So we've had a very long and grueling campaign."

"What are your plans after tonight?" the newscaster asked.

"Well, I continue on," Kennedy said. "The next primary is, of course, Indiana in the first part of May. Then I hit West Virginia, Maryland, and Oregon, and Nebraska all in the short period of two and a half weeks."

Back at the Kaiser Knickerbocker, Humphrey and his entourage also made their way to the newsroom. In the lobby, Humphrey was hounded by the press, and he made a show of smiling widely as the cameras and microphones crowded him.

When asked to comment on the tabulated results, a joy-filled Humphrey replied, "This has been a great election and the people of Wisconsin are to be congratulated on their genuine interest in this election. This is the best voice America can have when the people participate in their government and their politics."

"How are you going to come out in this election?" a reporter cut in.

"I say I've been in politics too long to make any predictions when one-third of the precincts are in," Humphrey said. "Only reckless people do that, and radicals, and I'm a conservative and prudent man."

Indeed, the precincts were still coming in, though the outcome was growing increasingly clear.

"Would you be satisfied with the result right now, Senator?" a reporter asked.

"I'm pleased, I'm pleased," Humphrey said after a beat. "You see, if somebody relegates you to what you call a 'hard bread and cold water' diet and you come up with bouillon and biscuits, then it seems pretty good."

No one could turn hard bread into biscuits quite like Humphrey. Though he'd been advised to drop out if he lost Wisconsin, he was reluctant to do so given the results. Humphrey had turned a potential blowout into a squeaker, after all. It made it easier for Humphrey to believe that destiny was calling. Or at least not hanging up on him altogether.

As Philleo and the others surrounded Humphrey, they couldn't help but peg him as the best loser in history. He was taking it extraordinarily well, probably because the outcome allowed him to fight another day.

As Humphrey made his way down the hotel corridor toward a cheering crowd, his victorious spin momentarily slipped away from him.

"Just imagine if we'd have won how much noise there would've been here," he chuckled merrily.

"We won," someone from the entourage reminded him.

Yes. Of course. How had he forgotten?

Humphrey had won, in a sense, by not losing by a larger margin.

The following day, shortly after sunup, paper carriers across the state took to their posts and began delivering their newspapers to doorsteps and street corners. Kennedy had won with 56.5 percent of the vote, claiming 476,024 votes to Humphrey's 366,753. It was the highest turnout in Wisconsin presidential primary history. Per the newly passed delegate rules, Kennedy earned twenty convention votes, Humphrey earned ten, and the thirty-first vote would be split by the state's national committee members. Yet no matter how you measured it—in terms of districts, delegates, or popular vote—the victory failed to meet the Kennedy team's expectations, particularly given Lou Harris's January polling that had predicted Kennedy winning 63 percent of the vote. Had Kennedy lost one more district, the tie would have been considered a defeat.

Though Ivan had doubts about Jack having much chance in the ninth and tenth, Lou Harris's polling had shown otherwise. Long-shots though they were, the polls had convinced Jack to keep fighting there, and had encouraged men like Chuck Spalding and Pete Dugal to keep up their full press in the western districts, even though victory there seemed elusive.

Publicly, Bobby and Jack had played up their so-called underdog status, but they both knew better. In the days leading up to the primary, Bobby was said to have remarked, "It's in the bag," while Jack himself thought he'd win the state by a margin of nine districts to one. Pat Lucey went so far as to predict a clean sweep of all ten districts. These were hardly the tempered expectations of an underdog, not that too many insiders believed that bit of bull anyway.

In the primary's aftermath, perhaps nothing better symbolized the outcome than what street cleaners discovered that Wednesday morning along West Doty Street in Madison. Someone—a broken-hearted Humphrey volunteer, no doubt—had dumped thousands of "Humphrey for President" handbills along the street. The handbills were scattered everywhere—a sea of green, blue, white, and yellow drifting in all directions. Madison's street department crew chased after them as best they could to collect the trash.

But the wind got the better of them, blowing them in all directions.

Including east, toward West Virginia.

PART III

AFTER

MAY 1960–NOVEMBER 1963

"John Kennedy was my colleague, my opponent, my president, and my friend. . . . As an opponent in the presidential primaries, I had envied him—his charm, his grace, his money, his success. As president of the United States, I grew to respect his intelligence and how he put it to work. . . . As a friend, I grew to love him for his warmth and wit and compassion."
—HUBERT H. HUMPHREY, FROM *THE EDUCATION OF A PUBLIC MAN: MY LIFE AND POLITICS*

HUMPHREY'S LAST STAND

Jerry Bruno, Hubert Humphrey, and Bobby Kennedy
May 10, 1960

One month and five days after the Wisconsin primary

For the rest of his life, Jerry Bruno would never forget the girl from Crum, West Virginia. A speck of a town along the state's southwestern border, Crum was a place you could barely find on a map, let alone on a census. The kind of place most political candidates skipped over, thinking they knew better than to waste their time on the coal miners who called the place home.

But Jerry didn't know any better, which was why he and Jack Kennedy's cousin, Joe Gargan, drove to Crum one late spring day to do some advance work. Jack's narrow victory in Wisconsin had been a wake-up call for Jerry, and he didn't want to repeat the same mistakes here in West Virginia. Winning six out of Wisconsin's ten districts had been disappointing, given the time and resources they'd expended in the state. Worse still, the press was reporting less on Kennedy's win and more on the thin margin by which he'd achieved it.

Humphrey's claims of near victory hardly helped matters. With all his upbeat optimism, you'd have thought he'd buried Jack.

"I suppose numerically I'm the defeated candidate," Humphrey cheerily told the press, "but if I'm defeated, I certainly don't hurt."

Jerry hoped Humphrey would receive his rude awakening in West Virginia, though in the days leading up to the state's May 10 primary, that remained very much in question.

According to Lou Harris's polling back in December of '59, Jack was on track to take West Virginia 70 percent to 30 percent over Humphrey. But by April 1960, those numbers had nearly flipped, 60 percent to 40 percent, in favor of Humphrey.

The difference?

The voters of West Virginia had recently learned that Jack Kennedy was Catholic, which was a problem in a state with a Catholic population somewhere between 2 and 3 percent. After Wisconsin, the campaign had planned to win big in West Virginia, then move on to Los Angeles for the nomination. But Lou's most recent polling threw cold water on that strategy.

Behind the scenes, Bobby had called upon Irish Mafia member Kenny O'Donnell to urge Humphrey to drop out. Nationally, Humphrey was polling at 5 percent to Kennedy's 34 percent, so why the hell continue the charade? For starters, because Humphrey's staying in the race greatly benefited Adlai Stevenson II and Lyndon Johnson—both of whom were enjoying the view from the sidelines. Humphrey admired both men and particularly appreciated where the Stevensonian wing of the party might be headed. But in the end, Humphrey's decision to stay in the race may not have been solely political. The campaign in Wisconsin had turned personal, and Humphrey wasn't yet ready to throw in the towel, no matter how much Kenny O'Donnell begged.

So, it had come to this: Jerry Bruno and Joe Gargan, in a place called Crum.

As they hung posters announcing Kennedy's upcoming visit, Jerry and Joe were approached by a young girl with stringy hair, wearing a dress sewn together from flour sacks. She had taken a keen interest in the posters, and Jerry encouraged her to come out and meet the next president in a few days.

"You know," she said shyly, "I ain't never seen anybody like that. Am I really going to be able to see him?"

"Yes," Jerry assured. "Bring all your friends."

The girl stared at the men, then back at Kennedy's face on the sign.

"Do you think I'll ever get out of Crum?" she asked.

Jerry didn't have much in the way of an answer. He couldn't know what the world had in store for her. Though in a place like Crum, it seemed few people made it much beyond the mines.

By 1960, West Virginia had lost tens of thousands of coal mining jobs, partly because of mechanization and partly because of the rise of oil and gas. Here in Crum and all over much of the state, people were out of work, struggling, and hungry. With so many hardships, it was difficult to see how a child could ever hope to escape.

Days later, on April 25, Jack Kennedy descended upon Crum just as the posters promised. He visited the local high school, the nearby Veterans Hospital, and the Wayne County Courthouse. Jerry was pleased by the turnout: in all, five hundred or so folks had shown up for Jack in a town that didn't even have that many residents. Jerry wondered if the little girl in the flour sack dress was among them.

After his brief remarks at the courthouse, Kennedy stayed for quite some time, greeting the people who had come to hear him speak and shaking hands with everyone in sight. It was a personal touch that became commonplace in West Virginia, where Jack went out of his way to meet with anyone who would meet with him—including miners, for whom he regularly rolled up his sleeves, shaking one dusty hand after another. They made for an odd pairing: men with miner's lights affixed to their helmets alongside the carefully coiffed Kennedy. Yet somehow, he seemed to be winning them over. In one particularly memorable exchange, a steely eyed miner approached Kennedy and asked, "Is it true you're the son of one of our wealthiest men?"

Kennedy sheepishly confirmed it.

"Is it true that you've never wanted for anything and had everything you wanted?"

This, too, he could not deny.

"Is it true you've never done a day's work with your hands all your life?"

The miner knew it was true, as did the country.

"Well, let me tell you this," the miner said, "you haven't missed a thing."

In truth, though, Kennedy had missed something important, and West Virginia helped him see it. As Kennedy traveled across the state, he became increasingly dismayed by the extent of the suffering he witnessed there. For the first time in his life, he saw what it meant to be hungry, and he was shocked when he learned that many families subsisted on bags of government surplus corn meal and powdered milk. In every hill and holler he encountered new, eye-opening indignities— shacks with boards over the windows, rampant unemployment, malnourished children.

As he campaigned across West Virginia, Kennedy increasingly spoke out about what he saw. "No community is an island, cut off from the rest of America," he said in a speech in Charleston. "What happens in West Virginia happens to all of us. And America has failed in its responsibilities to you. This is a fact, a fact of terrible urgency and a challenge to the leadership of the next president of the United States."

Kennedy continued: "I know what you face here. I know that something must be done, that something can be done. And I know that it is not being done by the present Administration in Washington."

Rather than blaming West Virginians for their plight, Kennedy promised to bear the burden with them and do his best to ease it—a promise he was destined to make good on.

As the May 10 primary approached, the tide began to turn Kennedy's way. His emotional outspokenness on matters of economic hardship inspired many West Virginia voters to feel like someone finally cared about what happened to them. The campaign's hardball politics certainly helped, too. The Kennedys let it be known that anyone funding Humphrey's campaign would be blackballed from all future political appointments. It was time for people to bet on the horse who could win, not the horse who was well-liked back in the stable.

Contributing to his rise in the polls was the fact that days before the primary, Kennedy at last effectively neutralized the Catholic issue. He addressed the issue head-on, taking to West Virginia television to remind voters that when a president takes the oath of office, "he is swearing to support the separation of church and state" and does so while placing one hand on the Bible and lifting the other toward God. It was a less-than-subtle reminder to Protestant voters that the Bible—*their* Bible—would be the book upon which he would take his oath.

But also, there was the money. The under-the-table money most of all. West Virginia was notorious for buying and selling votes to the highest bidder. Whether Jerry liked it or not, such shenanigans had become standard practice in cities and towns throughout the state. If you could buy off the town's sheriff, a lot of votes came with him. If you could buy off a church, there were votes hiding there as well. On more than one occasion, Jerry himself had been confused for the "bag man." It was politics at its worst—an exchange of money rather than ideas. But it was part of the winning formula, and the Kennedys didn't shy away from the practice. Since 1958, Jack had openly joked about his father's alleged buying of votes. "I have just received the following wire from my generous daddy," Kennedy told a Washington, DC, crowd that year. "Dear Jack—Don't buy a single vote more than necessary—I'll be damned if I'm going to pay for a landslide."

But purse strings were no laughing matter for Humphrey, whose coffers were all but empty after the Kennedys began making their threats. When the Humphrey campaign couldn't even muster the $750 needed to host their election eve telethon, the candidate took the extraordinary step of writing the check himself—money he'd earmarked for his daughter's wedding the following Saturday. (He had to call his father and brother to help cover it.)

None of it seemed particularly fair, but politics never was. Who could forget the Wisconsin Democratic Administrative Committee's last-minute rule change to alter the state's delegate math in Humphrey's favor? If you wanted fairness, try Little League. Or the Scouts. Just about anything was fairer than politics, especially in West Virginia.

By nightfall on May 10, the presumptive Democratic nominee was now clear. Kennedy received 61 percent of the vote, besting Humphrey by a margin nearly five percentage points higher than his victory in Wisconsin. In doing so, Kennedy effectively closed Humphrey's path to the nomination. Humphrey didn't have the delegates, the appeal, the money, or the fight.

No one was more surprised by the size of the victory than Jack Kennedy, who'd left West Virginia for Washington that morning to steer clear of the hoopla. After dinner and a movie with friends, Jack returned to his Georgetown home where he learned of his victory. He raced to the airport, boarding the first plane for West Virginia. While airborne, Jack celebrated with a bowl of tomato soup.

Back at the Humphrey camp, there was no celebrating. After his loss in Wisconsin, Humphrey had been too stubborn to leave the race. But after West Virginia, stubbornness alone wasn't enough to power him on. Instead, he handled the loss with the dignity and grace that a lesser man might never have mustered.

Years later, reporter Theodore White described how Humphrey huddled in his room at Charleston's Ruffner Hotel on that rain-slicked West Virginia night, and watched with growing sadness as his impending defeat became clear: "By 9:20, with ten precincts out of 2,750 in the state having reported, the first faint trend became visible: Kennedy, 638; Humphrey 473—a 60-to-40 break."

The trend continued for the next hour, until shortly after ten o'clock, when Humphrey knew he was sunk.

Though just because he wouldn't be accepting the nomination, that didn't mean Humphrey hadn't left his mark. "Maybe I was just consoling myself," Humphrey later reflected, "but I felt that, at least, we made an impact on the party." According to Humphrey, when the Democrats later met to adopt their party platform in Los Angeles, "every single candidate . . . came to our position on every issue." Pushing moderate Democrats like Jack Kennedy and Lyndon Johnson to the left was no small feat, and without Humphrey, they might never have made it there. But for Humphrey, those silver linings were all but invisible in the late hours of May 10, when the sting of defeat was still fresh.

From his room in the Ruffner, Humphrey wrote his concession letter, then sent it via Western Union to the Kennedy headquarters at the Kanawha Hotel a few blocks away. Jack hadn't yet returned from DC, so Bobby read the letter and then turned to Larry O'Brien and Dave Powers.

"God," Bobby said, "this must be awful for poor Hubert, ending up this way after working so hard in two states."

And then Bobby stood and left the room, walking through the rain toward the Ruffner Hotel and Hubert Humphrey.

What was said that night in the Ruffner between Bobby and Humphrey is lost to history. But shortly after their talk, Humphrey joined Bobby in walking back to the Kanawha Hotel, where Jack was set to arrive. Humphrey wanted to congratulate his adversary in person, and Kennedy's supporters, too. But on the way to the Kanawha, Humphrey first made a stop at his campaign headquarters, where—to the loyal volunteers who still remained—a teary-eyed Humphrey announced that his quest for the Democratic nomination had come to its end.

Wrapping an arm around the defeated candidate, Bobby joined Humphrey in walking the rest of the way through the rain to the Kanawha.

It was there that Jack and Humphrey met sometime before three o'clock in the morning.

"It was very nice of you to come over, Hubert," Jack said.

When the formalities had concluded and there was little left to do, Bobby pulled Jerry aside and said, "Why don't you bring the senator back to his headquarters?"

It was an unenviable task, one that Jerry performed with the solemnity of a monk. Humphrey wept for most of the drive back to the hotel. It was a difficult moment for Jerry, who'd known Humphrey since his Proxmire days and had been asked, and refused, to join Humphrey's campaign. "Maybe if I'd had you," Humphrey lamented to Jerry that night, "it would have been different."

After returning Humphrey to his hotel, Jerry double-timed it back to the Kanawha Hotel, where he heard piano music coming from the hotel's basement. He followed the music, which led him to Bobby Kennedy and Dave Powers, thoroughly enjoying the victory. Wine glasses lined the piano's perimeter, as Dave plinked out a few Irish songs and the men sang loudly. Jerry was used to a different Bobby Kennedy—the workhorse, the mastermind, the man who, on occasion, got himself lost in middle-of-nowhere Wisconsin, desperate for directions back home. But in the predawn hours of May 11, Jerry saw a different side of him. This was Bobby reveling in his hard-fought success. Jerry glanced at his watch. They'd be on the plane to Oregon within hours. But before all that, there were songs to sing, and a bottle or two in need of uncorking.

At dawn, as the Kennedy team hustled on to Oregon, Humphrey returned east to Washington, where he immediately got to work shepherding a tax bill on the Senate floor. At lunch, he met with journalist Geri Joseph to reflect on the hard-fought primary race that had just ended for him. The Minnesota senator had plenty of reasons to despise Kennedy—from the Kennedy campaign's insinuations of anti-Catholic sentiment to their false claims of Humphrey dodging the draft. Yet before the dust even settled, Humphrey turned stoically to the journalist seated across the table and said, "I'm going to do whatever I can to make Jack Kennedy a good president."

Not only did Humphrey release his delegates at the convention, but he also spent a portion of the fall of 1960 helping Jack squeak out a win in Minnesota, earning him the state's eleven electoral votes. Because Humphrey was beloved in Wisconsin, particularly in the state's ninth district, he hosted a "Senator Humphrey for Kennedy Bean Feed" at a local high school in Eau Claire, where he strongly endorsed Kennedy to a crowd one thousand strong. Joining Humphrey at the bean feed was the state's lieutenant governor, Philleo Nash, who in a one-line speech made his intentions known: "Let's elect Jack Kennedy."

When it was his turn at the microphone, Humphrey echoed Nash's sentiments with his more loquacious style, and then, as a newspaper reported, "unblushingly took credit for training Senator Kennedy in the Wisconsin primary for the fall campaign."

Indeed, the most important gift Humphrey bestowed upon Kennedy was a tough primary fight. In early April 1960, Jerry Bruno and the rest of the Kennedy campaign had viewed Humphrey's stubborn insistence in continuing on to West Virginia as a frustrating setback that risked imperiling—or at least delaying—Kennedy's path to the nomination. Later, many Kennedy insiders began to view it differently. Far more damaging than Humphrey's foot-dragging exit from the primary would have been his refusal to carry on just as he had.

What encouraged him to continue to West Virginia? His performance in Wisconsin, and the state's second district, including Madison, most of all. "I think that if Humphrey had not carried the second district, he would not have gone to West Virginia," Pat Lucey remarked in 1964. "And if he had not gone to West Virginia and provided the competition that Kennedy needed to prove that he could win where there were no Catholics in a contested primary, I'm not sure whether Kennedy would have been nominated."

By staying in the race, Humphrey provided Kennedy the platform he needed to prove his electability on a national level. Moreover, by the conclusion of the West Virginia primary, the Catholic question had been dealt with handily, removing it from Nixon's arsenal.

Years later, once the wounds healed, Jack Kennedy and Hubert Humphrey would be able to reflect more fondly on their shared primary season. During a particularly difficult moment in his presidency, as President Kennedy and Senate Majority Whip Humphrey huddled in the Oval Office, Kennedy paused and said, "Hubert, if I'd known it was going to be like this, I would have let you win."

"Well, Mr. President, I knew it might be like this," Humphrey quipped, "and that's why I let you win."

Though it took time, their relationship would eventually transform into one of gratitude and admiration. "As a friend," Humphrey would reflect later, "I grew to love [Jack Kennedy] for his warmth and wit and compassion, and for what he gave me personally by sharing those qualities."

In West Virginia, Kennedy began to understand what Humphrey had long known—that poverty in rural America was real, and that the people there needed federal assistance. It wasn't just about helping the girl from Crum in the flour-sack dress; it was about acknowledging that there were children like her all over the country. Children who had never known the luxury of a cold glass of milk, or three meals a day. Kennedy never forgot what he saw there.

On January 21, 1961, in his first executive order on his first full day as president, President Kennedy authorized a food stamp program to support hungry families. He made certain, too, that unemployed West Virginian coal miners were the first to receive it.

Flying High with Jack

Hubert Humphrey
June 4, 1960

One month and thirty days after the Wisconsin primary

From thousands of feet up in the air, Hubert Humphrey peered out the window of the *Caroline* at the state that had let him down.

Wisconsin. Beautiful, devastating Wisconsin.

The combination of altitude and darkness made it impossible to see the roads, but had the conditions been different, Humphrey would have seen an all-too-familiar terrain.

Had the conditions been different . . .

Now that was a phrase that would long haunt him. After all, had any number of conditions been even slightly different, the primary race might've been his. Instead, the clear favorite for the Democratic nomination was now the forty-three-year-old senator seated beside him on the plane. This was a far cry from Humphrey's freezing campaign bus—the plane cabin had tables, comfortable chairs, a private bedroom, and a flight attendant ready to serve.

How could anyone compete with all that?

How could anyone compete . . .

Hubert thanked the flight attendant who brought them chicken noodle soup and sandwiches, trying hard to pretend as if this was all business as usual for him. Though it wasn't. Not by a long shot.

"Well, Hubert, now you know why I never offered you a ride during the Wisconsin primary period," Jack said. "I suppose the smartest thing that I did during the primary was to deny you a ride on the plane that day both of us had to get back to Washington to vote. You would have painted me as a man enjoying the luxuries of life while the people down below were struggling. You would have torn me apart."

"Had I been able to see the inside of this plane," Hubert agreed, "I would have described you even better than I did as one of the rich, above the masses, who enjoyed the super luxuries of life while the rest of us were traveling around in buses."

After a four-and-a-half-hour flight, the *Caroline* landed in Minneapolis. Hubert and Jack made their way to the Nicollet Hotel, where they arrived late for the Jefferson-Jackson Dinner—the Democratic party's annual fundraising event.

For purposes of party unity, it was important that they arrived together. Minnesota was shaping up to be a tight race in the general election, and the sooner voters could rally around Jack, the better. Not that Hubert was quite ready to offer such a full-throated rallying cry. But he was getting there. And he had his own political future to think about. After all, Jack Kennedy wouldn't be the only one on Minnesota's ballot; Humphrey had his own Senate reelection to win. Maybe Humphrey lacked the clout to win a national election, but in Minneapolis, the people would come out in droves.

Hubert took his seat in the audience of the hotel's grand hall as Jack made his way to the mic.

"Emerson once said that 'Men are conservatives when they are least vigorous. That is why they are conservatives after dinner,'" Jack began, rousing a chuckle from the crowd.

> But here in Minnesota—the stronghold of progressive liberalism in the Democratic Party—we need not fear being lulled into conservatism at this dinner. Any drift toward conservative principles here will run headlong into the fighting liberal tradition of the Democratic-Farmer-Labor Party—the fighting liberal tradition of Orville Freeman and Gene McCarthy—and, above all, the great, fighting liberal tradition of my friend and colleague, Hubert Humphrey.

Kennedy might've stopped there, but he didn't. Much to Humphrey's surprise, he was just getting started.

I think you will all agree that there is no man in the Democratic Party
who knows more about the fighting liberalism of Hubert Humphrey
than I do—and there is no man in the Democratic Party who is happier that Hubert Humphrey is a Democrat than I am. For after seeing
how Hubert Humphrey campaigns in the spring, I know that the
Republican Party will never survive his campaigning in the fall. This
November, no matter who the Democratic candidate may be, the high
principles, the courage and the fighting spirit of Hubert Humphrey
are going to lead the way to a great, national Democratic victory.

They were kind words, Humphrey knew, though the line about "no
matter who the Democratic candidate may be" seemed more than a little disingenuous. After wins in ten primaries, Kennedy's growing delegate count made him the clear frontrunner. Of course, all of that could
change at the convention, but the odds of Johnson, or Symington, or Stevenson pulling off an upset were becoming more and more unlikely. But
none of that was Humphrey's concern. For now, all he had to do was sit
back, listen to Jack's speech, and let the convention work out the details.
Jack continued,

Hubert Humphrey and I fought, and fought hard, this spring. As he
so often pointed out, we were not making love. And I never thought
we were. But throughout those long, hard arduous battles—from the
farms of Wisconsin to the hills of West Virginia—Hubert Humphrey
never once retreated from those liberal principles to which he has
devoted his public life. He never once neglected the larger interests of
the Democratic Party for the advantage of the moment. And he never
once stopped his ceaseless, lifelong courageous battle against the vi-
cious forces of bigotry and intolerance.

It was the truth, Humphrey knew. Even if the Kennedy campaign had,
on occasion, used those qualities against him. Jack went on:

In the larger sense, Hubert Humphrey won a great victory this
spring—a victory for his own convictions—a victory for the Democratic Party, and a victory for the future of America. While others

retreated to the sidelines—hoping for a good, clean fight with no survivors—Hubert Humphrey brought the fight for liberalism to the people. He engaged in a great debate on the vital issues of our times. He helped to arouse and awaken the people of America to the critical challenges which our nation now faces. And he helped lay the groundwork for a smashing Democratic victory in November.

While Democratic presidential hopefuls like Johnson and Symington had watched the primary prizefight from the safety of their Senate offices, Humphrey and Kennedy had taken their messages directly to the people. And not just any people, but people who were too often overlooked. Like the dairy farmer in Eau Claire. And the miner from Morgantown. These were the folks who most needed to know that someone was listening to their concerns. These were the people who made all those miles on that frigid campaign bus worth it.

Senator Humphrey, Vice President Lyndon B. Johnson, and President John F. Kennedy gather for the Legislative Leaders Breakfast Meeting in the Oval Office, on February 7, 1961. ABBIE ROWE, WHITE HOUSE PHOTOGRAPHS, JOHN F. KENNEDY PRESIDENTIAL LIBRARY AND MUSEUM, BOSTON

"We Democrats need Hubert Humphrey," Jack said. "We need his vision, his vigor, his intellect and his fighting heart. And we need the guidance of his broad, human liberal principles if we are to recapture the White House and again govern the nation in the great tradition of Franklin Roosevelt and Harry Truman."

Though flattered, Humphrey couldn't help but note that the presidents Jack had referenced weren't exactly Kennedy fans themselves. Though Roosevelt died a year before Jack won his congressional seat, Roosevelt's widow, former First Lady Eleanor Roosevelt, had made no secret of her disdain for Jack Kennedy. And Truman was so put off by Kennedy's pre-ordained status as frontrunner that he would resign as a delegate in the days leading up to the convention. (That Truman was a major Symington supporter might've also played a role in his decision.)

To invoke their names that night in Minneapolis was ostensibly a compliment to Humphrey. But Jack knew that by doing so, he was also laying the groundwork for Eleanor Roosevelt and Harry Truman to warm to his general election campaign. Their support wouldn't come easily, but it was necessary if the party had any hope of beating Nixon.

For the remainder of the speech, Jack turned his attention to four policy goals that he believed would play well in Humphrey territory: recommitting the United States to "the great social welfare programs of Franklin Roosevelt and Harry Truman"; equal opportunities for all; support for farmers; and, finally, arms control and disarmament.

"For, as Franklin Roosevelt said in his first Inaugural," Jack concluded, "'In every dark hour of our national life, a leadership of frankness and vigor has met with that understanding and support of the people themselves which is essential to victory.'"

The crowd cheered appreciatively, and Humphrey joined them. It was a fine speech, and one that hit all the right notes. More importantly, it signaled Jack's slight lean to the left. It was too slow for Hubert's liking, but at least the transformation was underway.

From start to finish, the entire speech clocked in at around fifteen minutes—too short for the crowd that was accustomed to Senator Humphrey's more meandering style. But Hubert didn't mind Jack's short speech. Sometimes less really was more; he had learned that lesson the hard way.

Had Hubert been bested by another man, perhaps his defeat wouldn't have hurt so much. He was most bothered that all the goodwill he'd accumulated from Wisconsinites during his years in the Senate seemed to evaporate when Kennedy entered the race. Kennedy's money, organization, and charisma ultimately proved overwhelming. There wasn't a moment throughout that entire primary season when the Humphreys and their supporters hadn't given it their all, but their all was not enough.

Muriel, God bless her, had spent countless days passing out campaign literature for as long as the cold allowed. Some days she brought along her five-gallon coffee urn so she could hand out cups of hot coffee to the factory workers during shift change. Their four children had helped, too. Hubert would never forget how his youngest son, twelve-year-old Douglas, had huddled alongside him at the gates of one factory or another, hawking campaign literature with the best of them.

Hubert had missed so much of his children's lives during his political career. Perhaps winning the highest office in the land would have confirmed that the personal sacrifices had been worth it. But it was not to be—at least not now.

After Jack's speech, Hubert smiled politely and clapped as Jack offered a friendly wave to the crowd.

Perhaps someday he'd have another crack at it. Who knew what the future held.

BOLD ENOUGH TO TRY

Vel Phillips
July 10, 1960

Three months and five days after the Wisconsin primary

Jack Kennedy had clearly won the primaries, but anything could happen at the Democratic National Convention. The preceding week, Senate Majority Leader Lyndon B. Johnson had formally announced his candidacy for the presidency. Though hardly surprising, his announcement complicated the delegate math. By going the primary route, Kennedy was entering the convention with a strong advantage in pledged delegates. But compromise candidates like Johnson imperiled the clean victory Kennedy hoped for.

The convention was scheduled to begin on July 11; and for the first three days, Bobby Kennedy and the rest of the team would arm-twist and horse trade with anyone willing to deal. Political insiders knew Kennedy was the man to beat, but such predictions meant nothing until the delegate vote secured the nominee. Throughout the primaries, Senator Kennedy's image had taken a bruising—he was too young, too rich, and too Catholic. Some delegates considered him too liberal, others not liberal enough. Threading the needles to please a majority of delegates was no small task, and most delegates wanted something in return.

July 10, the day before the convention officially began, was a jam-packed day for Kennedy, beginning with a *Meet The Press* interview and ending with a celebrity gala featuring Frank Sinatra. In between, Kennedy would pick up nearly sixty pledged delegates from Illinois and an endorsement from California governor Pat Brown. But the biggest wild card of the day centered on how Kennedy would be received that afternoon at a rally organized by the NAACP.

Kennedy had agreed to speak at the rally, but as racial tensions continued to grow in the leadup to the convention, he began second-guessing himself. If the predominantly Black crowd responded unfavorably toward him, it could further complicate his ability to clinch the nomination. At such a critical time, such negative optics would do little to reassure northern liberals of his ability to win over Black voters.

Jack asked Vel Phillips to accompany him. Vel had traveled from Milwaukee to Los Angeles to attend the convention, but it was clear the senator first needed her support on the eve of the convention itself.

During the car ride to the rally, Vel listened as Jack called a colleague who was already there and learned that a representative from Johnson's campaign had immediately been booed from the stage. Blood drained from the senator's face as he realized he was about to enter a potentially hostile environment.

"I'm still not sure that it's wise to go," Jack told Vel.

"Well, we can't ever really be sure," Vel said, "but I would say we should go." It wasn't the reassurance Kennedy had hoped for, but it was enough.

Once they arrived, Vel and Jack exited the car to see a crowd of thousands of people, far more than could safely fit into the main auditorium.

"Vel, it would be a very bad thing at this point," Jack confided, "if . . . they just booed me right out."

"Oh, I know it would," Vel agreed. "[But] they wouldn't do that to you." The senator gave her a look. Just how sure was she?

As they made their way inside and toward the front of the auditorium, they overheard a perturbed Clarence Mitchell, NAACP regional director, shouting to the crowd, "For God's sake, let your good manners rule." But the crowd seemed to have little patience for a parade of representatives sent on behalf of pandering politicians.

"We have invited all of these people here so you can hear them and go away better informed for the good not only of you, but this being covered all over, and we want this to be for everyone's benefit," Mitchell pled. "And we will never be able to get them here again if you don't treat . . ." Mitchell trailed off, and the crowd remained unmoved.

Jack turned toward Vel. "Vel," he said, "I'm afraid."

"It's going to be fine, you'll see," Vel assured him, though she had no such assurances herself. Perhaps it wouldn't be fine. Perhaps the crowd would boo him off the stage as quickly as they had Johnson's representative. But they'd come this far, Vel knew, and they might as well see how the rest played out.

As soon as Senator Kennedy was introduced, low rumblings of boos emitted from the crowd. But by the time he began to speak, the boos quietly silenced. The man standing before the crowd wasn't some campaign representative, but the candidate himself who had bothered to show up. Kennedy offered a few introductory remarks, and then spoke candidly to his audience.

"While we point with pride to the strides we have made in fulfilling our forefathers' dream of the equality of man," he said, "let us not overlook how far we still have to go." For a man whose civil rights record remained thin, it was an acknowledgment of potential growth—both individually and for the country.

> Let us bear in mind that this is not merely a regional problem—it is not merely a national problem—it is international in scope and effect. For the average American of Caucasian descent does not realize that it is he who is a member of a minority race—and a minority religion—and a minority political system—and that he is regarded with some suspicion, if not hostility, by most of that restless, envious, surging majority. The tide of human dignity is world-wide—and the eyes of that world are upon us.

On matters of civil rights, Jack Kennedy was no Hubert Humphrey. But the primaries—both in Wisconsin and beyond—had forced Kennedy to begin reckoning with one of the most vital issues of the era. For most of his life, Kennedy's race, wealth, and privilege precluded him from fully understanding civil rights on a fundamental level. But he knew to show up, try, and withstand the boos if they were hurled his way.

Peering out at the sea of faces, most of them Black, Kennedy concluded his remarks:

Francis Bacon once wrote, "There is hope enough and to spare—not only to make a bold man try—but also to make a sober-minded man believe." My friends, if you are sober-minded enough to believe—then—to the extent that these tasks require the support, the guidance, and the leadership of the American presidency—I am bold enough to try.

He'd done it. He'd won over the crowd.

Vel cheered along with the audience as Kennedy pushed past the press, the photographers, and his newest supporters. Vel caught the future president's eye.

Relieved, he gave her a wink.

INAUGURATION DAY

Ivan Nestingen, Pat Lucey, and Pete Dugal
January 20, 1961

Nine months and fifteen days after the Wisconsin primary

The bright sun glinted across the inauguration crowd as eighty-six-year-old poet Robert Frost—wearing a dark overcoat, scarf, and glasses—made the short, stilted walk from his seat near the front of the presidential box to the lectern, his fists filled with papers.

Frost had publicly supported Kennedy since March 1959—back when Kennedy's presidential run was still a whisper. By inviting him to read at the inauguration, Kennedy was giving Frost the biggest platform poetry had received in recent history. The crowd offered its rapt attention as the seasoned poet, born just a decade after the Civil War, attempted to usher in a new generation of leadership. The inaugural committee, meanwhile, held its collective breath. Frost was the first poet in US history to participate in an inauguration, and if things didn't go smoothly, he might also be the last.

The inauguration committee had already dealt with a few headaches. The previous day, as almost a million Americans began to descend upon the nation's capital to witness history, a light afternoon snowfall had suddenly transformed into a nor'easter that froze the city solid. Thousands of people got stuck in the storm, abandoning their trapped cars in the streets in what the National Weather Service later described as "the most crippling traffic jam" on record. More than fourteen hundred cars were scattered among the streets; tow truck drivers couldn't work fast enough. Hopeful inauguration attendees tried to walk the rest of the way, pushing through eight inches of snow and creating their own pre-inauguration parade.

On the eve of the inauguration, Jack Kennedy had peered out the window of his Georgetown home and lamented his bad luck. Besting Humphrey had been hard enough, then Nixon, but how on earth was he supposed to beat a blizzard? Already he'd had to cancel dinner, though he refused to cancel Frank Sinatra's pre-inauguration ball at the DC Armory. Anyone who was anyone would be there. Sinatra had even persuaded a couple of Broadway shows to take the night off so that the stars could attend the ball and add to the glitz and the glamour.

The morning of the inauguration, Kennedy woke after four hours of sleep to drag himself to morning mass at Holy Trinity Church just a few minutes before nine o'clock. Though the church was less than a quarter mile away, the previous night's snowfall had made travel difficult. Nevertheless, he found his way to the pews.

Meanwhile, in their nearby hotel, Madison mayor Ivan Nestingen and his wife, Geraldine, readied themselves for the inauguration. Ivan reached for his tuxedo pants, then his crisp white dress shirt, then his sterling silver cuff links, which he fed through their slots. And finally came his tuxedo coat—a perfect fit. Ivan peered into the mirror at the tall Norwegian man looking back at him. He adjusted the part on the right side of his hair, stood tall, and smiled. To think that Jack Kennedy had been pushing Ivan's car up Kenosha's snow-slicked Washington Street hill just fourteen months earlier. And now he was preparing to become the United States' thirty-fifth president.

Ivan turned from the mirror to spot Geraldine in her full-length turquoise taffeta dress. She pulled white gloves toward her elbows and then reached for her silk-lined pearl clutch. With her blonde hair freshly styled and sprayed, thirty-six-year-old Geraldine looked as beautiful as she had nearly a decade and a half prior when Ivan first met her at a law school picnic on the Madison campus. Now they had three daughters, two of whom were old enough to join their father on his campaign tours throughout Madison.

President Kennedy honors the fiftieth anniversary of the nation's first Worker's Compensation Law, enacted in Wisconsin in 1911. The White House ceremony featured a commemorative stamp created for the occasion. Seated behind President Kennedy is Ivan Nestingen. ABBIE ROWE, WHITE HOUSE PHOTOGRAPHS, JOHN F. KENNEDY PRESIDENTIAL LIBRARY AND MUSEUM, BOSTON

A few hours later, Ivan and Geraldine found their seats on the East Portico of the Capitol, just a few rows behind the president-elect and soon-to-be First Lady. Ivan had agreed to serve that day as inaugural parade marshal. But the bigger question on Ivan's mind was what role he might play within the administration. For the past few weeks, Ivan had been approached by several people in Kennedy's inner circle, all men he'd come to know throughout the campaign. His name had been floated for undersecretary of the Department of Health, Education, and Welfare. This wide-sweeping role would include oversight of the Office of Education, the Social Security Administration, the Welfare Administration, the Food and Drug Administration, and the Vocational Rehabilitation Administration. The position interested Ivan enormously. It would be a major leap up the ladder—replacing his Madison mayor's office and its thirty-million-dollar budget with four billion dollars and the chance to make a national impact. As a reporter later pointed out, he would oversee some sixty-five thousand employees—nearly half the population of Madison. But at the same time, moving to Washington to work in the Kennedy administration would almost certainly derail Ivan's future political plans, including a potential run for governor.

Ivan Nestingen's family celebrates his appointment as undersecretary of the US Department of Health, Education, and Welfare. Seated with Ivan are (left to right) daughters Leslie, Marcia, and Laurel, and Ivan's wife, Geraldine. WHI IMAGE ID 143672

Days after the inauguration, Ivan would officially put his political ambitions on hold by accepting the undersecretary role at the Department of Health, Education, and Welfare. In March 1961, a newspaper article would praise Ivan for a "most unbureaucratic and un-Washington" approach to the job; he refused handlers, for example, and preferred to greet his guests personally and at the appointed time (thereby breaking "two bureaucratic traditions at once"). Ivan "did not leave Wisconsin when he gave up his position as mayor of Madison to come to Washington," the article would note. "He brought Wisconsin with him, and Washington is delighted."

Sitting alongside Geraldine, Ivan watched as Robert Frost squinted at his poem. The bright sun made it difficult for Frost to read the words. Ivan watched as vice president elect Lyndon Johnson intervened, using his hat to try to block the sun.

"Give me that," Frost said, snatching Johnson's hat and attempting to block the sun himself. It was no use.

"I just have to get through this," Frost said irritably as the microphone broadcast his mutterings throughout the crowd.

Seated not far from the presidential box, Pat Lucey and his wife, Jean, willed the poet back on track. Pat had been named assistant deputy grand marshal for the inauguration parade; like Ivan, it was the only position he had been willing to commit to by Inauguration Day. Jockeying for roles in the Kennedy administration had begun shortly after the election, but Pat had stayed out of the fray. In early January, Kennedy had called Pat, wondering why on Earth he hadn't sought an appointment within the administration. Pat had thanked the president-elect but noted his preference to stay in Madison, where he could more easily raise his family and continue his lucrative work in the real estate market.

What he could do, Pat had offered, was compile a list of fellow Wisconsinites who were deserving of such appointments. Pat's friend Ivan ranked high on that list, but the Kennedy administration already knew that. Pat's more unlikely recommendation was to find a role for Philleo Nash. Philleo, who'd fought fiercely for Humphrey throughout the primary, had come around to support Kennedy in the general election. Such an about-face hadn't been easy for Philleo, and Pat knew that Philleo's hustling on Kennedy's behalf had likely cost him his lieutenant governorship in the election that fall—all the more reason to find Philleo a safe place to land. Later that year, Philleo would be named President Kennedy's Commissioner of Indian Affairs, a near-perfect fit for the cranberry-farmer-turned-lieutenant-governor who'd earned a PhD for his work in the Pacific Northwest on tribal cultures. It might never have happened if it hadn't been for Pat's recommendation.

Far below on the Capitol grounds, another Wisconsinite tilted his ear toward Frost as the poet tried to find his bearings. Pete Dugal had made the trek from Cadott to witness what had once seemed impossible: Jack Kennedy, the man Pete had driven all over northwestern Wisconsin, was suddenly the most powerful man in the world. Pete would never forget the St. Patrick's Day they spent crisscrossing the western half of the state. How they'd met the nuns outside Ladysmith, the priest in Phillips, and the tiny crowd of eight sipping coffee at the N-Joy Cafe in Cornell. That such a modest campaign had snowballed into this—a jampacked inauguration nearly a million people strong—filled Pete with pride. Of course, things hadn't always gone smoothly—like the time Pete had accidentally locked the keys in the trunk, imperiling Kennedy's schedule—but somehow, they always found their way through.

What remained to be seen, however, was whether Robert Frost would.

Seated directly behind Frost, the president-elect remained expressionless; though sitting to Kennedy's right, Jackie looked worried, whispering frantically to the person on her other side. It was momentarily excruciating for Pete and the many others in the crowd.

Frost, who'd had quite enough of Johnson's hat and Kennedy's phalanx of handlers, finally decided to right the problem himself.

"This was to be a preface to the poem I can say to you without seeing it," he said. "The poem goes like this."

Tossing his papers aside, Frost recited from memory "The Gift Outright" in perfect hymnal grace. It was the performance everyone had hoped for, even if it had come in the least expected way.

As Frost spoke of salvation and surrender, Pete listened to the silence that surrounded him. When was the last time one million Americans had gathered to hear a poet? Had it ever happened? Was this, too, history in the making?

Pete watched Kennedy—or was it President Kennedy now?—as he listened to the poet's words. And then, as the final line left Frost's brittle lips, the crowd turned somehow even more silent than before.

Amid that silence, Frost remarked that his poem was dedicated to "president-elect, Mr. John Finley." Which wasn't exactly John Kennedy, but no matter. It was close enough.

Jack Kennedy leaped to his feet and began clapping, and the crowd joined him—Ivan and Pat on the portico, and Pete far below in the crowd.

Patrick Lucey, state Democratic chairman of Wisconsin, meets with President Kennedy in the Oval Office, August 8, 1961. ROBERT KNUDSEN, WHITE HOUSE PHOTOGRAPHS, JOHN F. KENNEDY PRESIDENTIAL LIBRARY AND MUSEUM, BOSTON

More Than a Face in the Crowd

Ira Kapenstein and Bobby Kennedy
May 12, 1962

Two years, one month, and seven days after the Wisconsin primary

Jockeying alongside President Kennedy's hordes of well-wishers, journalist Ira Kapenstein secured his place near the front entrance of Milwaukee's Schroeder Hotel. Ira checked his watch. If President Kennedy was on schedule, he was due to arrive any minute. Not that President Kennedy stuck tightly to schedules. Throughout the Wisconsin primary, Kennedy's tardiness was so consistent that you could set your watch by it. Ira didn't mind. The anticipation was half the fun.

Ira was looking forward to catching a glimpse of President Kennedy—who was returning to Wisconsin to speak at the Jefferson-Jackson Day Dinner later that night at the Milwaukee Arena—but he knew the moment would be bittersweet. The president would be arriving, after all, with his entourage—an entourage that might've included Ira if things had gone differently.

Ira was first approached about joining the Kennedy campaign in January 1960. Jerry Bruno had been the first to mention it, gauging Ira's interest in the campaign by jokingly encouraging Ira to leave his beat at the *Milwaukee Journal* to work for him at the Kennedy for President Club of Wisconsin. They'd shared a laugh, though Ira couldn't help but wonder if the offer had been serious.

Weeks later, Ira received a second salvo, this one from Ivan Nestingen, who'd heard from Jerry that Ira might be interested in joining the cam-

John F. Kennedy and Ira Kapenstein, date unknown. COURTESY OF JAMES KAPENSTEIN

paign. They were looking for someone to work alongside Pierre Salinger—Kennedy's future press secretary—to handle the press, Ivan told Ira. It sounded like an ideal position, but Ira declined. He and his wife, Betty, had one young child at home and a second on the way. The prospect of giving up his stable position at the *Milwaukee Journal* for the unpredictability of a presidential campaign seemed too large a gamble. Not that Ira wouldn't have loved every second working with the Kennedys. It was, he knew, a once-in-a-lifetime opportunity. A chance not to report the news, but to help make it.

The third salvo came days later when Ira was directed to Milwaukee's Wisconsin Hotel for a meeting with Bobby Kennedy himself. Ira had never met Bobby Kennedy before, and his first impression was quite memorable. Ira entered the hotel suite to find Bobby half dressed in a shirt and boxers. As he pulled on pants and finished dressing, Bobby explained that he'd heard great things about Ira and wanted to know what it would take to get him to join the campaign.

Ira was grateful, he assured Bobby, and honored, too, but he wasn't sure he was the right man for the job. He was too young, for starters, only twenty-four, and he didn't have any experience in politics beyond reporting on it. Surely someone more qualified was available.

Bobby quickly dismissed Ira's worries—if Ivan and Jerry believed he was the right person, then he was—and asked what salary Ira would need.

"A thousand a month," Ira said.

Bobby agreed without skipping a beat. Now that the money had been settled, Bobby expected a quick yes. But Ira hesitated. He needed three days, he explained, to think it over.

It was an excruciatingly difficult decision, complicated even further by some dire health news. Ira had just been diagnosed with melanoma. Giving up his job now was too great a risk, especially since Bobby had been upfront with him about not being able to guarantee Ira a job beyond the convention in July.

Three days later, Ira called Bobby to decline the offer, explaining that the uncertainty was simply too great. Bobby turned quiet. And then he uttered the words that Ira would long remember: "Don't you know that Jack takes care of his friends?"

Now, as Ira stood amid the crowd outside of the Schroeder Hotel, the pang of regret was palpable. He longed for those days of reporting on the campaign trail, stretching all the way back to Kennedy's 1959 visit to the Milwaukee Press Club's Gridiron Dinner and the speech in Beloit's Eaton Chapel. As a member of the press corps, Ira had followed Kennedy from one district to another—observing from close range as the candidate gained statewide momentum, from the primary announcement in the second district to the nuns of Ladysmith in the tenth.

If Ira had said yes to Jerry and Ivan and Bobby, he'd have been on the inside track for whatever came next. He might've followed Salinger to DC to become Jack's deputy press secretary. Instead, he was still covering the political beat in Wisconsin.

"I think they just could not understand why a young man would turn down such an opportunity," Ira would remark later. "And looking back on it, I can understand why they felt that way."

The crowd suddenly cheered as the presidential motorcade pulled up before the hotel. A moment later, President Kennedy stepped smoothly from the car. There was the hearty wave, the boyish grin, and the much-written-about "tousled hair." Ira watched from his place among the crowd, a tinge of regret fluttering within him.

The president worked the line, nodding and hobnobbing all the way to the door. Along the way, President Kennedy's eyes fixed on Ira's. Suddenly, a different smile emerged, one that was more sincere. President Kennedy pulled himself away from the crowd and detoured Ira's way.

"Ira, how are you getting along?" the president asked. "I hear you've been ill. How are you feeling?"

At a loss for words, Ira managed the little response he could. President Kennedy nodded, listened carefully, and wished him well. As the president turned back to the crowd, Ira was flummoxed by what had just occurred. Here was the president of the United States—a man whose head was overflowing with ten thousand names—and yet, he'd remembered Ira. Not only remembered him, but knew enough about him to ask about his health.

Ira no longer felt regret as much as humility.

His work mattered. And his words did, too. You needed only to ask the president.

One year later, Ira would finally take a job from President Kennedy. Working directly underneath Irish Mafia member Larry O'Brien, Ira would serve as Special Assistant to the Postmaster General for Public Information, where, among other things, he would help roll out the nation's zip code system. He would stay in that role even after President Kennedy's death. And in 1968, Ira would once again be asked to join a political campaign—this time he would say yes, serving alongside Larry O'Brien on Bobby Kennedy's 1968 presidential run.

Shortly after midnight on June 5, 1968—in the moments following Bobby Kennedy's victories in both the South Dakota and California primaries—Ira, Larry, and Bobby shared a congratulatory moment in Bobby's room at Los Angeles's Ambassador Hotel. Bobby was eager to go to the ballroom to thank his campaign workers, though Ira and Larry encouraged him to stay in the room instead. It had been a long day, and they had an even longer one ahead of them.

But Bobby insisted. He'd go downstairs, make a few remarks, and be back up in no time.

If only it were true.

After speaking to a ballroom crowded with supporters, Bobby Kennedy turned away from the brightly lit podium and left through the service area. Moments later, as Ira and Larry waited in Bobby's hotel room, shots rang out in the narrow passageway just beyond the hotel's kitchen.

Ira, like so many of the Kennedy faithful, had endured the assassination of not one but two Kennedy brothers.

At the time of Bobby's death, Ira was thirty-two years old, the father of three, happily married, with his whole life ahead of him. On March 1, 1971, he died of cancer at age thirty-five.

As President Kennedy wished Ira well outside the Schroeder Hotel on May 12, 1962, neither man knew their lives would be cut so short. That day, the world was still theirs for the shaping.

As President Kennedy gave his remarks at the Milwaukee Arena that evening, he spoke about the Wisconsin primary and the role it played in his success. Seated beside him was Vel Phillips, whose initial lukewarm feelings toward Jack Kennedy had warmed tremendously throughout the primary season and beyond.

"Whatever other qualifications I may have had when I became president," Kennedy said, "one of them at least was that I knew Wisconsin better than any other president of the United States."

The crowd laughed.

"That is an unchallengeable statement," President Kennedy said. "My foot-tracks are in every house in this state, and what I don't know about the state, the Majority Whip, our distinguished friend Senator Humphrey, he knows the rest of it."

The crowd laughed louder still. It had taken a few years, but Jack and Hubert's war had evolved into a friendship. They were no longer opponents but compatriots, two men who'd endured a long winter that at last gave way to spring. President Kennedy continued:

When they talk about a cold wind, I look north to Superior and the Tenth Congressional District, and I know the difference between the kind of farms they have in the Seventh District and the First District, and I know what a distinguished University can be in Madison, Wisconsin—and I know all about Vince Lombardi and Green Bay, long before they won. And I knew all about the Braves before you did, when they were back in Boston.

And then he spoke the line that would've produced smiles from Ivan, Pat, Jerry, Pete, and every other member of Kennedy's Wisconsin team: "I suppose that there's no training ground for the presidency, but I don't think it's a bad idea for a president to have stood outside of Mayer's meat factory in Madison, Wisconsin, just because Senator Proxmire always did it, at five-thirty in the morning, with the temperature ten above."

As the speech continued, he offered remarks on everything from higher education to the space program. It was a speech chock full of potential, a promise of what the United States could be.

"I don't know with certainty what the future will bring," President Kennedy said, "but I am certain that if we are willing to continue to play our proper part, that it can be happy for all of us."

The crowd cheered. And Ira, his heart soaring, halted his pencil just long enough to join them.

A Band on Every Corner

Jerry Bruno, Hubert Humphrey, and Pat Lucey
November 22–25, 1963

Three years, seven months, and seventeen days
after the Wisconsin primary

R ule No. 1 of advance work: always bring the crowd. Not occasionally. Not sometimes. Always. Especially when you worked for Jack
Kennedy.

Jerry Bruno's first glimpse of Jack's near-obsessive interest in crowds
began in November of '59. The cranberry scare was quickly heating up, and
with Thanksgiving right around the corner, all sorts of political jockeying
was underway. The presidential primary hadn't officially begun, but neither Kennedy nor Nixon was waiting around for the starter pistols. And
so, the future candidates for their respective parties were squaring off at
dueling dinners in Wisconsin.

One might think a sitting senator would have little time for micro-
managing a dinner in a small Wisconsin town. Yet micromanage Jack did,
calling Jerry every day for more than a week, asking about the number of
tickets sold and strategizing ways to increase turnout.

"The guy was a very detailed guy," Jerry later said. "You would think
that he had other things to do, but he was so zeroed in on that first event,
[and] he had such a knack for knowing that the national press was going
to try to compare the two visits."

Just think of it: two presidential hopefuls speaking thirty miles apart
on the very same night in the heart of Wisconsin—an early and tide-

turning primary state. What happened that night would be widely reported, setting the stage for all that would come. Crowd size was the new straw poll, and if Jack could lure a few hundred more supporters than Nixon, that would be the story. One that would be printed again and again in newspapers across the state, ideally above the fold.

At the dinner in Marshfield—where Kennedy's crowd was indeed larger—Jerry learned a lesson that Jack already knew. Every event was a proxy war. And the best weapon in their arsenal was a crowd.

President Kennedy's interest in crowd size remained firmly intact, even after the primaries and the general election. With Jerry now in the role of presidential advance man, it was up to him to handle the logistics of the president's trips—finalizing every detail to ensure a proper crowd everywhere President Kennedy went. Experience was Jerry's teacher, but Kennedy was, too. Throughout his many years of campaigning, Jack had devised a surefire way to assemble a crowd, a strategy he insisted Jerry adopt.

"He'd look around, and he'd look to see where I was, and he'd count the bands," Jerry recalled. "This was his big thing, bands. He wanted bands at every corner, at every stop. . . . He was big on bands because for every band there were sixty players, they each had a mother and father, so they all came out to see them. And then their friends. So, if you put a band at every corner, you automatically get a crowd."

As Jerry learned, the strategy worked both at home and abroad. From June 23 to July 2, 1963, President Kennedy took his final trip to Europe. By every measure, it was a grand success. With the help of Jerry's advance work, the president traveled across western Europe for nine days, leaving a wave of patriotic fervor in his wake. In Berlin on June 26, he stood before an enthusiastic crowd over a million strong and famously proclaimed, "Ich bin ein Berliner!"

The show of solidarity resonated with the West and put the rest of the world on notice: Democracy would reign supreme, whether the Communists liked it or not. Jerry had never seen anything like it—such an outpouring of support for a US president on foreign soil. It was electric, emboldening, and proof of the power of a crowd.

That evening, as they left Berlin and flew toward Ireland, Jack turned to Ted Sorensen and said, "We'll never have another day like this one as long as we live."

He was right, though on a personal level, the following three-day sprint across Ireland would resonate, too. Jack's visit to his ancestral homeland reminded all those watching at home that the United States was, indeed, a nation of immigrants. As for the Irish, they were thrilled to welcome the first Irish-Catholic US president. Everywhere Jack went—from Dublin to Dunganstown, Galway to Cork—he was greeted by adoring crowds.

"The stories about huge outpouring[s] of people in Berlin, the crush of people, and Ireland, it was just unbelievable," Jerry recalled later.

Yet President Kennedy's European trip wasn't all adoring crowds. During Jack's July visit to Rome, he confronted a problem he hadn't faced since the Wisconsin primary: near-empty streets. The Italian press had recently reported on President Kennedy's enormous crowd size, warning that anyone interested in catching a glimpse of the president should stay home and turn on their televisions. So stay home they did.

It was an advance man's worst nightmare. Unfortunately, Jerry wasn't there to fix it. He was sunning himself on the nearby Isle of Capri—a short break that was interrupted by a frantic phone call from press secretary Pierre Salinger.

"The president is up in arms," Pierre shouted. "Nobody showed up in Rome. Naples is the last European stop. He wants this trip to be remembered by the last stop. It's got to be a success, or the whole trip's going to be a failure. And he's counting on Naples."

Jerry hustled back to Naples, where he quickly arranged a meeting with the city's Communist mayor. "Do you have any bands?" Jerry asked, with the help of an interpreter.

"Bands?" the mayor asked, turning to his interpreter.

"Lots of bands," Jerry repeated.

At last, the message got through.

"Oh, no problem," the mayor said, throwing his hands into the air. "Lots of bands! Lots of bands. Yes, we can do that."

Jerry was astonished by the mayor's agreeable nature; the man adopted every idea Jerry had. From inviting nearby mayors to occupy the streets of Naples to releasing the children from school—the mayor said yes to it all. Only later did Jerry realize the reason.

"Somehow this mayor . . . figured that *I* was somehow the expert on protocol," Jerry said.

The following day, President Kennedy arrived in Naples and pulled Jerry aside. "How's the crowd going to be?" the president asked. "How's the bands?"

"I think we're doing alright," Jerry said. "I think we're doing alright."

Jerry, who had made it his practice to underestimate all crowd expectations to more easily please the president, offered no further detail.

Minutes later, as the motorcade began rumbling through the streets of Naples, Jerry's prediction proved true. The crowds were so great that the press corps got separated from the motorcade, making it impossible to capture the scene entirely. In the photos that remain, President Kennedy stands in the back of an open-air convertible, waving to throngs of well-wishers while passing buildings lined with American flags.

President Kennedy stands in a convertible, facing away from the camera, and waves to the crowd at Capodichino Airport in Naples, Italy, on July 2, 1963. Seated next to Kennedy is Italian president Antonio Segni. ROBERT KNUDSEN, WHITE HOUSE PHOTOGRAPHS, JOHN F. KENNEDY PRESIDENTIAL LIBRARY AND MUSEUM, BOSTON

"They swarmed all over the motorcade," Jerry recalled. "They yelled; they screamed; they cheered. They wouldn't let Kennedy get more than ten feet at a time before they jumped into the path of the car to cheer him and greet him."

Upon arriving at the airport in Naples, a grinning Jack threw an arm around Jerry and asked how they'd managed such a turnout. The answer, of course, was the bands. But that day, Jerry offered another explanation: "Mr. President, it's all my cousins who came out to see you."

Jack chuckled as the pair boarded Air Force One together, preparing for the long flight home.

In the weeks leading up to President Kennedy's trip to Dallas on November 22, 1963, Jerry traveled to Texas to begin his advance work. No sooner had he arrived than he realized he was dealing with a wasp's nest of political infighting. Texas governor John Connally was at war with Texas senator Ralph Yarborough. Though both Democrats, their feuding threatened to tear the state's Democratic Party apart. If Kennedy hoped to win reelection in 1964, he needed Texas. Jack's visit was meant to mend the rift between the state's governor and senator and, hopefully, give Texans someone to rally behind in '64.

Jerry kept getting caught in the middle as they tried to map out the president's visit. Much of the disagreement centered on the venue: Governor Connally demanded an easily manageable private luncheon for the president at the Trade Mart shopping mall, while Senator Yarborough wanted a large rally at the fairgrounds. Politically, it boiled down to a difference in access. A luncheon at the Trade Mart would allow Governor Connally to handpick the crowd, giving the impression to his financial backers that Kennedy supported him over Yarborough. By contrast, a fairgrounds rally would grant access to ten thousand Texans—many of whom were expected to back Yarborough.

Jerry examined both locations and leaned strongly toward the fairgrounds for safety reasons. "The first impression we had [of the Trade Mart] was that it didn't look safe because of the catwalks," Jerry later said.

But Governor Connally was adamant. "This is my show," he told Jerry at lunch later that day. "If the president doesn't want to do it my way, the president doesn't have to come."

When Jerry wouldn't budge, Governor Connally abruptly called the White House, returning to the table moments later. "They want you to go back to Washington and they'll tell you what we're going to do," the governor told him.

Despite Jerry's reservations, it eventually was decided that the president would attend the luncheon at the Trade Mart.

"The thing that, 'til this day it disturbs me," Jerry said, "had we gone to the fairgrounds, the president would have come to the downtown from a different direction. We would have still done the motorcade downtown. But instead of driving in front of the book building where [Lee Harvey] Oswald worked and had positioned himself, we would have been over a block away from that building where Oswald was."

The alternative route wouldn't have guaranteed the president's safety, but it would have complicated Oswald's plans by removing his ability to take aim from the Texas School Book Depository's sixth-floor window.

There was yet another way President Kennedy's death in Dallas might have been avoided. According to Jerry, Governor Connally's proposed schedule for the visit had noted that Texas Christian University would be granting President Kennedy an honorary degree following the president's planned commencement address. But when Jerry visited the university's football field where the event was to be held, he was informed of a mix-up.

"There must be some misunderstanding," a university official explained. "The president's welcome to give a speech, but we're not going to give him an honorary degree."

"Why not?" Jerry asked.

"We have never ever in the history of the university given an honorary degree to a Catholic," the official said.

And so, the commencement address was scrapped.

Had Texas Christian University conferred the president with an honorary degree, the motorcade would have taken a different route downtown. And had they taken a different route, the book depository might again have been avoided.

"If I had to blame anybody for that trip," Jerry said, "I would have to blame [Texas Christian University] and the board of regents for rejecting a president of the United States based on his religion."

Rather than accompany the president on his two-day, five-city tour of Texas, Jerry stayed behind at the Democratic National Committee headquarters in DC to monitor the entire trip more easily from a single location. Everything seemed to be going smoothly at the start. On November 21, the president and First Lady touched down in Fort Worth right on schedule, where Jack delivered a well-received speech at Brooks Air Force Base. From there, they continued on to Houston for a testimonial dinner for Congressman Albert Thomas before concluding the day at the Hotel Texas back in Fort Worth.

The following morning—President Kennedy's last—began with a few impromptu remarks to well-wishers in the parking lot outside the Hotel Texas. From there, he entered the hotel's grand ballroom, where Kennedy delivered the last public remarks of his life before two thousand Fort Worth Chamber of Commerce members and their guests.

To watch the footage of that speech today is to be crushed with the painful knowledge of what was about to come. How that vibrant, jovial president—always quick with a joke, as he proved in the opening minutes of his final remarks—would be gunned down within hours.

"Two years ago, I introduced myself in Paris by saying that I was the man who had accompanied Mrs. Kennedy to Paris," Jack told the crowd, a twinkle in his eye. "I'm getting somewhat that same sensation as I travel around Texas."

The crowd laughed as Jack paused before delivering his next punchline: "Nobody wonders what Lyndon [Johnson] and I wear."

Next, Jack and Jackie took the motorcade to Carswell Air Force Base, boarding Air Force One for the eighteen-minute flight to Dallas. Upon landing at Love Field, the president and First Lady worked the crowd of twenty-five hundred people near the fence line.

Back in DC, Jerry monitored everything from his headquarters. A few minutes before twelve thirty central time, Jerry tried to place a call to a fellow advance man on the ground in Dallas. He reached a Secret Service agent instead.

"How's it going?" Jerry asked.

The Secret Service agent confirmed that all was going as planned.

But then, the agent's voice turned frantic.

"I got to get off, I got to get off. There's trouble with the motorcade, trouble in the motorcade, I got to get off."

"There were a dozen things I was imagining," Jerry later wrote, "a blown tire . . . , a wrong turn, a right-wing nut that had run out to spit on the president—everything except what happened."

But what exactly had happened?

Moments later, a secretary ran down the hall screaming that the president had been shot.

Reaching for the phone, Jerry shouted for the White House switchboard. Rather than put the call through, the operator wept.

At around one thirty eastern time on November 22, Senate Majority Whip Hubert Humphrey glanced up from his lunch at the Chilean Embassy as a stricken Ed Morgan from ABC approached and whispered the terrible news into his ear:

"The president's been shot in Dallas. But he's still alive."

Humphrey excused himself, slipping discretely into his car where he could listen to the news bulletins in private. In 1901, when President McKinley was assassinated, such up-to-the-minute coverage would've been impossible. But now, the full measure of horror could be reported in real time. TV, radio, and teletype ensured that every American—and, in fact, everyone worldwide—could receive the dramatic news almost as it happened. That Friday afternoon, nearly 50 percent of American households with televisions tuned in. For the funeral that followed, that number leaped to 81 percent—the country's collective grief would earn one of the highest TV ratings in history.

Returning to the luncheon, Humphrey peered out at the forty or so guests, all of whom remained blissfully unaware of the seismic shift that had just occurred. He stood, commanding the attention of the guests. He had some difficult news to share, he explained. Though Humphrey had never been a man of few words, on this day he was, as he simply stated that Kennedy had been shot.

But by 2:30 p.m. eastern time, a new and devastating reality had taken hold across the nation. Television, radio, and teletype all were reporting the same tragic story: the president was dead.

For the next few hours, Hubert roamed the White House alone, witnessing the cascade of grief that soon consumed everyone. The pain was palpable, from the press offices to the switchboards. Wails went up throughout the White House. There was not enough comfort to go around. Then came the long hours when everyone tried to make themselves useful, but there was nothing anyone could do. For a time, Hubert cloistered himself in his Senate office, reuniting with Muriel later that afternoon so the pair could hold vigil at Andrews Air Force Base. The plane carrying the president's body landed at around six in the evening, Kennedy's entourage stepping forth from the plane's interior to surround the casket like an honor guard.

There were too many people and not enough jobs. Everyone wanted to play some part in transporting the casket from the plane to the ambulance. Jackie was there, and Bobby, too. Huddled alongside the casket was Kennedy's Irish Mafia: Dave Powers, Kenny O'Donnell, and Larry O'Brien—all men who had dedicated most of their adult lives to helping Jack fulfill his dream of becoming president. Military personnel didn't know whether to salute or bear the weight of the casket. All protocols, for the moment, were forgotten.

The following day, Senator Humphrey appeared opposite reporter Bob McCormick for a televised interview on NBC. He recounted his last interaction with President Kennedy, which had occurred the previous Wednesday as the pair enjoyed a stroll around the White House Rose Garden. It was a "wonderful, wonderful visit," Hubert told McCormick, "just like two friends would have."

The news reached other members of the Wisconsin team in its own way. Ivan Nestingen's wife, Geraldine, was at her home in DC when a neighbor

EXTRA! EXTRA!

THE MILWAUKEE JOURNAL

Eighty-second Year—76 Pages   Circulation Thursday . 386,910   **Friday, November 22, 1963**   Daily, per copy, 10 cents   By carrier, 45 cents weekly   Latest Edition ††

Kennedy Is Slain

Shot to Death in Dallas Motorcade

Lyndon B. Johnson, President

Johnson OK; Bullets Also Hit Connally

President's Wife Unhurt, Leaves Hospital With Husband's Body; Rifle Used in Assassination Is Found by Police on Fifth Floor of Near-By Building

President John F. Kennedy

Suspect Captured in Dallas Gunfight

Policeman Is Slain in Theater After Tip Is Received in Assassination

Cabinet Officers Fly Back to US

The Weather

Bulletins

Last Rites Administered

Soviets Blame Death on 'Right Wingers'

Ethiopia, Somalia Exchange Blasts

Romanian Visits Tito

Infant Develops Taste for Beauty, Shakes Up Mom

Word Spreads Fast Along Wisconsin Av.

City Truck Drivers Accept Maier Plan

Zinos States 'Union Meeting' Will End if Council Agrees to Proposals

Other Strike Stories

Meet With Mayor

The front page of the *Milwaukee Journal*, announcing President Kennedy's assassination on November 22, 1963. WHI IMAGE ID 78148

banged on her door to deliver the news. Geraldine did what came naturally: she ran to her nearby church. It was the only sanctuary she could
find, the only chance to soothe the many emotions roiling within her.

"You could not stop crying or having tears in your eyes for days," Geraldine said later. "There was sheer gloom everywhere in this city. No one
on the street seemed to act the same anymore. . . . I felt the world was
falling apart."

Meanwhile, as Geraldine ran to the church that Friday afternoon, Pat
Lucey boarded a plane for Ohio to attend a planning session for Jack's re-
election campaign. Politically, things were looking up. If Jack could hold
Texas in '64, then his reelection would be all but ensured.

Pat was excited to help the president get reelected and was hopeful
about his own chances at winning Wisconsin's lieutenant governorship
that same year. But all Pat's optimism faded in the moments before take-
off, when he began to hear rumblings of what he hoped were merely un-
substantiated reports.

The president had been shot. The president was dead.

In the predawn hours of November 23, Jerry took his place in the East
Room of the White House alongside much of Kennedy's inner circle. "I
guess I stayed there all night," he said later, "and it was never real, none
of it: the floodlights, the announcers, the body being brought back to the
White House—it was all like a bad dream."

At 4:30 a.m. on November 23, the Marine Corps honor guard met
President Kennedy's casket at the North Portico. The White House staff
remained at attention as they saw what had not been seen in more than
half a century—the body of an assassinated president being placed in the
East Room. When William McKinley's body had lain there in September
of 1901, it was a very different country. It seemed somehow inconceivable
that such a tragedy could befall a modern president. Yet here they were. In
the same room where McKinley and Abraham Lincoln had lain. And where
Teddy Roosevelt's children had roller skated. And where Truman had once
played a Steinway piano on live television. Golden curtains draped the
windows as those present shuffled their feet against the decorative wood

flooring. A trio of Bohemian glass chandeliers hung low overhead, while golden-encrusted eagles stood guard over the dual doorways. In the quiet solemnity of that historic room, the enormity of the moment began to sink in.

Jack's inner circle wept. Despite his flaws and missteps, Jack Kennedy had served as their north star, a guiding light toward a brighter America. That light had been snuffed out, and his dream, they feared, had died with him. But it hadn't. For decades, a generation of civil servants whom President Kennedy had inspired would bear that light within them.

Over the course of a single day, the nation had changed immeasurably. Jack Kennedy was dead, Lyndon Johnson was president, and the whiplash had left the country reeling. At last, it was time to sleep. Shortly before dawn, when even the silence was more than they could bear, Bobby encouraged those in the East Room to get some rest.

Nobody wanted to leave, but what choice did they have? Soon enough, the sunrise would cast its terrible light on the scene, solidifying it once and for all.

On Monday, November 25, 1963, the biggest crowd yet gathered for President Kennedy. The route was simple enough: the funeral processional began with the president's horse-drawn caisson clicking through the streets from the Capitol to the White House, then to St. Matthew's Cathedral, and finally to Arlington Cemetery.

There were plenty of bands, just as Jack would've liked it.

First up was the Coast Guard Academy Band, which at 10:48 a.m. played "Ruffles and Flourishes," "Hail to the Chief," and "O God of Loveliness." At 11:00 a.m., as the cortege left Capitol Plaza, the Marine Band, the Navy Band, and the Air Force Band took turns playing a repertory of three songs each. Then the Naval Academy Catholic Choir took its turn, followed by nine Scottish bagpipers from the Black Watch of the Royal Highlanders Regiment, whom Kennedy had watched perform on the White House Lawn just twelve days before.

It was little comfort, at least for Jerry, who watched heartbroken. He couldn't shake the belief that had he fought harder for his preferred route

in Dallas, the president might still be alive. "This was the one time," Jerry later lamented, "I didn't just stick up and fight like a son of a bitch for the place I wanted to go."

The reverberations would weigh heavily upon him.

Jerry wanted nothing more than to put a band on every corner for the president. And to keep doing it for as long as the president required. But after the funeral, there would be no more bands for President Kennedy. No dinners, rope lines, or press events. No jam-packed schedules. No ballrooms. No nothing.

At Arlington Cemetery, the crowd turned silent as the US Army bugler lifted his instrument to his lips. Pressing his gloved fingers to the bugle, the

Jackie Kennedy, flanked by Attorney General Robert F. Kennedy and Senator Edward Kennedy, leads the president's funeral processional from the White House to St. Matthew's Cathedral, November 25, 1963. ABBIE ROWE, WHITE HOUSE PHOTOGRAPHS, JOHN F. KENNEDY PRESIDENTIAL LIBRARY AND MUSEUM, BOSTON

hauntingly beautiful notes of "Taps" rang out throughout the cemetery. The bugler had probably played the call a thousand times, Jerry figured, but on this day—as the world listened—he flubbed the sixth note.

It was proof, Jerry knew, that you could plan everything down to the last detail and still not get the outcome you desired.

The seventh and final note reverberated past the cemetery's oak trees. And then, just like that, the music ended.

Madison, Wisconsin, October 23, 1960

BIBLIOGRAPHY

Books

Bishop, Jim. *A Day in the Life of President Kennedy*. New York: Random House, 1964.

Bradlee, Benjamin C. *Conversations with Kennedy*. New York: W. W. Norton, 1975.

Bruno, Jerry, and Jeff Greenfield. *The Advance Man*. New York: William Morrow, 1971.

Christopherson, Ed. *"Westward I Go Free": The Story of J.F.K. in Montana*. Missoula, MT: Earthquake Press, 1964.

Dallek, Robert. *An Unfinished Life: John F. Kennedy, 1917–1963*. New York: Back Bay Books, 2004.

Dresang, Dennis J. *Patrick J. Lucey: A Lasting Legacy*. Madison: Wisconsin Historical Society Press, 2020.

Gellman, Irwin. *The Contender*. New York: Free Press, 1999.

Hersh, Burton. *Edward Kennedy: An Intimate Biography*. Berkeley, CA: Counterpoint, 2010.

Humphrey, Hubert H. *The Education of a Public Man: My Life and Politics*. New York: Doubleday, 1976.

Kennedy, Edward M. *True Compass: A Memoir*. New York: Twelve, 2011.

Kennedy, Jacqueline, Michael Beschloss, Caroline Kennedy. *Jacqueline Kennedy: Historic Conversations on Life with John F. Kennedy; Interviews with Arthur M. Schlesinger Jr., 1964*. New York: Hyperion, 2011.

Kenney, Charles. *John F. Kennedy: The Presidential Portfolio*. New York: Public Affairs, 2000.

Kunhardt Jr., Philip B., ed. *LIFE in Camelot: The Kennedy Years*. Boston: Little, Brown, 1988.

Levingston, Steven. *The Kennedy Baby: The Loss That Transformed JFK*. New York: Diversion Books, 2013.

Lowe, Jacques. *Remembering Jack: Intimate and Unseen Photographs of the Kennedys*. New York, Bulfinch Press, 2003.

Matthews, Chris. *Jack Kennedy: Elusive Hero*. New York: Simon & Schuster, 2011.

Newseum, Cathy Trost, and Susan Bennett. *President Kennedy Has Been Shot: The Inside Story of the Murder of a President*. Naperville, IL: Sourcebooks Media Fusion, 2004.

O'Donnell, Helen. *A Common Good: The Friendship of Robert F. Kennedy and Kenneth P. O'Donnell*. New York: William Morrow, 1998.

O'Donnell, Kenneth, and David Powers, with Joe McCarthy. *Johnny, We Hardly Knew Ye: Memories of John Fitzgerald Kennedy*. Boston: Little, Brown, 1970.

Pietrusza, David. *1960: LBJ vs. JFK vs. Nixon: The Epic Campaign That Forged Three Presidencies*. New York: Union Square Books, 2008.

Salinger, Pierre. *P.S.: A Memoir*. New York: St. Martin's Press, 2001.

Solberg, Carl. *Hubert Humphrey: A Biography*. St. Paul, MN: Borealis Books, 1984.

Sorensen, Ted. *Kennedy: The Classic Biography*. New York: Harper Perennial Political Classics, 2009.

Tye, Larry. *Demagogue: The Life and Long Shadow of Senator Joe McCarthy*. New York: Mariner Books, 2020.

White, Theodore H. *The Making of the President 1960*. New York: Harper Perennial Political Classics, 2009.

Articles

"The Almost Sinful Strike: Four Years & Stubbornness Have Torn a Town." *Time Magazine*, March 17, 1958. https://content.time.com/time/subscriber/article/0,33009,863137,00.html.

Alsop, Joseph. "Lesson in Wisconsin 'Religious Issue.'" *Madison Capital Times*, April 2, 1960.

Ambrose, Kevin, and Jason Samenow. "How a Surprise Snowstorm Almost Spoiled Kennedy's Inauguration 60 Years Ago." *Washington Post*, January 19, 2021. www.washingtonpost.com/weather/2021/01/19/kennedy-inauguration-weather-1961/.

Associated Press. "Both Nixon, Kennedy Visit State." *Kenosha Evening News*, November 13, 1959.

———. "Humphrey Asks Bold and Honest Look at Issues." *Wisconsin State Journal*, November 15, 1959.

———. "Kennedy Enters Primaries in Nebraska and Wisconsin." *Eau Claire Leader*, January 22, 1960.

———. "Kennedy Sees Bill Curbing Labor Abuses." *Wisconsin State Journal*, April 11, 1959.

———. "Kennedy Plunges into State Contest." *Kenosha Evening News*, January 21, 1961.

———. "Proxmire Will Win Senate Election, Kennedy Predicts." *Sheboygan Press*, August 22, 1957.

———. "Senator Kennedy Touring State." *Kenosha Evening News*, April 10, 1959.

——. "Two Leaders Split on Jack, Hubert Backing." *Monroe Evening Times*,
    March 28, 1960.
——. "Wiley Predicts Kohler Will Beat Proxmire in Tuesday's Election."
    Sheboygan Press, August 23, 1957.
"Awards Presented at Annual Jaycees Meeting." *Eau Claire Leader-Telegram*,
    January 26, 1960.
Barnes, Bart. "Philleo Nash Dies at 77." *Washington Post*, October 13, 1987.
    www.washingtonpost.com/archive/local/1987/10/13/
    philleo-nash-dies-at-77/fab5543f-8a04-479a-8123-e8c1ae3c2d14/.
Bartelt, James. "Senator Kennedy Undecided on Presidential Race Entry."
    Appleton Post-Crescent, April 10, 1959.
Brown, Andrew. "November in Lawrence History." *Lawrentian*, November 7,
    2016. www.lawrentian.com/archives/1009256.
Burwell, Fred. "Fridays with Fred: Kennedy Impresses Campus, 'Tousled
    Hair and All.'" Beloit College, October 21, 2010. www.beloit.edu/live/
    news/1635-fridays-with-fred-kennedy-impresses-campus-tousled.
Byrne, Jeb. "The Hours before Dallas." *Prologue Magazine* 32, no. 3 (Summer
    2000), 75-85. www.archives.gov/publications/prologue/2000/summer/
    jfk-last-day-1.
"Charles Spalding." *SF Gate*, December 30, 1999. www.sfgate.com/news/
    article/Charles-Spalding-2888010.php.
"Cheers and Boos Greet Kennedy at Rights Rally; Senator Calls for Action
    against Racial Discrimination at White House Level." *Los Angeles Times*,
    July 11, 1960.
Coe, Alexis. "Portrait of a Troublemaker: A Rare Glimpse of John F.
    Kennedy's Life at Boarding School." *Town & Country*, May 26,
    2017. www.townandcountrymag.com/society/politics/a9923248/
    john-f-kennedy-student-life-at-choate-rosemary-hall/.
Congressional Quarterly. "For a Sale in '60: Cover the Territory." *Wisconsin
    State Journal*, April 9, 1959.
Dallek, Robert. "The Medical Ordeals of JFK." *The Atlantic*, December 2002.
    www.theatlantic.com/magazine/archive/2013/08/
    the-medical-ordeals-of-jfk/309469/.
Diamond, Jason. "Where Daisy Buchanan Lived." *The Paris Review*,
    December 25, 2012. www.theparisreview.org/blog/2012/12/25/
    where-daisy-buchanan-lived/.

Eisele, Albert. "How Gerald Heaney Might Have Changed the Course of
    History." *Minn. Post*, June 24, 2010 www.minnpost.com/politics-policy/
    2010/06/how-gerald-heaney-might-have-changed-course-history/.
"Enthusiastic Crowd Sees Kennedy." *Kenosha Evening Press*, February 17, 1960.
Fiedler, Carl. "New Leadership Needed to Solve U.S. Problems, Kennedy
    Declares." *Sheboygan Press*, April 11, 1959.
Frost, Robert. "The Gift Outright." In *The Poetry of Robert Frost*, edited by
    Edward Connery Lathem. New York: Henry Holt and Company, 1969.
Goodman, Jay. "Senator Kennedy Speaks in Chapel; Urges Students to Political
    Careers." *Round Table*, April 14, 1959.
"Handbills 'Distributed' a Little Too Late." *Wisconsin State Journal*, April 7, 1960.
Haney, Richard C. "The Rise of Wisconsin's New Democrats: A Political
    Realignment in the Mid-Twentieth Century." *Wisconsin Magazine of
    History* 58, no. 2 (Winter 1974–1975): 90–106. https://content.wisconsin
    history.org/digital/collection/wmh/id/46999.
Hersey, John. "Survival." *New Yorker*, June 17, 1944. www.newyorker.com/
    magazine/1944/06/17/survival.
Herskovitz, Jon. "How the JFK Assassination Transformed Media Coverage."
    Reuters, November 21, 2013. www.reuters.com/article/us-usa-jfk-
    media/how-the-jfk-assassination-transformed-media-coverage
    -idUSBRE9AK11N20131121.
"How 'Favorite Son' Politics Works." *Pittsburgh Post-Gazette*, January 12, 1928.
"Humphrey Plans Final State Drive." *Eau Claire Daily Leader*, March 28, 1960.
"Humphrey Throws Support to Kennedy in Speech Here." *Eau Claire Daily
    Telegram*, October 19, 1960.
John F. Kennedy Presidential Library Staff. "Campaign of 1960." John F.
    Kennedy Presidential Library and Museum. www.jfklibrary.org/learn/
    about-jfk/jfk-in-history/campaign-of-1960.
———. "High Hopes." John F. Kennedy Presidential Library and Museum.
    www.jfklibrary.org/learn/about-jfk/life-of-john-f-kennedy/
    fast-facts-john-f-kennedy/high-hopes.
———. "Results of 1960 Presidential Election Primaries." John F.
    Kennedy Presidential Library and Museum. www.jfklibrary.org/
    learn/about-jfk/life-of-john-f-kennedy/fast-facts-john-f-kennedy/
    results-of-1960-presidential-election-primaries.

"Kennedy Address Wayne Audience; Town Put in National TV Spotlight."
    Wayne County (Virginia) News, April 29, 1960. https://archive.wvculture.
    org/history/1960presidentialcampaign/newspapers/19600429
    waynecountynews.html.
"Kennedy Nears End of District Campaign." *Eau Claire Daily Leader*,
    March 29, 1960.
Kohler Co. National Labor Relations Board-Board Decisions. 128 N.L.R.B. 1062
    (N.L.R.B-BD 1960). *Casetext*, https://casetext.com/admin-law/kohler-co-10.
Labaton, Stephen. "Philleo Nash, at 77; Was a U.S. Official in 3 Administra-
    tions." *New York Times*, October 27, 1987. www.nytimes.com/1987/10/27/
    obituaries/philleo-nash-at-77-was-a-us-official-in-3-administrations.html.
Lister Jr., Walter. "Kennedy Campaign Money Coming from East; Humphrey
    Minnesota Contributions Placed at 85,000." *Janesville Daily Gazette*,
    March 26, 1960.
"The Lost Inaugural Gala for JFK: Never-Before-Seen Performances."
    Thirteen, February 18, 2020. www.thirteen.org/blog-post/
    the-lost-inaugural-gala-for-jfk-never-before-seen-performances/.
Lowens, Irving. "Accurate Listing of Funeral Music." *Washington Star*,
    December 1, 1963.
Mallon, Thomas. "Trying to Remember JFK." *New Yorker*, May 15, 2017.
    www.newyorker.com/magazine/2017/05/22/trying-to-remember-jfk.
Maraniss, Elliot. "Kennedy Margin Is 100,000." *Madison Capital Times*,
    April 6, 1960.
Martin, Lou. "Invoking Noble Coal Miners Is a Mainstay of American Pol-
    itics." *The Conversation*, April 25, 2018. https://theconversation.com/
    invoking-noble-coal-miners-is-a-mainstay-of-american-politics-94281.
Matthews, Chris. "Once an Awkward Loner, RFK Found His Footing on the
    Football Field." *Boston Globe*, September 28, 2017. www.bostonglobe.com/
    opinion/2017/09/28/once-awkward-loner-rfk-found-his-footing
    -playing-field/2UrBoFjW7446Y58FNovdtM/story.html.
McFadden, Robert, "Lou Harris, Pollster at Forefront of American Trends,
    Dies at 95." *New York Times*, December 19, 2016. www.nytimes.com/
    2016/12/19/us/louis-harris-pollster-at-forefront-of-american-trends
    -dies-at-95.html.
McKusick, Frances. "City's Ex-Mayor Scores a Hit on Big New Job in
    Washington." *Wisconsin State Journal*, March 12, 1961.

Miller, John. E. "The Making of Theodore H. White's 'The Making of the President 1960.'" *Presidential Studies Quarterly* 22, no. 2 (June 1999): 389–406.

"Minneapolis Mayor." Our Campaigns. www.ourcampaigns.com/RaceDetail .html?RaceID=563282.

Morin, Relman. "Nixon, Unopposed, Trails Presidential Aspirants." *Racine Journal-Times*, April 6, 1960.

"Mrs. Kennedy Makes Campaign Debut Here; Has Overflow Crowd," *Wisconsin Rapids Daily Tribune*, March 11, 1960.

"Nation: The Golden Handshake." *Time Magazine*, December 24, 1965. https://content.time.com/time/subscriber/article/0,33009,834841,00.html.

"National Affairs: New Rules in Wisconsin." *Time Magazine*, February 8, 1960. http://content.time.com/time/subscriber/article/0,33009,828622,00.html.

NCC Staff. "Term Limits for American Presidents." *Constitution Center*, February 27, 2023. https://constitutioncenter.org/blog/ how-we-wound-up-with-the-constitutions-only-term-limits-amendment.

"Obituary: Peter J. Dugal." *Chippewa Valley Herald*, February 11, 2017. https:// chippewa.com/news/local/obituaries/obituary-peter-j-dugal/article _c11b3981-2253-5ebd-b274-aa404651ab59.html.

O'Brien, Shane. "Who Was Arabella Kennedy?" *Irish Central*, July 26, 2020. www.irishcentral.com/roots/who-was-arabella-kennedy.

Ott, Tim. "Why Robert Frost Didn't Get to Read the Poem He Wrote for John F. Kennedy's Inauguration." *Biography*, June 1, 2020. www.biography.com/ news/john-f-kennedy-inauguration-robert-frost-poem.

"'Perfect' Weather Aids Ski Tourney. *Madison Capital Times*, February 15, 1960.

Perry, Barbara. "How John F. Kennedy and Eleanor Roosevelt Went from Rivals to Allies." *Dallas Morning News*, August 30, 2020. www.dallasnews.com/opinion/commentary/2020/08/30/ how-john-kennedy-and-eleanor-roosevelt-went-from-rivals-to-allies/.

Price, Christopher. "The Impact of the Mechanization of the Coal Mining Industry on the Population and Economy of Twentieth Century West Virginia." *West Virginia Historical Society* 22, no. 3 (July 2008): 1–14. https://archive.wvculture.org/history/wvhs/wvhs2203.pdf.

"Robert Frost Lets JFK Do the Unthinkable." *New England Historical Society*. https://newenglandhistoricalsociety.com/robert-frost-lets-jfk-unthinkable/.

Roberts, Llewelyn G. "Winner Kennedy Pockets Six of Ten State Districts." *Wisconsin State Journal*, April 6, 1960.

Roos, Dave. "How John F. Kennedy Overcame Anti-Catholic Bias to Win the Presidency." History.com, November 20, 2019. www.history.com/news/jfk-catholic-president.

Ross Joynt, Carol. "Five Georgetown Locations Rich in Kennedy History." *Washingtonian*. August 22, 2012. www.washingtonian.com/2012/08/22/5-georgetown-locations-rich-in-kennedy-history/.

Shafer, Ronald G. "Before 'Stop Bernie,' a Brokered Democratic Convention Stopped Estes Kefauver." *Washington Post*, February 27, 2020. www.washingtonpost.com/history/2020/02/28/bernie-sanders-brokered-convention-kefauver/.

Starr, J. Barton. "Birmingham and the 'Dixicrat' Convention of 1948." *Alabama Historical Quarterly* 32, no. 1&2 (spring and summer 1970): 23–50. https://archive.org/stream/alabama-historical-quarterly-v32n0102/AHQ_v32_n1_2_1970_djvu.txt.

"State Leaders Recall JFK Tragedy." *Wisconsin State Journal*, November 19, 1983.

"Strategic Warpath in Wisconsin," *LIFE* magazine, March 28, 1960.

Summers, Candace. "Stevenson, Adlai E. II." McLean County Museum of History, 2014. www.mchistory.org/research/biographies/stevenson-adlai-e-ii.

"Ted Kennedy Campaigning in This Area." *Eau Claire Daily Leader*, March 28, 1960.

Thelan, David P., and Esther S. "Joe Must Go: The Movement to Recall Senator Joseph McCarthy." *Wisconsin Magazine of History* 49, no. 3 (spring 1966): 185–209.

Thornton, Denise. "Cranberries Past Present and Future." *Digging in the Driftless*, November 22, 2011. https://digginginthedriftless.com/2011/11/22/cranberries-past-present-and-future/.

"'Twas a Great Day for Rock County Democrats—U.S. Senator, Congressman, and Governor Here," *Janesville Daily Gazette*, April 11, 1959.

UPI. "Humphrey Backers Win Edge in Delegate Fight." *Eau Claire Sunday Leader*, January 31, 1960.

Vargas, Theresa. "Thanksgiving Panic: How a Cranberry Crisis Changed the Way Americans See Food." *Washington Post*, November 20, 2017.

www.washingtonpost.com/news/retropolis/wp/2017/11/20/thanksgiving
-panic-how-a-cranberry-crisis-changed-the-way-americans-see-food/.

"Vel Phillips." *Wisconsin Historical Society.* www.wisconsinhistory.org/
Records/Article/CS14781.

Walker, Norman. "NLRB Orders Kohler To Rehire Striking Workers."
Stevens Point Daily Journal, August 26, 1960.

White, William. "Stevenson Nominated on the Third Ballot; Pledges Fight
'With All My Heart and Soul'; Truman Promises to 'Take Off Coat' and
Help." *New York Times*, July 26, 1952.

Widmer, Ted. "Eich Bin Ein Berliner." *New York Times*, June 25, 2013.
www.nytimes.com/2013/06/26/opinion/ich-bin-ein-berliner.html.

"WI U.S. Senate." Our Campaigns. www.ourcampaigns.com/RaceDetail
.html?RaceID=46910.

Wolfe, Lisa Reynolds. "The Cranberry Scare of 1959." *Cold War Studies*,
November 19, 2020. https://coldwarstudies.com/2020/11/19/
the-cranberry-scare-of-1959/.

Wyngaard, John. "Price of Strategy Win Could Be High." *Appleton Post-Crescent*,
February 1, 1960.

Archival Materials

Address at Jefferson Jackson Day Dinner, Milwaukee, Wisconsin, May 12, 1962.
Papers of John F. Kennedy. Presidential Papers. President's Office Files.
John F. Kennedy Presidential Library. www.jfklibrary.org/asset-viewer/
archives/JFKPOF/038/JFKPOF-038-014.

Address in Milwaukee, Wisconsin at a Jefferson-Jackson Day Dinner, May 12,
1962. WH-094-001. White House Audio Collection. White House Audio
Recordings, 1961–1963. John F. Kennedy Presidential Library.
www.jfklibrary.org/asset-viewer/archives/JFKWHA/1962/
JFKWHA-094-001/JFKWHA-094-001.

Address to the Greater Houston Ministerial Association. IFP-140. Historic
Speeches. John F. Kennedy Presidential Library. www.jfklibrary.org/
learn/about-jfk/historic-speeches/address-to-the-greater-houston
-ministerial-association.

Bruno, Gerald J. "Jerry." Recorded interview, October 29, 2002. JFKOH
-GJB-01. John F. Kennedy Oral History Collection. John F. Kennedy
Presidential Library.

DiSalle, Michael V. Recorded interview by Ken Mack, November 24, 1964. JFKOH-MVD-01. John F. Kennedy Oral History Collection. John F. Kennedy Presidential Library.

Dugal, Peter J. Recorded interview by Charles T. Morrissey, January 14, 1966. JFKOH-PEJD-01. John F. Kennedy Oral History Collection. John F. Kennedy Presidential Library.

Humphrey, Hubert H. Recorded interview by Max Kampelman, December 14, 1964. JFKOH-HHH-01. John F. Kennedy Oral History Collection. John F. Kennedy Presidential Library.

"Introducing: Senator Proxmire's Staff." *Wisconsin Historical Society.* February 1, 1949. https://content.wisconsinhistory.org/digital/api/collection/proxmire/id/9092/download.

Kapenstein, Ira. Recorded interview by Charles T. Morrissey, December 15, 1965. JFKOH-IK-01. John F. Kennedy Oral History Collection. John F. Kennedy Presidential Library.

"Kennedy Assassination Statement, NBC-TV with Robert McCormick." Hubert H. Humphrey: An Inventory of His Speech Text Files at the Minnesota Historical Society Manuscripts Collection. www2.mnhs.org/library/findaids/00442/pdfa/00442-01227.pdf.

Kitzman, Harvey. Recorded interview by Charles T. Morrissey, December 6, 1965. JFKOH-KT-01. John F. Kennedy Oral History Collection. John F. Kennedy Presidential Library.

Knudsen, Robert. White House Photographs. JFKWHP-1963-07-02-F. John F. Kennedy Presidential Library. www.jfklibrary.org/asset-viewer/archives/JFKWHP/1963/Month%2007/Day%2002/JFKWHP-1963-07-02-F.

Lucey, Patrick J. Draft Card. Draft Registration Cards for Wisconsin, 10/16/1940-03/31/1947. Records of the Selective Service System, 147. Box 436. National Archives in St. Louis, Missouri.

Lucey, Patrick J. Recorded interview by Leon D. Epstein, August 1, 1964. JFKOH-PJL-01. John F. Kennedy Oral History Collection. John F. Kennedy Presidential Library.

Nash, Philleo. Recorded interview by Charles T. Morrissey, January 28, 1966 (Interview #1). JFKOH-PN-01. John F. Kennedy Oral History Collection. John F. Kennedy Presidential Library.

Nash, Philleo. Recorded interview by Charles T. Morrissey, March 8, 1966 (Interview #2). JFKOH-PN-02. John F. Kennedy Oral History Collection.

John F. Kennedy Presidential Library.

Nash, Philleo. Recorded interview by William W. Moss, February 26, 1971 (Interview #3). JFKOH-PN-03. John F. Kennedy Oral History Collection. John F. Kennedy Presidential Library.

Nestingen, Ivan A., Draft Card. Draft Registration Cards for Wisconsin, 10/16/1940-03/31/1947. Records of the Selective Service System, 147. Box 511. National Archives in St. Louis, Missouri.

Nestingen, Ivan Arnold, Papers, 1942–1961. Wisconsin Historical Society. Mss 350; Disc 139A; AD 031.

Nestingen, Ivan Arnold, Papers, 1942–1961. *The John F. Kennedy Wisconsin Presidential Campaign*. Wisconsin Historical Society, Division of Library, Archives, and Museum Collections.

Nestingen, Ivan. Recorded interview by Charles T. Morrissey, March 3, 1966 (Interview #1). JFKOH-IAN-01. John F. Kennedy Oral History Collection. John F. Kennedy Presidential Library.

Nestingen, Ivan. Recorded interview by John F. Stewart, May 29, 1968 (Interview #2). JFKOH-IAN-02. John F. Kennedy Oral History Collection. John F. Kennedy Presidential Library.

Nelson, Gaylord. Recorded interview by Edwin R. Bayley, July 1, 1964, John F. Kennedy Library Oral History Program. John F. Kennedy Presidential Library.

"Opening Statement by Senator John F. Kennedy for the Wisconsin Presidential Primary, Press Conference, Madison, Wisconsin, February 16, 1960." Papers of John F. Kennedy. Pre-Presidential Papers. Senate Files, Box 906, "Wisconsin Presidential Primary Opening Statement, Press Conference, Madison, Wisconsin, February 16, 1960." John F. Kennedy Presidential Library. www.jfklibrary.org/archives/other-resources/john-f-kennedy-speeches/madison-wi-19600216.

Phillips, Vel. Recorded interview by Charles T. Morrissey, January 13, 1966. JFKOH-VRP-01. John F. Kennedy Oral History Collection. John F. Kennedy Presidential Library.

"Press Conference Concerning Resignation as a Delegate to the 1960 National Democratic Convention." July 2, 1960. Harry S. Truman Library. www.trumanlibrary.gov/soundrecording-records/sr60-719-press -conference-concerning-resignation-delegate-1960-national.

"Remarks by Senator John F. Kennedy at the Democratic National Convention, International Amphitheatre, Chicago, Illinois, August 16, 1956." Papers of John F. Kennedy. Pre-Presidential Papers. Senate Files, Box 895, "Nominating Stevenson for President, Chicago, Illinois, August 16, 1956." John F. Kennedy Presidential Library. www.jfklibrary.org/archives/other-resources/john-f-kennedy-speeches/ chicago-il-democratic-national-convention-19560816.

"Remarks of Senator John F. Kennedy, Annual Convention, Democratic Party of Wisconsin, Milwaukee, Wisconsin, November 13, 1959." Papers of John F. Kennedy. Pre-Presidential Papers. Senate Files, Box 905, "Democratic Party of Wisconsin Convention, Milwaukee, Wisconsin, November 13, 1959." John F. Kennedy Presidential Library. www.jfklibrary.org/archives/other-resources/john-f-kennedy-speeches/ milwaukee-wi-19591113.

"Remarks of Senator John F. Kennedy at Charleston, West Virginia, April 11, 1960." David F. Powers Personal Papers, Box 33, "Economic Issues, Charleston, WV, April 11, 1960." John F. Kennedy Presidential Library. www.jfklibrary.org/archives/other-resources/john-f-kennedy-speeches/ charleston-wv-19600411.

"Remarks of Senator John F. Kennedy at Jefferson-Jackson Dinner, Minneapolis, Minnesota, June 4, 1960." Papers of John F. Kennedy. Pre-Presidential Papers. Senate Files, Box 909, "Jefferson-Jackson Day dinner, Minne-apolis, Minnesota, June 4, 1960." John F. Kennedy Presidential Library. www.jfklibrary.org/archives/other-resources/john-f-kennedy-speeches/ minneapolis-mn-19600604.

"Remarks of Senator John F. Kennedy at the Gridiron Club, Washington, DC, March 15, 1958." Papers of John F. Kennedy. Pre-Presidential Papers. Senate Files, Box 899, "Gridiron Club, Washington, DC, March 15, 1958." John F. Kennedy Presidential Library. www.jfklibrary.org/archives/ other-resources/john-f-kennedy-speeches/washington-dc-19580315.

"Remarks of Senator John F. Kennedy, Gridiron Dinner Club, Milwaukee, Wisconsin, April 9, 1959." Papers of John F. Kennedy. Pre-Presidential Papers. Senate Files, Box 902, "Milwaukee Gridiron Dinner, Milwaukee, Wisconsin, April 9, 1959." John F. Kennedy Presidential Library. www.jfklibrary.org/archives/other-resources/john-f-kennedy-speeches/ milwaukee-wi-19590409.

"Remarks of Senator John F. Kennedy at NAACP Rally, Los Angeles, California, July 10, 1960." Papers of John F. Kennedy. Pre-Presidential Papers. Senate Files, Box 910, "NAACP rally, Los Angeles, California, July 10, 1960." John F. Kennedy Presidential Library. www.jfklibrary.org/archives/other-resources/john-f-kennedy-speeches/los-angeles-ca-naacp-rally-19600710.

Riggins, William J. Recorded interview by Charles T. Morrissey, December 6, 1965. JFKOH-WJR-01. John F. Kennedy Oral History Collection. John F. Kennedy Presidential Library.

Spalding, Charles. Recorded interview by John F. Stewart, on March 14, 1968 (JFK Interview). JFKOH-CHS-01. John F. Kennedy Oral History Collection. John F. Kennedy Presidential Library.

Spalding, Charles. Recorded interview by John F. Stewart, on March 22, 1968 (RFK Interview). RFKOH-CHS-01. Robert Kennedy Oral History Collection. John F. Kennedy Presidential Library.

Treanor, John H. Recorded interview by William J. Hartigan, September 28, 1977. JFKOH-JHT-01. John F. Kennedy Oral History Collection. John F. Kennedy Presidential Library.

"West Virginia Primary Announcement." Papers of John F. Kennedy. Pre-Presidential Papers. Senate Files, Box 906, "West Virginia primary announcement, February 4, 1960." John F. Kennedy Presidential Library. www.jfklibrary.org/archives/other-resources/john-f-kennedy-speeches/west-virginia-primary-19600204.

U.S., *School Yearbooks, 1880–2012*. Nestingen, Ivan A. School Name: Sparta High School, Year: 1939. Ancestry.com.

U.S., *World War II Draft Cards Young Men, 1940–1947*. Bruno, Gerald Joseph, Draft Card. Ancestry.com.

U.S., *World War II Draft Cards Young Men, 1940–1947*. Dugal, Peter, Draft Card. Ancestry.com.

U.S., *World War II Draft Cards Young Men, 1940–1947*. Spalding, Charles, Draft Card. Ancestry.com.

U.S., *World War II Draft Cards Young Men, 1940–1947*. Yasko, Karel, Draft Card. Ancestry.com.

Wisconsin: Primary: Results. JFKCAMP1960-0973-019-p0001. Campaigns by State: Pre-Convention Political Files, 1960. Papers of John F. Kennedy. Pre-Presidential Papers. Presidential Campaign Files, 1960. John F.

Kennedy Presidential Library. www.jfklibrary.org/asset-viewer/archives/
    JFKCAMP1960/0973/JFKCAMP1960-0973-019.

Yasko, Karel H. Recorded interview by William McHugh, December 14, 1966.
    JFKOH-KHY-01. John F. Kennedy Oral History Collection. John F.
    Kennedy Presidential Library.

Online Resources

"720 College St." Wisconsin Historical Society. www.wisconsinhistory.org/
    Records/Property/HI58033

"1956 Presidential General Election Results-Wisconsin." Dave Leip's Atlas
    of U.S. Elections. https://uselectionatlas.org/RESULTS/state
    .php?fips=55&year=1956&f=0&off=0&elect=0

Ameche, Alan. Pro Football Reference. www.pro-football-reference.com/
    players/A/AmecAl00.htm.

"Annotated Timeline of Campaign Stops, June 1958–May 10, 1960." West
    Virginia Archives and History. https://archive.wvculture.org/history/
    1960presidentialcampaign/annotatedtimeline.html.

"Brokered Convention." Political Dictionary. 2002. https://politicaldictionary
    .com/words/brokered-convention/.

Coleman, David. "JFK Explains Why He Wants to Be President." 14th Day.
    https://jfk14thday.com/jfk-tape-political-career/.

"Daniel Shaw Lumber Company." Historical Marker Database.
    www.hmdb.org/m.asp?m=76025.

"The East Room." White House Historical Association.
    www.whitehousehistory.org/white-house-tour/the-east-room.

"Eau Claire, Eau Claire County." Wisconsin Historical Society.
    www.wisconsinhistory.org/Records/Article/CS7315.

"Favorite Son." Political Dictionary. https://politicaldictionary.com/words/
    favorite-son/.

Govtrack. "HR. 6127. Civil Rights Act of 1957. Amendment to Guarantee Jury
    Trials in All Cases of Criminal Contempt and Provide Uniform Methods
    for Selecting Federal Court Juries." August 2, 1957. www.govtrack.us/
    congress/votes/85-1957/s73.

"Have You No Sense of Decency?" United States Senate. www.senate.gov/
    about/powers-procedures/investigations/mccarthy-hearings/have-you-
    no-sense-of-decency.htm.

Holleran, Scott. "Lake Forest: A History." *Daily North Shore*, November 22, 2015. https://jwcdaily.com/2015/11/22/lake-forest-a-history/.

"Hotel Loraine." Historical Marker Database. www.hmdb.org/m.asp?m =48309.

"Hotel Loraine." Wisconsin Historical Society. www.wisconsinhistory.org/ Records/Image/IM136261.

Humphrey, Hubert H. 1948 Democratic National Convention Address. AmericanRhetoric.com. www.americanrhetoric.com/speeches/ huberthumphey1948dnc.html.

Humphrey, Hubert Horatio Jr., Biographical Directory of the United States Congress. https://bioguideretro.congress.gov/Home/ MemberDetails?memIndex=h000953.

"JFK Early Campaign." Pop History Dig. https://pophistorydig.com/topics/ jfks-early-campaign1959/.

Kamarack, Elaine: "The 1960 West Virginia Primary: Can It Happen Again?" *Brookings*, May 10, 2006. www.brookings.edu/blog/fixgov/2016/05/10/ the-1960-west-virginia-primary-can-it-happen-again/.

LIFE. March 28, 1960. https://oldlifemagazine.com/march-28-1960-life -magazine.html.

McCarthy, Joseph R., Death Certificate. www.dcdave.com/article5/ deathcertificate.JPG.

"Presidential Primaries, 1960." CQ Researcher. https://library.cqpress.com/ cqresearcher/document.php?id=cqresrre1960010600.

Stevenson, Adlai, 1952 Democratic National Convention Address. American Rhetoric.com. www.americanrhetoric.com/speeches/adlai stevenson1952dnc.html.

"Uniroyal, Inc. Records,1917–1990." University of Wisconsin–Eau Claire. www.uwec.edu/kb/article/uniroyal-inc-records-1917--1990/.

US Senate. "John Sparkman: A Featured Biography." www.senate.gov/ senators/FeaturedBios/Featured_Bio_SparkmanJohn.htm.

US Senate. "Senator William Proxmire." www.senate.gov/artandhistory/ history/minute/Senator_William_Proxmire.htm.

"William McKinley's Coffin in State in the East Room." www.whitehouse history.org/photos/william-mckinley-coffin-in-state-in-the-east-room.

Wisconsin Congressional Districts, 1933–1963 (map), https://commons .wikimedia.org/wiki/File:WisCongMap1933.jpg.

Personal Interviews

Dugal, Dan. Telephone interview by B.J. Hollars. September 3, 2020.

Kapenstein, James. Telephone interview by B.J. Hollars. February 8, 2021.

Nestingen, Leslie. Telephone interview and correspondence with B.J. Hollars. October 23, 2020.

Nestingen Rock, Marcia. Telephone interview and correspondence with B.J. Hollars. November 10, 2020.

Videos

Drew, Robert, director. *Primary*. Time Life Television, 1960.

Frost, Robert. "January 20, 1961–Poet Robert Frost Reads Poem at John F. Kennedy's Inauguration." January 15, 2021. Youtube.com. www.youtube.com/watch?v=AILGO3gVlTU.

Kennedy, John F. "John F. Kennedy Wisconsin Primary 1960." July 23, 2011. Youtube.com. www.youtube.com/watch?v=IJDWkTwAag8.

NOTES

The Gathering

Indeed, Jack Kennedy was the reason: White, *Making of the President*, 49.

a nickname he'd earned: Gellman, *The Contender*, 303.

For the next three hours, Jack demonstrated just that: White, *Making of the President*, 54.

"How does he do that?" marveled Pierre Salinger: Salinger, *P.S.: A Memoir*, 71.

Until as late as 1972, candidates routinely skipped state primaries: "Brokered Convention," Political Dictionary.

often dismissing them as "beauty contests": Kamarack, "The 1960 West Virginia Primary."

just fifteen states plus the District of Columbia: John F. Kennedy Presidential Library Staff, "Results of 1960 Presidential Election Primaries."

"favorite son" strategy: "Favorite Son," Political Dictionary; "Presidential Primaries, 1960," CQ Researcher; "How 'Favorite Son' Politics Works," *Pittsburgh Post-Gazette*.

Following a lunch of roast turkey: White, *Making of the President*, 56.

Ted Kennedy was given the task: Edward M. Kennedy, *True Compass*, 128; White, *Making of the President*, 57.

it was in Wisconsin . . . that he learned the necessary skills: Sorensen, *Kennedy*, 133–138.

Dispatches from the Cranberry Bog

Though Philleo remained hopeful: Nash, recorded interview #1, January 28, 1966.

along with sixty million other radio listeners: Solberg, *Hubert Humphrey*, 19.

Humphrey had distinguished himself: Humphrey, Hubert Horatio Jr., Biographical Directory of the United States Congress.

staggering 66 percent of the vote: "Minneapolis Mayor," *Our Campaigns*.

Philleo would've liked to have known Humphrey better: Nash, recorded interview #1, January 28, 1966.

left Wisconsin for Washington, DC: Nash, recorded interview #1, January 28, 1966.

Klamath Indians' ghost dances: Barnes, "Philleo Nash Dies at 77."

Since his father's death: Nash, recorded interview#1, January 28, 1966.

The Democrats' Platform Committee had defeated: Solberg, *Hubert Humphrey*, 11.

"My friends," Humphrey bellowed: Humphrey, 1948 Democratic National
   Convention Address.
working with NAACP lawyer: Nash, recorded interview #1, January 28, 1966.
"My good friends": Humphrey, 1948 Democratic National Convention
   Address.
lead author of the 1964 Civil Rights Act: Solberg, *Hubert Humphrey*, 226–227.
For eight minutes, delegates from various states engaged in a shouting match:
   Solberg, *Hubert Humphrey*, 11.
the delegates voted 651½ to 582½: Solberg, *Hubert Humphrey*, 19.
Wisconsin delegates cast the deciding votes: Solberg, *Hubert Humphrey*, 19.
formed the States' Rights Democratic Party: Starr, "Birmingham and the
   'Dixicrat' Convention of 1948."

Locking Horns at the Stock Yard Inn

Pat Lucey stepped outside: Lucey, recorded interview, August 1, 1964.
Pat had high hopes: Lucey, recorded interview, August 1, 1964; Dresang,
   Patrick J. Lucey, 95.
deputy quartermaster: Dresang, *Patrick J. Lucey*, 29–32.
Pat liked the idea: Dresang, *Patrick J. Lucey*, 4, 20, 95–96.
"undecided, the hesitant, or the merely cautious": White, "Stevenson
   Nominated."
Truman had been exempted: NCC Staff, "Term Limits."
had won twelve of the fifteen primaries: Shafer, "Before 'Stop Bernie.'"
Kennedy strongly supported Stevenson: Lucey, recorded interview,
   August 1, 1964.
"I understand that you Stevenson people": Lucey, recorded interview,
   August 1, 1964.
an outspoken segregationist: US Senate, "John Sparkman."
"if you northern liberals": Lucey, recorded interview, August 1, 1964.
Stalking off, Pat thought: Lucey, recorded interview, August 1, 1964.
Senator Kefauver cast Tennessee's twenty-eight: White, "Stevenson
   Nominated."
From 1919 to 1933: Dresang, *Patrick J. Lucey*, 45.
Pat met with several statewide Democratic leaders at the Retlaw Hotel:
   Dresang, *Patrick J. Lucey*, 46.
They'd grown weary: Haney, "The Rise of Wisconsin's New Democrats."
Pat was hired as director: Dresang, *Patrick J. Lucey*, 56.
grassroots politicking: Dresang, *Patrick J. Lucey*, 59.
Democrats dramatically improved their odds: Dresang, *Patrick J. Lucey*, 56–79.
Senator Kennedy endured blizzard-like conditions: Associated Press,

"Both Nixon, Kennedy Visit State."

"years the locusts have eaten": "Remarks of Senator John F. Kennedy,"
   November 13, 1959.

"I think we can close the gaps": "Remarks of Senator John F. Kennedy,"
   November 13, 1959.

"fallen for a kind of 'pitch'": Associated Press, "Humphrey Asks Bold and
   Honest Look."

"This has happened to us": Associated Press, "Humphrey Asks Bold and
   Honest Look."

Thirty-one-year-old Sorensen cornered Pat: Dresang, *Patrick J. Lucey*, 95–96.

the man was smart and likable: Dresang, *Patrick J. Lucey*, 95–96.

Sorensen argued that the party: Dresang, *Patrick J. Lucey*, 95–96; Lucey,
   recorded interview, August 1, 1964.

A Politician Rises

Sitting in his living room: Nestingen, recorded interview, March 3, 1966.

"The ordeal of the twentieth century": Stevenson, 1952 Democratic National
   Convention Address.

Stevenson's great-grandfather: Summers, "Stevenson, Adlai E. II."

Childish pranks: Matthews, *Jack Kennedy*, 13–23; Dallek, *An Unfinished Life*,
   38–39; Coe, "Portrait of a Troublemaker."

in 1934 was diagnosed as colitis: Dallek, *An Unfinished Life*, 73.

"most likely to succeed": Dallek, *An Unfinished Life*, 38.

Born in Sparta, Wisconsin: Nestingen Rock, personal interview.

Nestingen's Quality Grocery: Nestingen Rock, personal interview.

In his senior photo: "U.S., School Yearbooks, 1880–2012."

"We have come here today": "Remarks by Senator John F. Kennedy,"
   August 16, 1956.

"Sometimes in the heat": "Remarks by Senator John F. Kennedy,"
   August 16, 1956.

thirty-eight votes short: Dallek, *An Unfinished Life*, 207.

After a moment's hesitation: O'Donnell and Powers, *Johnny*, 122; Dallek,
   An Unfinished Life, 206–210.

Bobby Kennedy later blamed: Dallek, *An Unfinished Life*, 207.

"These are problems that cry out": "Remarks by Senator John F. Kennedy,"
   August 16, 1956.

Everyone who subscribed: Pietrusza, *1960*, 8.

In the aftermath of PT-109's collision: Hersey, "Survival."

He enlisted in the army: Nestingen Rock, personal interview.

a sleek-framed, 138-pound: Nestingen, Draft Card.

rarely spoke of his war years: Nestingen Rock, personal interview.

In 1954, as a thirty-three-year-old alderman: Nestingen Rock, personal
     interview.

"The Senator Joseph McCarthy of March 1954": Thelan and Thelan, "Joe Must Go."

With eight hundred members: Thelan and Thelan, "Joe Must Go."

the most signatures ever on a notarized petition: Thelan and Thelan,
     "Joe Must Go."

On December 2, 1954, in a bipartisan vote: Dallek, *An Unfinished Life*, 189.

McCarthy had even vacationed: Tye, *Demagogue*, 226.

Joe Sr. gave generously to McCarthy's reelections: Tye, *Demagogue*, 227.

Jack Kennedy had attended McCarthy's wedding: Pietruska, *1960*, 11.

godfather for Bobby's first child: Pietruska, *1960*, 11.

Throughout Jack's three days: Dallek, *An Unfinished Life*, 206.

"He had made such a very outstanding": Nestingen, recorded interview,
     March 3, 1966.

Kennedy for Proxmire

On the ground, Philleo Nash: Nash, recorded interview #1, January 28, 1966.

After his time in the Truman administration: Nash, recorded interview #1,
     January 28, 1966.

Proxmire wasn't necessarily Philleo's favorite: Dresang, *Patrick J. Lucey*, 70.

Four years earlier, on an evening in 1953: Bruno, recorded interview, October
     29, 2002; Bruno and Greenfield, *Advance Man*, 32.

Curious, Jerry started up the stairs: Bruno, recorded interview, October 29,
     2002; Bruno and Greenfield, *Advance Man*, 32.

"This guy Proxmire was somebody": Bruno and Greenfield, *Advance Man*, 32.

emigrants from Cosenza, Italy: Bruno and Greenfield, *Advance Man*, 31.

From 1945 to 1947, Jerry served in the navy: Bruno and Greenfield,
     Advance Man, 31.

secretary of the Kenosha County Proxmire: Proxmire Campaign Literature.

to improve their wages and other portions of their contract: Walker, "NLRB
     Orders Kohler to Rehire Striking Workers."

the nation's second-largest plumbing supply company: "The Almost Sinful Strike."

The strike eventually led to hundreds of arrests: "Nation: The Golden Handshake."

Jerry returned to the picket line: Bruno, recorded interview, October 29, 2002.

In 1960, the National Labor Relations Board: Kohler Co., National Labor Relations Board-Board Decisions.

when the red-baiting Senator Joseph McCarthy died: "Have You No Sense of Decency?"

"hepatitis, acute, cause unknown": McCarthy, Death Certificate.

"Until this moment, Senator": "Have You No Sense of Decency?"

"Have you no sense of decency?": "Have You No Sense of Decency?"

Proxmire's divorce weakened his support: Bruno, recorded interview, October 29, 2002.

The winners of two special elections: Bruno, recorded interview, October 29, 2002; Bruno and Greenfield, *Advance Man*, 33.

"I think I had the same feeling": Bruno and Greenfield, *Advance Man*, 35.

"I laid this wreath": Bruno, recorded interview, October 29, 2002.

"never wanted to have anybody involved": Bruno, recorded interview, October 29, 2002.

If this was how Proxmire was going to behave: Bruno, recorded interview, October 29, 2002.

"You know, the senator": Bruno, recorded interview, October 29, 2002.

"Get on the plane": Bruno, recorded interview, October 29, 2002.

Following McCarthy's death, the *Journal*: Nash, recorded interview #1, January 28, 1966.

"But something else was accomplished": Nash, recorded interview #1, January 28, 1966.

"one of the most impressive ad lib performances": Nash, recorded interview #1, January 28, 1966.

"The party that is in [power] doesn't care too much": Associated Press, "Wiley Predicts Kohler."

the first woman and first Black person: "Vel Phillips," Wisconsin Historical Society.

Vel believed Kennedy: Vel Phillips, recorded interview, January 13, 1966.

guaranteed jury trials: Govtrack, "HR. 6127."

"You know, I have been a great fan": Phillips, recorded interview, January 13, 1966.

Well, what can you say: Phillips, recorded interview, January 13, 1966.

Citing the following day's commitments: Nash, recorded interview #1, January 28, 1966; Associated Press, "Wiley Predicts Kohler."

how might Wisconsin voters respond: Nash, recorded interview #1, January 28, 1966.

Sorensen shrouded his question: Nash, recorded interview #1, January 28, 1966, 2002.

"And that ended one of the most interesting days": Nash, recorded interview #1, January 28, 1966.

William Proxmire defeated Walter Kohler: "WI U.S. Senate," Our Campaigns.

first Democratic senator elected: US Senate, "Senator William Proxmire."

The Unannounced Campaign Begins

Since 1953, Ira had taken on any assignment: Kapenstein, personal interview.

taken Kennedy to forty-seven states since 1957: *Congressional Quarterly*, "For a Sale in '60."

For three days Kennedy would crisscross Wisconsin: Kapenstein, recorded interview, December 15, 1965.

lengthy remarks by Wisconsin governor: Kapenstein, recorded interview, December 15, 1965.

"an extremely important state": Bartelt, "Senator Kennedy Undecided."

"look like a campus telephone booth": Bartelt, "Senator Kennedy Undecided."

"fraught with interest": Associated Press, "Senator Kennedy Touring State."

"I have chosen this forum": "Remarks of Senator John F. Kennedy," April 9, 1959.

"We have been speaking lightly": "Remarks of Senator John F. Kennedy," April 9, 1959.

"For we in this country": "Remarks of Senator John F. Kennedy," April 9, 1959.

"For what we need now": "Remarks of Senator John F. Kennedy," April 9, 1959.

a luncheon at Sheboygan's Foeste Hotel: Fiedler, "New Leadership Needed."

the nineteenth-century chapel: "720 College St," Wisconsin Historical Society.

As Kennedy entered to find a crowd: "'Twas a Great Day."

"It is the basic responsibility": Burwell, "Fridays with Fred"; Goodman, "Senator Kennedy Speaks."

"It has not been a hindrance: Associated Press, "Kennedy Sees Bill Curbing Labor Abuses."

"Contrary to common newspaper usage": Address to the Greater Houston Ministerial Association.

"But if this election is decided": Address to the Greater Houston Ministerial Association.

"If somebody doesn't ask about it": Kapenstein, recorded interview, December 15, 1965.

How does the senator respond: Kapenstein, recorded interview, December 15, 1965.

Kennedy ought to have shown "less profile": Mallon, "Trying to Remember JFK"; Perry, "How John F. Kennedy and Eleanor Roosevelt."

refused to support Jack Kennedy's bid: Dallek, *An Unfinished Life*, 233–234.

"The one regret I have": Kapenstein, recorded interview, December 15, 1965.

Later, the pieces came together: Kapenstein, recorded interview, December 15, 1965.

Breakfast at Kennedy's

to serve as Proxmire's "Wisconsin secretary": Bruno and Greenfield, *Advance Man*, 34.

"Hey Jerry, how's Wisconsin?": Bruno, recorded interview, October 29, 2002.

"Listen," Jack said, changing the subject: Bruno, recorded interview, October 29, 2002.

"Well, Humphrey's very viable": Bruno, recorded interview, October 29, 2002.

At five foot five: *U.S., World War II Draft Cards*, Bruno.

"I'm not going to be able to talk": Bruno, recorded interview, October 29, 2002.

At eight thirty the following morning: Bruno, recorded interview, October 29, 2002.

3307 N. Street: Joynt, "Five Georgetown Locations."

eighteen-month-old Caroline: O'Donnell, *A Common Good*, 167.

"I'd had experience in Wisconsin": Bruno and Greenfield, *Advance Man*, 35.

for Jack generally consisted of orange juice: Bishop, *A Day in the Life*, 9.

"Go to work for [Ivan and Pat]": Bruno, recorded interview, October 29, 2002.

"taking a real gamble": Bruno, recorded interview, October 29, 2002.

"I've got a pretty good chance": Bruno, recorded interview, October 29, 2002.

"what the hell have I got to lose?": Bruno, recorded interview, October 29, 2002.

Jerry informed Proxmire of his decision: Bruno, recorded interview,
    October 29, 2002.

"Bruno is on his own": Bruno, recorded interview, October 29, 2002.

The Uphill Battle

Ivan Nestingen, the mayor of Madison: Nestingen, recorded interview #1,
    March 3, 1966.

By 1948, Republicans had run the table: Dresang, *Patrick J. Lucey*, 48.

reelect President Dwight D. Eisenhower: "1956 Presidential General Election
    Results-Wisconsin."

had been engaged in a shadow campaign: Nestingen, recorded interview #1,
    March 3, 1966.

As chairman of Chippewa County's Democratic Party: Dugal, recorded inter-
    view, January 14, 1966.

making lofty speeches about the role of the United States: Associated Press,
    "Both Nixon, Kennedy Visit State"; Brown, "November in Lawrence
    History."

Flemming's timing could not have been worse: Vargas, "Thanksgiving Panic."

Kennedy at the Hotel Charles in Marshfield: "JFK Early Campaign,"
    Pop History Dig.

Philleo had been conspicuously not invited: Nash, recorded interview #1,
    January 28, 1966.

he and Humphrey shared a political base: Nash, recorded interview #1,
    January 28, 1966.

"I see no reason for hysteria": Vargas, "Thanksgiving Panic."

Jerry Bruno, now working with Ivan Nestingen: Bruno, recorded interview,
    October 29, 2002.

When a photographer encouraged Kennedy: Nash, recorded interview #2,
    March 8, 1966.

"Well, [Nixon and I] have both eaten them": Vargas, "Thanksgiving Panic."

Ivan watched in his rearview mirror: Riggins, recorded interview,
    December 6, 1965.

Kenny and Dave were at Jack's side: O'Donnell, *Common Good*, 178.

Ira Kapenstein watched the scene: Riggins, recorded interview,
    December 6, 1965.

Making It Official

"Wisconsin was uppermost in the minds": White, *Making of the President*, 55.

Though Wisconsin had been the first state: White, *Making of the President*, 80.

low poll numbers nationwide: Pietruska, *1960*, 132.

"Kennedy would have been finished": O'Donnell and Powers, *Johnny*, 148.

"the crisis of the campaign": Dallek, *An Unfinished Life*, 248.

"we should get out of the fight": Dallek, *An Unfinished Life*, 248.

"If I am beaten": Pietruska, *1960*, 92.

At the behest of Harry Truman: O'Donnell and Powers, *Johnny*, 150–152; DiSalle, recorded interview, November 24, 1964.

whose groundbreaking polling techniques: McFadden, "Lou Harris, Pollster at Forefront of American Trends, Dies at 95."

After polling twenty-three thousand: White, *Making of the President*, 93; Sorensen, *Kennedy*, 134.

"I believe that any Democratic aspirant": Kennedy, "John F. Kennedy Wisconsin Primary 1960."

would touch down at Milwaukee's Mitchell Field: Associated Press, "Kennedy Plunges into State Contest."

Some candidates, like Humphrey: John F. Kennedy Presidential Library Staff, "Results of 1960 Presidential Election Primaries."

Wisconsin governor Gaylord Nelson: Dresang, *Patrick J. Lucey*, 96.

They certainly hadn't been in 1928: Dresang, *Patrick J. Lucey*, 20.

32 percent of the state's population: Solberg, *Hubert Humphrey*, 204.

Joe Sr. had purchased the plane: Pietruska, *1960*, 86.

reached for her coat collar: Associated Press, "Kennedy Plunges into State Contest."

And there were other early supporters, too: Dresang, *Patrick J. Lucey*, 97–98.

An eager press awaited them, including Ira Kapenstein: Kennedy, "John F. Kennedy Wisconsin Primary 1960."

Ivan Nestingen positioned himself: Kennedy, "John F. Kennedy Wisconsin Primary 1960."

"I shall run": Kennedy, "John F. Kennedy Wisconsin Primary 1960."

"I am fully aware": Kennedy, "John F. Kennedy Wisconsin Primary 1960."

Jack would end up running: John F. Kennedy Presidential Library Staff, "Results of 1960 Presidential Election Primaries."

"Well, there are several polls": Kennedy, "John F. Kennedy Wisconsin
    Primary 1960."
Vel Phillips arrived: Phillips, recorded interview, January 13, 1966.
"Vel, it is so good to see you,": Phillips, recorded interview,
    January 13, 1966.
Vel had paid a personal price: Phillips, recorded interview, January 13, 1966.
"[M]y mother puts Jackie Robinson": Phillips, recorded interview,
    January 13, 1966.
"Think nothing of it": Phillips, recorded interview, January 13, 1966.
"I understand that we have a suit alike": Phillips, recorded interview,
    January 13, 1966.
By the end of the primary season: John F. Kennedy Presidential Library Staff,
    "Results of 1960 Presidential Election Primaries."
"which binds its delegates": "West Virginia Primary Announcement."
"rather provincial view": Lucey, recorded interview, August 1, 1964.
"Well," Jack said wryly,: Lucey, recorded interview, August 1, 1964.
"Well," Pat managed: Lucey, recorded interview, August 1, 1964.
"Well, don't feel that way about it": Lucey, recorded interview, August 1, 1964.

A Stroll through the Snow

For the past few hours, Bobby and Chuck had watched: Spalding, recorded
    interview JFK, March 14, 1968.
Chuck had regularly joined Bobby: Spalding, recorded interview JFK,
    March 14, 1968.
He was known to sail his boat: Spalding, recorded interview JFK,
    March 14, 1968.
with his gangly six-foot-four-inch frame: U.S., World War II Draft Cards,
    Spalding.
Chuck first met Jack Kennedy: Spalding, recorded interview JFK, March 14, 1968.
"It was just a wonderful disarray": Spalding, recorded interview JFK,
    March 14, 1968.
"[H]e was the most engaging person that I've ever known": Spalding, recorded
    interview JFK, March 14, 1968.
From California to Cape Cod: Spalding, recorded interview JFK, March 14, 1968.
"You know," Jack lamented: Spalding, recorded interview JFK, March 14, 1968.
"One politician was enough": Coleman. "JFK Explains Why."

"That would be wonderful,": Spalding, recorded interview JFK, March 14, 1968.

"Listen," Chuck told Bobby: Spalding, recorded interview RFK, March 22, 1968.

For his part, though, Bobby still had his doubts: White, *Making of the President*, 55.

third-largest meatpacking company: "Charles Spalding," *SF Gate*.

the wealthy town that had inspired F. Scott Fitzgerald's *The Great Gatsby*: Diamond, "Where Daisy Buchanan Lived." www.theparisreview.org/blog/2012/12/25/where-daisy-buchanan-lived/.

Lake Forest was born from pious Presbyterians: Holleran, "Lake Forest: A History."

German and Norwegian lumbermen: "Eau Claire, Eau Claire County," Wisconsin Historical Society.

upwards of 989 million board feet: "Daniel Shaw Lumber Company."

provided jobs for two hundred and fifty: "Uniroyal, Inc. Records,1917–1990."

employed close to three thousand: "Uniroyal, Inc. Records,1917–1990."

Consisting of eleven counties: Wisconsin Congressional Districts, 1933–1963 (map).

"aren't you really glad you came?": Spalding, recorded interview JFK, March 14, 1968.

Fuzzy Math

State election rules dictated: "National Affairs: New Rules in Wisconsin."

The thirty-first vote would be divided: "National Affairs: New Rules in Wisconsin."

But in January 1960, Sam Rizzo: "National Affairs: New Rules in Wisconsin."

Even if Kennedy won the popular vote: Wyngaard, "Price of Strategy Win."

a vote of fourteen to twelve: "National Affairs: New Rules in Wisconsin."

the Humphreyites were scared: Wyngaard, "Price of Strategy Win."

Ivan wrote an angry letter: *Nestingen Papers, 1942–1961*, letter dated February 3, 1960.

"Your leadership in the effort": *Nestingen Papers*, letter dated February 3, 1960.

"The eyes of the entire United States": *Nestingen Papers*, letter dated February 5, 1960.

"If as a result of this kind": *Nestingen Papers*, letter dated February 5, 1960.

swing fifty thousand additional votes: Eisele, "How Gerald Heaney."

"It is both puzzling and disturbing": *Nestingen Papers*, letter dated
     January 26, 1960.
Even Wisconsin governor Gaylord Nelson: Wyngaard, "Price of Strategy Win."
"Sen. Humphrey enjoys many advantages": UPI, "Humphrey Backers Win Edge."
"I think this matter will be settled": "National Affairs: New Rules in
     Wisconsin."
"For anyone to accuse": "National Affairs: New Rules in Wisconsin."
"Let me make it completely clear": "Opening Statement by Senator John F.
     Kennedy," February 16, 1960.
"The Kennedy campaign was": Lucey, recorded interview, August 1, 1964.

Ted Takes the Leap
Standing at the top of Tomahawk Ridge: " 'Perfect' Weather Aids Ski Tourney";
     Kennedy, *True Compass*, 140.
"look like part of the crowd": Kennedy, *True Compass*, 140.
"Why don't you go over": Kennedy, *True Compass*, 140.
odds of him voluntarily launching himself: Kennedy, *True Compass*, 141.
suddenly began to play "The Star-Spangled Banner": Kennedy, *True Compass*, 141.
"Now at the top of the jump" Kennedy, *True Compass*, 141.
"Here he comes, ladies and gentlemen!": Kennedy, *True Compass*, 141.
Far below, the Marine Band: Kennedy, *True Compass*, 141.
"It was either jump," Ted recounted: Christopherson, *Westward I Go Free*, 36.
"Did anyone see Hubert Humphrey": Kennedy, *True Compass*, 141.
which Joan described as "a perfect memento": Nestingen Rock, personal
     interview.
"It is a great deal more pleasant": "Mrs. Kennedy Makes Campaign Debut."

Jackie Steals the Show
twelve hundred supporters: "Enthusiastic Crowd Sees Kennedy."
Later, Jackie would admit: Kennedy, *Jacqueline Kennedy*, 67.
suspicious of anyone sort of gregarious": *Jacqueline Kennedy*, 67.
Some days she and Jack would enter: Kennedy, *Jacqueline Kennedy*, 67.
"In Wisconsin, those people would stare": Kennedy, *Jacqueline Kennedy*, 67.
Tolstoy's *War and Peace*: Kennedy, *Jacqueline Kennedy*, xii.
Kerouac's *The Dharma Bums*: Lowe, *Remembering Jack*, 2003.
Tragically, that grief was compounded: O'Brien, "Who Was Arabella Kennedy?"

"You better haul your ass": O'Brien, "Who Was Arabella Kennedy?"

"Jackie's drawing more people": O'Donnell and Powers, *Johnny*, 156.

"Just keep on with your shopping": O'Donnell and Powers, *Johnny*, 156–157.

"Please," she said, "vote for him": O'Donnell and Powers, *Johnny*, 157.

twenty-six-year-old Alan Ameche: Alan Ameche, Pro Football Reference.

"in a way to make you feel proud": "Enthusiastic Crowd Sees Kennedy."

"I apologize for my husband's tardiness": "Enthusiastic Crowd Sees Kennedy."

"Let's sing a song": O'Donnell and Powers, *Johnny*, 157; Bruno, recorded
     interview, October 29, 2002.

"Everyone is voting for Jack": John F. Kennedy Presidential Library Staff,
     "High Hopes."

suit and dotted floral tie: "Enthusiastic Crowd Sees Kennedy."

"the most significant in the United States": "Enthusiastic Crowd Sees Kennedy."

Chance Encounters

Forty-eight-year-old Karel: *U.S., World War II Draft Cards*, Yasko.

brick box on West Washington: "Hotel Loraine," Wisconsin Historical Society.

example of the Beaux Art tradition: "Hotel Loraine," Historical Marker
     Database.

Completed in 1924: "Hotel Loraine," Historical Marker Database.

Milwaukee-based architect Herbert Tullgren: "Hotel Loraine," Historical
     Marker Database.

Karel was sitting at the front table: Yasko, recorded interview,
     December 14, 1966.

That sounded wonderful, Karel said: Yasko, recorded interview,
     December 14, 1966.

"Would you care to say a word or two": Yasko, recorded interview,
     December 14, 1966.

"an extemporaneous, spontaneous talk": Yasko, recorded interview,
     December 14, 1966.

"The great regret of my life": Yasko, recorded interview, December 14, 1966.

"We have with us tonight": Yasko, recorded interview, December 14, 1966.

"Yesterday I was in Eau Claire": Yasko, recorded interview, December 14, 1966.

"Just before that I'd been up": Yasko, recorded interview, December 14, 1966.

"The best of all": Yasko, recorded interview, December 14, 1966.

"And he took me off the hook": Yasko, recorded interview, December 14, 1966.

about twenty degrees below zero: Yasko, recorded interview, December 14, 1966.

he was hatless: Yasko, recorded interview, December 14, 1966.

"Bobby Kennedy's the name": Yasko, recorded interview, December 14, 1966.

"You know," Jack smiled: Yasko, recorded interview, December 14, 1966.

"I'm Jack Kennedy": Yasko, recorded interview, December 14, 1966.

"If I fall asleep": Yasko, recorded interview, December 14, 1966.

"Bob, Bob it's time to go": Yasko, recorded interview, December 14, 1966.

The Candidates Square Off in Clintonville

photographer Stan Wayman: "Strategic Warpath in Wisconsin."

most of the money was coming from out East: Lister Jr., "Kennedy Campaign
    Money."

By 1926, both of the town's banks: Solberg, *Hubert Humphrey*, 44.

that terrible day in 1927: Solberg, *Hubert Humphrey*, 44.

infuse his son's campaign: Pietruska, *1960*, 90.

$17,000 in debt: White, *Making of the President*, 109.

Humphrey and his staff froze: Humphrey, *Education*, 207; Solberg, *Hubert
    Humphrey*, 205.

"Come down here, Jack": Humphrey, *Education*, 207.

nearly seven million readers peered: "Masthead." *LIFE* magazine,
    March 28, 1960.

"I think I saw in the Wisconsin primary": Humphrey, recorded interview,
    December 14, 1964.

"To this day it astounds me": Humphrey, recorded interview, December 14, 1964.

"I would be interpreted as being brash": Humphrey, recorded interview,
    December 14, 1964.

"If you're going to run": Humphrey, recorded interview, December 14, 1964.

"to fish or cut bait": Humphrey, recorded interview, December 14, 1964.

the latter of whom he tried to win over: Bruno, recorded interview,
    October 29, 2002.

"I think in Wisconsin one of the drawbacks Hubert had": Kitzman, recorded
    interview, December 6, 1965.

"It was," Humphrey later lamented: Humphrey, recorded interview,
    December 14, 1964.

"Thank God, thank God," he said: Kenney, *John F. Kennedy*, 39.

"It was a stupid thing": Humphrey, recorded interview, December 14, 1964.

His wife, Muriel, was passing out: Humphrey, *Education*, 219.

"the only legitimate kind of politics": Associated Press, "Two Leaders Split."

president of the United States, not some star: Associated Press, "Two
    Leaders Split."

Driving Senator Kennedy

At six thirty on a Thursday morning: Dugal, recorded interview, January 14,
    1966; Treanor, recorded interview, September 28, 1977.

Pete sometimes struggled: Dugal, recorded interview, January 14, 1966.

the best orator in the Senate: Dugal, recorded interview, January 14, 1966.

Pete's first drive with Jack: Dugal, recorded interview, January 14, 1966.

Pete was a few inches shorter: *U.S.*, *World War II Draft Cards*, Dugal.

a green and white cake she'd baked: Treanor, recorded interview,
    September 28, 1977; White, *Making of the President*, 83.

Though internal polling continued to show: White, *Making of the President*, 83.

Despite enduring the one-on-one handshakes: Nestingen, recorded interview
    #1, March 3, 1966.

"Stop the car," Jack said: Dugal, recorded interview, January 14, 1966.

"Did you arrange this [stop], too, John?": Treanor, recorded interview,
    September 28, 1977.

"I died a thousand deaths": Treanor, recorded interview, September 28, 1977.

their Mother Superior even attempting to pin: Treanor, recorded interview,
    September 28, 1977.

Kapenstein hopped from a trailing car: Kunhardt Jr, *LIFE in Camelot*, 100.

"Why the hell did you stop?": Dugal, recorded interview, January 14, 1966.

"Gee, he told me to": Dugal, recorded interview, January 14, 1966.

"That'll be the only press": Dugal, recorded interview, January 14, 1966.

"the dirtiest looking Roman Catholic priest": Treanor, recorded interview,
    September 28, 1977.

"shaking hands, and saying in a very loud, guttural accent": Treanor, recorded
    interview, September 28, 1977.

For many voters, anti-Catholic sentiment: Roos, "How John F. Kennedy
    Overcame."

"forlorn and lonesome young man": White, *Making of the President*, 83.

"grunted and let him pass": White, *Making of the President*, 84.

"which was totally indifferent to the fact that a presidential candidate": White,
    Making of the President, 84.

"was as careless of his presence as of a cold wind": White, *Making of the
    President*, 84.

"hatless, trudging like a trooper": Salinger, *P.S.: A Memoir*, 71.

"My name is John Kennedy": O'Donnell and Powers, *Johnny*, 153.

"President of what?": O'Donnell and Powers, *Johnny*, 153.

"We were trying to pin buttons": Dugal, recorded interview, January 14, 1966.

crowd of up to eight hundred people: Dugal, recorded interview, January 14, 1966.

"Are there really a lot of whores": Dugal, recorded interview, January 14, 1966.

"That's what they say": Dugal, recorded interview, January 14, 1966.

"What a hell of a way to spend": O'Donnell and Powers, *Johnny*, 153.

acquired a board for him: Dugal, recorded interview, January 14, 1966.

"seen no more than sixteen hundred": White, *Making of the President*, 84.

"it did not seem preposterous": White, *Making of the President*, 85.

Lost in the Pasture

Back in Milwaukee, Jerry Bruno: O'Donnell, *Common Good*, 184.

"Yeah, what's up?": O'Donnell, *Common Good*, 184.

"Um, well, describe it, describe the town": O'Donnell, *Common Good*, 184.

But no such path existed: White, *Making of the President*, 55–56.

barely measuring in in at five foot nine: Matthews, "Once an Awkward Loner."

So what if he broke his leg: Matthews, "Once an Awkward Loner."

In 1952, Democrats were falling: Dallek, *An Unfinished Life*, 174.

"an independent merchant": Pietrusza, *1960*, 86.

At Jack's invitation: Kennedy, *True Compass*, 115.

"standing ovation after standing ovation": Dallek, *An Unfinished Life*, 245.

Their mother, Rose Kennedy, and their sisters: "Mrs. Kennedy Makes
    Campaign Debut Here."

"Well, I'm looking out the window": O'Donnell, *Common Good*, 184.

"This is just great": O'Donnell, *Common Good*, 185.

"We shouldn't have even": O'Donnell, *Common Good*, 185.

"What the hell am I doing": O'Donnell, *Common Good*, 185.

"Did you say prize bull": O'Donnell, *Common Good*, 185.

"Watertown, Wisconsin!": O'Donnell, *Common Good*, 185.

At the Gates

"Shake hands with the senator": Alsop, "Lesson in Wisconsin 'Religious Issue.'"

"Happy to meet you," Jack said, extending: "Kennedy Nears End of District Campaign."

Men who wore ball caps: "Kennedy Nears End of District Campaign."

The plant employed thirty-two hundred employees: "Uniroyal, Inc. Records, 1917–1990."

his beige suitcoat in contrast to Jack's: "Kennedy Nears End of District Campaign."

A slow afternoon drizzle: Alsop, "Lesson in Wisconsin 'Religious Issue.'"

the dozen or so journalists who'd joined: "Kennedy Nears End of District Campaign."

They'd started early: "Kennedy Nears End of District Campaign."

enthusiastic crowd in a Methodist Church: Alsop, "Lesson in Wisconsin 'Religious Issue.'"

like Roosevelt had built: John F. Kennedy Presidential Library Staff, "Campaign of 1960."

Folks like Senator Eugene McCarthy: "Humphrey Plans Final State Drive."

Dave, who'd accompanied Jack: O'Donnell and Powers, *Johnny*, 154.

"God, Dave, I don't have the guts": O'Donnell and Powers, *Johnny*, 154.

"What the hell are you doing": O'Donnell and Powers, *Johnny*, 154.

A single fur-lined glove: O'Donnell and Powers, *Johnny*, 154.

"I'm John Kennedy, candidate for president": O'Donnell and Powers, *Johnny*, 154.

"God, if I had his money": O'Donnell and Powers, *Johnny*, 154.

Instead, Jack shook hands until his own hand bled: O'Donnell and Powers, *Johnny*, 155.

ordering coffees in tall paper cups: O'Donnell and Powers, *Johnny*, 155.

"Happy to meet you," Jack said: "Kennedy Nears End of District Campaign."

"But I like Humphrey, too": "Kennedy Nears End of District Campaign."

"Meet the senator": "Kennedy Nears End of District Campaign."

Primary Day

Philleo Nash walked through the door: Nash, recorded interview #1, January 28, 1966.

Philleo approached the table: Nash, recorded interview #1, January 28, 1966.

A break-even scenario would give Humphrey a psychological victory: Nash, recorded interview #1, January 28, 1966.

perhaps as high as 65 to 35 percent: Nash, recorded interview #1, January 28, 1966.

"Well, what do you think?" a voice called: Nash, recorded interview #1, January 28, 1966.

"I did not expect these returns": Nash, recorded interview #1, January 28, 1966.

No one knew whether the state's open primary rule: O'Donnell and Powers, *Johnny*, 150.

If Humphrey could hold the western ninth and tenth: Pietrusza, *1960*, 92–93; Nash, recorded interview #1, January 28, 1966.

"If I were to form an image of myself": Lucey, recorded interview, August 1, 1964.

Humphrey's strength in the second district: Dresang, *Patrick J. Lucey*, 96–97.

In all, there were 3,440 precincts to report: Pietrusza, *1960*, 92.

"Well, what do you think?" Teddy asked: Nash, recorded interview #1, January 28, 1966.

As the returns continued, Philleo listened: Nash, recorded interview #1, January 28, 1966.

Less than a mile away, Jack Kennedy sipped soup: Drew, *Primary*.

They monitored the information as best they could: White, *Making of the President*, 94.

A documentary film crew, led by director Robert Drew: Drew, *Primary*.

He had initially been hesitant about encouraging Jack: O'Donnell and Powers, *Johnny*, 149–150.

"The longer Ivan followed Kennedy's career": Nestingen, Leslie. Personal interview and correspondence.

"romantic, almost quaint faith in ordinary people": Miller, "The Making of Theodore H. White"; White, *Making of the President*, 87.

"Humphrey . . . may carry five districts": Drew, *Primary*.

"What does it mean?": Drew, *Primary*; Pietrusza, *1960*, 94.

Humphrey had won all of them: White, *Making of the President*, 95; Pietrusza, *1960*, 92–93.

Ultimately, the crossover vote . . . appeared to have: Solberg, *Hubert Humphrey*, 207.

Twelve thousand more people voted: Dresang, *Patrick J. Lucey*, 103–104, 108.

awarded Humphrey two additional delegates: Wisconsin: Primary: Results; "National Affairs: New Rules in Wisconsin."

It was difficult . . . to discern just what role religion had played: Pietrusza, *1960*, 93.

"in the beech tree and basswood counties": Sorensen, *Kennedy*, 138.

"Well, I was hopeful we could take six districts": Drew, *Primary*.

"Well, I continue on": Drew, *Primary*.

"This has been a great election": Drew, *Primary*.

"I say I've been in politics": Drew, *Primary*.

"You see, if somebody relegates you": Drew, *Primary*.

"Just imagine if we'd have won": Drew, *Primary*.

Kennedy had won with 56.5 percent: Robert, "Winner Kennedy"; John F. Kennedy Presidential Library Staff, "Results of 1960 Presidential Election Primaries."

Kennedy earned twenty convention votes: Wisconsin: Primary: Results.

predicted Kennedy winning 63 percent: Pietruska, *1960*, 92.

"It's in the bag": Pietrusza, *1960*, 91.

Pat Lucey went so far as to predict: Lucey, recorded interview, August 1, 1964.

"Humphrey for President" handbills: "Handbills 'Distributed' a Little too Late."

Humphrey's Last Stand

For the rest of his life, Jerry Bruno would never forget: Bruno, recorded interview, October 29, 2002.

"I suppose numerically": Morin, "Nixon, Unopposed."

According to Lou Harris's polling back: Pietrusza, *1960*, 109.

somewhere between 2 and 3 percent: Bruno, recorded interview, October 29, 2002.

Nationally, Humphrey was polling: Pietrusza, *1960*, 110.

"I ain't never seen anybody like that": Bruno, recorded interview, October 29, 2002.

"Do you think I'll ever get out": Bruno, recorded interview, October 29, 2002.

By 1960, West Virginia had lost: Price, "The Impact of the Mechanization."

He visited the local high school: "Annotated Timeline of Campaign Stops."

After his brief remarks: "Kennedy Address Wayne Audience."

"Is it true you're the son": Pietrusza, *1960*, 114.

"No community is an island": "Remarks of Senator John F. Kennedy," April 11, 1960.

"I know what you face here": "Remarks of Senator John F. Kennedy,"
	April 11, 1960.

His emotional outspokenness : Pietrusza, *1960*, 114.

anyone funding Humphrey's campaign: Pietrusza, *1960*, 118.

"he is swearing to support the separation of church and state": White, *Making
	of the President*, 107–108.

Jerry himself had been confused for the "bag man": Bruno, recorded
	interview, October 29, 2002; Pietrusza, *1960*, 125.

"I have just received the following wire": "Remarks of Senator John F. Kennedy,"
	March 15, 1958.

When the Humphrey campaign couldn't even muster: Pietrusza, *1960*, 127.

He had to call his father and brother: Humphrey, *Education*, 218.

Kennedy received 61 percent: Pietrusza, *1960*, 130.

left West Virginia for Washington that morning: White, *Making of the
	President*, 114.

celebrated with a bowl of tomato soup: White, *Making of the President*, 114.

"By 9:20, with ten precincts . . . having reported": White, *Making of the
	President*, 112.

"Maybe I was just consoling myself": Humphrey, recorded interview,
	December 14, 1964.

"God," Bobby said, "this must be awful": O'Donnell and Powers, *Johnny*, 171.

"It was very nice of you to come": White, *Making of the President*, 114.

"Why don't you bring the senator back": Bruno, recorded interview,
	October 29, 2002.

"Maybe if I'd had you," Humphrey lamented: Bruno and Greenfield, *Advance
	Man*, 45.

Bobby Kennedy and Dave Powers: Bruno, recorded interview, October 29,
	2002.

"I'm going to do whatever I can": Solberg, *Hubert Humphrey*, 212.

Not only did Humphrey release his delegates: Humphrey, recorded interview,
	December 14, 1964; Humphrey, *Education*, 232.

"Senator Humphrey for Kennedy Bean Feed": "Humphrey Throws Support."

"Let's elect Jack Kennedy": "Humphrey Throws Support."

"unblushingly took credit": "Humphrey Throws Support."

"I think that if Humphrey had not carried": Lucey, recorded interview, August 1, 1964.

"Hubert, if I'd known": Humphrey, *Education*, 249.

"As a friend," Humphrey would reflect later: Humphrey, *Education*, 258.

President Kennedy authorized a food stamp program: Martin, "Invoking Noble Coal Miners."

Flying High with Jack

chicken noodle soup and sandwiches: Humphrey, *Education*, 222.

"Well, Hubert, now you know": Humphrey, *Education*, 222.

"Had I been able to see: Humphrey, *Education*, 222.

After a four-and-a-half-hour flight: Humphrey, *Education*, 222.

"Emerson once said": "Remarks of Senator John F. Kennedy at Jefferson-Jackson Dinner," June 4, 1960.

"I think you will all agree": "Remarks of Senator John F. Kennedy," June 4, 1960.

"Hubert Humphrey and I fought": "Remarks of Senator John F. Kennedy," June 4, 1960.

"In the larger sense, Hubert Humphrey won": "Remarks of Senator John F. Kennedy," June 4, 1960.

"We Democrats need Hubert Humphrey": "Remarks of Senator John F. Kennedy," June 4, 1960.

Eleanor Roosevelt, had made no secret of her disdain: Dallek, *An Unfinished Life*, 233.

And Truman was so put off by Kennedy's preordained status: "Press Conference Concerning Resignation."

"the great social welfare programs of Franklin Roosevelt": "Remarks of Senator John F. Kennedy," June 4, 1960.

"For, as Franklin Roosevelt said in his first Inaugural": "Remarks of Senator John F. Kennedy," June 4, 1960.

Some days she brought along her five-gallon coffee urn: Humphrey, *Education*, 219.

his youngest son, twelve-year-old Douglas, had huddled alongside him: Humphrey, *Education*, 210.

Bold Enough to Try

Lyndon B. Johnson had formally announced: Pietruska, *1960*, 166.

would arm-twist and horse trade: Dallek, *An Unfinished Life*, 264–265.

"I'm still not sure": Phillips, recorded interview, January 13, 1966.

"Vel, it would be a very bad thing": Phillips, recorded interview, January 13, 1966.

"For God's sake": Phillips, recorded interview, January 13, 1966.

"We have invited": Phillips, recorded interview, January 13, 1966.

"It's going to be fine, you'll see": Phillips, recorded interview, January 13, 1966.

"While we point with pride": "Remarks of Senator John F. Kennedy," July 10, 1960.

"Let us bear in mind": "Remarks of Senator John F. Kennedy," July 10, 1960.

"Francis Bacon once wrote": Remarks of Senator John F. Kennedy," July 10, 1960.

gave her a wink: Phillips, recorded interview, January 13, 1966.

Inauguration Day

wearing a dark overcoat: Frost, "January 20, 1961–Poet Robert Frost Reads Poem."

Frost had publicly supported: "Robert Frost Lets JFK."

abandoning their trapped cars: Ambrose and Samenow, "How a Surprise Snowstorm."

"the most crippling traffic jam": Ambrose and Samenow, "How a Surprise Snowstorm."

Sinatra had even persuaded: "The Lost Inaugural Gala for JFK."

Kennedy woke after four hours: Dallek, *An Unfinished Life*, 323.

Ivan reached for his tuxedo pants: Nestingen Rock, personal interview.

turquoise taffeta dress: Nestingen Rock, personal interview.

law school picnic: Nestingen, personal interview.

inaugural parade marshal: Nestingen, recorded interview, May 29, 1968.

its thirty-million-dollar budget: Nestingen, recorded interview, May 29, 1968.

oversee some sixty-five thousand: McKusick, "City's Ex-Mayor."

"most unbureaucratic and un-Washington": McKusick, "City's Ex-Mayor."

"two bureaucratic traditions at once": McKusick, "City's Ex-Mayor."

"did not leave Wisconsin": McKusick, "City's Ex-Mayor."

"Give me that": Frost, "January 20, 1961–Poet Robert Frost Reads."

"I just have to get through this": Frost, "January 20, 1961–Poet Robert Frost Reads."

assistant deputy grand marshal: Dresang, *Patrick J. Lucey*, 109.

Pat had stayed out of the fray: Dresang, *Patrick J. Lucey*, 109–110.

likely cost him his lieutenant governorship: Dresang, *Patrick J. Lucey*, 110–111.
who'd earned a PhD: Nash, recorded interview #1, January 28, 1966.
Pete Dugal had made the trek: "Obituary: Peter J. Dugal."
St. Patrick's Day they spent: Dugal, recorded interview, January 14, 1966.
locked the keys in the trunk: O'Donnell, *Common Good*, 183.
"This was to be a preface": Frost, "January 20, 1961–Poet Robert Frost Reads."
"president-elect, Mr. John Finley": Ott, "Why Robert Frost Didn't Get To Read."

More Than a Face in the Crowd

Ira Kapenstein secured his place: Kapenstein, recorded interview,
    December 15, 1965.
Ira was first approached: Kapenstein, recorded interview, December 15, 1965.
Ira received a second salvo: Kapenstein, recorded interview, December 15, 1965.
work alongside Pierre Salinger: Kapenstein, recorded interview,
    December 15, 1965.
Milwaukee's Wisconsin Hotel: Kapenstein, recorded interview, December 15, 1965.
"A thousand a month": Kapenstein, recorded interview, December 15, 1965.
"Don't you know that Jack": Kapenstein, recorded interview,
    December 15, 1965.
He might've followed Salinger: Kapenstein, personal interview, February 8, 2021.
"I think they just could not understand": Kapenstein, recorded interview,
    December 15, 1965.
President Kennedy pulled himself away: Kapenstein, recorded interview,
    December 15, 1965.
"Ira, how are you getting along?": Kapenstein, recorded interview,
    December 15, 1965.
Working directly underneath Irish Mafia member Larry O'Brien: Kapenstein,
    personal interview.
he would help roll out the nation's zip code: Kapenstein, personal interview.
Ira, Larry, and Bobby shared a congratulatory moment: Kapenstein, personal
    interview.
Ira was thirty-two years old: Kapenstein, personal interview.
"Whatever other qualifications": "Address in Milwaukee, Wisconsin,"
    May, 12 1962.
"That is an unchallengeable statement": "Address in Milwaukee, Wisconsin,"
    May 12, 1962.

"When they talk about a cold wind": "Address in Milwaukee, Wisconsin,"
    May 12, 1962.
"I suppose that there's no training ground": "Address in Milwaukee,
    Wisconsin," May 12, 1962.
"I don't know with certainty": "Address in Milwaukee, Wisconsin," May 12, 1962.

A Band on Every Corner

"The guy was a very detailed guy": Bruno, recorded interview, October 29, 2002.
"He'd look around, . . . and he'd count the bands": Bruno, recorded interview,
    October 29, 2002.
"We'll never have another day like this": Widmer, "Eich Bin Ein Berliner."
"The stories about huge outpouring[s]": Bruno, recorded interview,
    October 29, 2002.
"The president is up in arms": Bruno, recorded interview, October 29, 2002.
"Do you have any bands?": Bruno, recorded interview, October 29, 2002.
"Oh, no problem": Bruno, recorded interview, October 29, 2002.
"Somehow this mayor . . . figured that": Bruno and Greenfield Advance Man, 75.
"How's the crowd going to be?": Bruno, recorded interview, October 29, 2002.
Minutes later, as the motorcade began: Knudsen, White House Photographs.
"They swarmed all over": Bruno and Greenfield, Advance Man, 76.
"Mr. President, it's all my cousins": Bruno, recorded interview, October 29, 2002.
Much of the disagreement centered on the venue: Bruno and Greenfield,
    Advance Man, 89–91; Bruno, recorded interview, October 29, 2002.
"The first impression we had": Bruno, recorded interview, October 29, 2002.
"This is my show": Bruno, recorded interview, October 29, 2002.
"The thing that, 'til this day it disturbs me": Bruno, recorded interview,
    October 29, 2002.
"There must be some misunderstanding": Bruno, recorded interview,
    October 29, 2002.
"If I had to blame anybody for that trip": Bruno, recorded interview,
    October 29, 2002.
his two-day, five-city tour: Byrne, "The Hours before Dallas."
"Two years ago, I introduced myself in Paris": Byrne, "The Hours before Dallas."
"How's it going?": Bruno and Greenfield, Advance Man, 93.
"I got to get off": Bruno and Greenfield, Advance Man, 94.

"There were a dozen things I was imagining": Bruno and Greenfield, *Advance Man*, 94.

the operator wept: Bruno and Greenfield, *Advance Man*, 94.

At around one thirty eastern time: Humphrey, *Education*, 258.

nearly 50 percent of American households: Herskovitz. "How the JFK Assassination Transformed Media Coverage."

Humphrey roamed the White House alone: Humphrey, *Education*, 259.

Jackie was there: Humphrey, *Education*, 260.

Huddled alongside the casket: Humphrey, *Education*, 260.

a stroll around the White House Rose Garden: "Kennedy Assassination Statement."

"wonderful, wonderful visit": "Kennedy Assassination Statement."

"You could not stop crying": "State Leaders Recall JFK Tragedy."

Pat Lucey boarded a plane: "State Leaders Recall JFK Tragedy."

winning Wisconsin's lieutenant governorship: Dresang, *Patrick J. Lucey*, 123.

"I guess I stayed there all night": Bruno and Greenfield, *Advance Man*, 95.

At 4:30 a.m. on November 23: Newseum, *President Kennedy Has Been Shot*, 172.

McKinley's body had lain there: "William McKinley's Coffin."

Teddy Roosevelt's children had roller skated: "The East Room."

Truman had once played a Steinway piano: "The East Room."

First up was the Coast Guard Academy Band: Lowens, "Accurate Listing of Funeral Music."

"This was the one time": Bruno and Greenfield, *Advance Man*, 94.

he flubbed the sixth note: "Taps at President Kennedy Funeral."

ACKNOWLEDGMENTS

While writing a book is hardly as complicated as running for national office, I couldn't help but draw occasional comparisons throughout this project. As a writer, the stakes were always much lower, and the voters irrelevant, but from the very first word, I knew—as presidential candidates do—that success is achieved through a well-built coalition.

First and foremost, a humble thank you to those who shared their family's stories with me: Dan Dugal, James Kapenstein, Leslie Nestingen, Marcia Nestingen Rock, and Michael Phillips.

To the journalists, whose bylines are far too often forgotten, though their words remain.

To the John F. Kennedy Presidential Library, archivist Stacey Chandler, and the many interviewers who captured the stories of the people included herein.

And to the people themselves—Jerry Bruno, Pete Dugal, Ira Kapenstein, Pat Lucey, Philleo Nash, Ivan Nestingen, Vel Phillips, Charles "Chuck" Spalding, Karel Yasko, Robert F. Kennedy, Edward "Teddy" Kennedy, First Lady Jacqueline Kennedy, and President John F. Kennedy, too. Though none of you will ever read these words, thank you for extending your hands across history.

And to the memory of the late Hubert H. Humphrey—a worthy adversary, a better ally.

Closer to home, thanks to my inspiring students, who provide me the vigor to hit the historical campaign trail.

To my colleagues and friends at the University of Wisconsin–Eau Claire: Chancellor Jim Schmidt, Provost Patricia Kleine, Executive Director Kimera Way, Interim President Julia Diggins, Dean Aleks Sternfeld-Dunn, Dean Carmen Manning, Chair Jan Stirm, Jon Loomis, Allyson Loomis, Molly Patterson, Brett Beach, Dr. Dorothy Chan, Dr. Asha Sen, Dr. Sarita Mizin, Dr. Kaia Simon, Dr. Jonathan Rylander, Dr. David Jones, Dr. David Shih, Dr. Bob Nowlan, Dr. José Alvergue, Dr. Stephanie Farrar, Dr. Stephanie Turner, Dr. Theresa Kemp, Dr. Karly Grice, Dr. Joel Pace, Dr. Cathy Rex, Dr. Matt Seymour, Dr. Stacy Thompson, Dr. Blake

Westerlund, Dr. Lynsey Wolter, Dr. Frank Fucile, Dr. Heather Fielding, Amy Fleury, Shelley Donnelly, Sara Monahan, Liz Kitzmann, Professor Arthur Grothe, Dr. Chiayu Hsu, Nick Butler, John Hildebrand, Max Garland, Bruce Taylor, Patti See, Greg Kocken, Dr. Justin Patchin, Dr. Jason Spraitz, Dr. Paul Thomas, Dr. Jeff DeGrave, Joanne Erickson, Candis Sessions, and Alaina Guns (and so many more).

Thanks to Dr. Catherine Chan and Dr. Erica Benson and the Office of Research and Sponsored Programs at the University of Wisconsin–Eau Claire, whose support proved vital to this project. Thanks, too, for the support provided by the University of Wisconsin–Eau Claire Academic Affairs Professional Development Program.

To my first family—Mom, Dad, Brother. And hi, Janae! And Howie!

To the Dayton family for kindling the good fires and extinguishing the bad ones.

To early readers, including Doug Mell, Robert Gough, and Dennis McBride.

To Don Steffen, the late Fred Steffen, and the *Eau Claire Daily Telegram* (currently the *Leader-Telegram*) for lending some photos.

To the *Volume One* team for publishing an early excerpt of this work.

Thank you to the Wait! What? Writers, and especially Eric Rasmussen, Ken Szymanski, Andy Patrie, and Julian Emerson, for reading this again and again.

To Jim Alf, who keeps the pages turning.

And to Pat McBride for connecting the dots.

To editor extraordinaire Carrie Kilman, whose work fundamentally transformed these pages for the better. And to Kate Thompson and the rest of the Wisconsin Historical Society Press team, too.

And finally, to my family, who, on the darkest days of this project, reminded me of the words of President John F. Kennedy: "Every accomplishment starts with the decision to try."

INDEX

and assassination of JFK, 177–178
attends Jefferson-Jackson Dinner, 147–152
background of, 99
benefits of tough primary fight from, 145–146
campaign funding and spending of, 99–101, 142
campaign surrogates of, 122
campaign weaknesses of, 102–103, 115, 132
and change in Wisconsin primary delegate math, 76–80, 128, 133, 135, 142
following West Virginia primary, 145
on JFK, 137
JFK on, 148–152
JFK questions Bruno about, 47
as JFK's campaign worry, 55–56
and JFK's entrance into Wisconsin primary, 58–59, 63–64
LIFE magazine photo shoot with JFK, 97–104, *100*, 123
Nash as supporter of, 52–53
at 1948 Democratic National Convention, 8–12
in Oval Office, *150*
and Phillips' support of JFK, 65–66
as presidential candidate, 60
on primary day, 127–130, 132, 134–135
relationship with JFK, 146, 168
speaks at Mid-West Conference of the Democratic Party, 17–18
strengths of, 115
support for civil rights, 10–12, 14, 65

support for, in Wisconsin, 74, 105, 111, 115
supports JFK, 145
talkativeness of, 97–98, 132
urged to drop out of primary, 139
and West Virginia primary, 143–144
Humphrey, Hubert Sr., 99
Humphrey, Muriel, 103, 152, 178
Hurley, Wisconsin, 112

Inauguration Day, 157–163
Ireland, 172
Irish Mafia, 1, 42, 56, 139, 167, 178

Jefferson-Jackson Dinner, 148–152
"Joe Must Go" Club, 24, 28
Johnson, Lyndon B., 19, 60, 139, *150*, 153, 161, 181
Joseph, Geri, 145

Kapenstein, Ira, 37–44, 56, 110, 164–168, *165*
Kefauver, Estes, 14, 15, 21–22
Kennedy, Arabella, 86
Kennedy, Edward (Ted)
    campaigns for JFK, 117, 119–126
    JFK mistaken for, 94
    and JFK's campaign strategy, 1, 6
    at JFK's funeral, *182–183*
    and ski jump competition, 82–84, 123
Kennedy, Eunice, 132
Kennedy, Jackie
    arrives in Wisconsin, 61
    and assassination of JFK, 176, 178
    and birth of Arabella Kennedy, 86
    campaigns for JFK, 85–91, *87*, 103, 117
    in Hyannis Port, *72*

ABOUT THE AUTHOR

BRIAN HOLLARS

B.J. Hollars is the author of several books, most recently *Year of Plenty: A Family's Season of Grief*; *Go West Young Man: A Father and Son Rediscover America on The Oregon Trail*; *Midwestern Strange: Hunting Monsters, Martians, and the Weird in Flyover Country*; and *The Road South: Personal Stories of the Freedom Riders*. In addition, Hollars is the editor of *Hope Is The Thing: Wisconsinites on Perseverance in a Pandemic*. His work has been featured in the *Washington Post*, *Parents Magazine*, NPR, and elsewhere. He is the recipient of the Truman Capote Prize for Literary Nonfiction, the Anne B. and James B. McMillan Prize, the Council of Wisconsin Writers' Blei-Derleth Award, and the Society of Midland Authors Award. He is the founder and director of the Chippewa Valley Writers Guild, as well as a professor of English at the University of Wisconsin–Eau Claire.